WOMEN

—of the—

KLONDIKE

WOMEN
—of the—
KLONDIKE

Frances Backhouse

Whitecap Books
Vancouver/Toronto

Edited by Elaine Jones
Cover design by Designgeist
Interior design by Warren Clark
Cover photograph by E.A. Hegg (B461), Special Collections Division,
University of Washington Libraries, Seattle
Typeset by Warren Clark

Printed and bound in Canada.

Care has been taken to trace the ownership of copyright material used in
the text. The author and publisher welcome any information enabling them
to rectify any reference or credit in subsequent editions.
p. 28: Quote reprinted by permission of Caxton Printers, Ltd. from
A Pioneer Woman in Alaska by Emily Craig Romig.
p. 104: Quote reprinted by permission of Alaska Northwest Books from "As Well As
Any Man" by Alice McDonald, *Alaska Journal,* Summer 1984, pp. 39–45.
p. 184: Quote reprinted with permission from *Guarding the Goldfields: The Story of
the Yukon Field Force,* edited by Brereton Greenhous, "Edward Lester's Diary,"
Dundurn Press, 1987: p. 90. © National Museums of Canada, 1987.

Canadian Cataloguing in Publication Data

Backhouse, Frances
  Women of the Klondike
  Includes bibliographical references and index.
  ISBN 1-55110-375-3

  1. Women—Yukon Territory—Klondike River Valley—
  History. 2. Klondike River Valley (Yukon)—Gold discoveries.
  3. Yukon Territory—History—1895-1918.* I. Title.
  FC4022.9.W6B32 1995   971.9'102'0922   C95-910688-X
  F1095.K5B32 1995

The publisher acknowledges the support of the Canada Council
and the Cultural Services Branch of the Government of British Columbia
in making this publication possible.

CONTENTS

FOREWORD

by Pierre Berton

This lively work is an essential addition to the growing bookshelf of Klondike history. I read it with enormous interest because I have known several of the major figures—such remarkable women as Emilie Tremblay, Martha Black, Belinda Mulrooney, Sadie Stringer, and Klondike Kate Rockwell. I bought my first mechanical toy in Madame Tremblay's famous emporium, now preserved as a heritage site by Parks Canada. I drank my first glass of ginger ale in Mrs. Stringer's kitchen. Martha Black was a regular visitor in our home. I interviewed Belinda Mulrooney at the end of her life in her house on the outskirts of Seattle. Kate Rockwell and her third husband were my shipmates on the *Princess Louise*, steaming down the panhandle of Alaska.

These women were not typical of their times. Nor were the others, whose stories are told so well in these pages. I have written of the men, such as Clarence Berry and Tom Lippy, two of the "Kings of Eldorado." Here they are shown from a different viewpoint, that of their wives. Ms. Backhouse's careful research has put a new spin on a familiar tale.

More and more new material is being turned up to enliven the history of the great stampede of 1898. There are many passages in Ms. Backhouse's chronicle that are new to me. It is rewarding to find that she has covered all the territory—not just the dance hall girls, who certainly deserve their own chapter, but also the other women who are part of the great saga, from nuns to natives.

The Klondike phenomenon swept the continent at a time when the only jobs open to the female sex were those of stenographer, nurse, and teacher. But here are stories of determined and resilient women who defied the strictures of society and marched to a different drum. They did so in search of wealth—at least that was the excuse. More accurately they went in search of adventure and also to prove they were as capable as men of doing the impossible.

Any member of the Yukon Order of Pioneers who reads this remarkable book must surely feel a sense of shame to realize that, even now, the membership of the Order remains exclusively male. Madame Tremblay, the first woman over the Chilkoot, could not join. Nor could Martha Black, who climbed the passes while pregnant; nor Kate Carmack, who helped start it all. Nor could my mother. In clinging to an outmoded and moth-eaten principle, the Order diminishes itself and all men who refuse to acknowledge the debt owed to the *real* pioneers, the ones who enliven the pages of this important and entertaining story.

PREFACE

"There are strange things done in the midnight sun by the men who moil for gold." So wrote Robert Service, poet laureate of the Klondike. Rereading those famous lines a few years ago I began to wonder about the women who moiled through the endless days of the Yukon summer and the dark winter months. Soon idle contemplation turned to obsession and I found myself poring over old newspapers, diaries, turn-of-the-century books, and memoirs. I discovered a wealth of references to women, many frustratingly brief, and a number of real gems: richly detailed stories that introduced me to some fascinating individuals. Most precious were the first-hand accounts written by women at the time of the gold rush or carefully recorded years later.

As I suspected, the women of the Klondike were more numerous and more diverse than most historians would have us believe. Not all were white or English-speaking. The majority were American, but some came from as far away as Europe, Australia, and Japan. Native women also played a part in gold rush society—some as active participants, others as silent observers.

The diversity of Klondike women is best revealed in the work they did. Although I did not find one who made her fortune by wielding a pick and shovel, a number of women did strike paydirt running successful businesses or shrewdly investing in mining properties. Many more simply managed to make a living, doing the same kinds of jobs they had done in the south—cooking, sewing, washing laundry, teaching, typing, nursing, and entertaining men.

The singers, dancers, and prostitutes attracted the most attention at the time and have since come to be considered archetypes of the gold rush woman. Yet they were never representative of the Klondike's female population. The majority of women living in Dawson and the surrounding gold fields were wives who accompanied their husbands or joined them later. Often they burned with gold fever just as intensely as their men. In some cases, however, they simply believed that a woman's place was at her husband's side and that her greatest reward came from making a comfortable, happy home for him.

Then there were the women who went questing for different kinds of gold. Some were seeking souls to save; others hoped to gain professional recognition. A few even travelled to the Klondike to bring back exotic tales to relate at dinner parties in New York City and San Francisco.

Compared to the tens of thousands of men, the number of women who joined the stampede was never high, probably no more than a few thousand. Nevertheless, they were a vital part of Klondike society, both during and after the gold rush. Nearly a century after the historic event, their words speak to me and their eyes meet mine as they stare out from faded photographs. This is their story.

ACKNOWLEDGEMENTS

My research on women of the Klondike was smoothed by helpful staff at a number of institutions including the British Columbia Archives and Records Services, Yukon Archives, Glenbow-Alberta Institute Library and Archives, University of Washington Libraries Special Collections Division, Dawson City Museum, National Archives of Canada, Provincial Archives of Alberta, and Vancouver Public Library. Special thanks are due to Michael Gates (Klondike National Historic Sites, Dawson), Sister Margaret Cantwell (Archives of the Sisters of St. Ann, Victoria), Captain Florence Curzon (Salvation Army Heritage Centre, Toronto), Dr. Julie Cruikshank (Department of Anthropology, University of British Columbia, Vancouver), and Katharine Martyn (Thomas Fisher Rare Book Library, University of Toronto). I was also fortunate to make links to the past through Emilie Tremblay's granddaughter, Joan White of Victoria, and Clare Boyntan Phillips's great-granddaughter, Virginia Nethercott of Starrucca, Pennsylvania. The Canada Council played a major role in seeing this project to completion by awarding me an Explorations grant.

The creation of a book is influenced by countless people. Without my parents, Helen and John Backhouse, who have always given me their loving and unconditional support, I may never have had the faith in myself to become a writer. While I cannot name all the others who inspired and encouraged me in writing this book, I am particularly grateful to Rick Stuart for first infecting me with Klondike fever; Dr. Sylvia VanKirk for taking time to discuss my idea in relation to her work on women of the Cariboo gold rush; Rosemary Neering for reviewing my proposal and portions of the manuscript; and Blair Marshall for his enthusiasm during the early days of this project and for his ongoing interest.

For the sake of brevity, I have to ask most of my dear friends who kept me going through this venture to accept a collective acknowledgement. I would, however, like to thank Laura Markle and Jim Gilpin for kindly opening their home to me in Whitehorse; Warren Ford for his generous hospitality in Dawson; and three delightful women—Suzanne Thuir, Guri Slagsvold, and Sue Carr—for joining me on a spectacular hike over the Chilkoot trail. Thanks also to Mark Zuehlke who helped me over some equally steep and rocky ground with wise words and unwavering support.

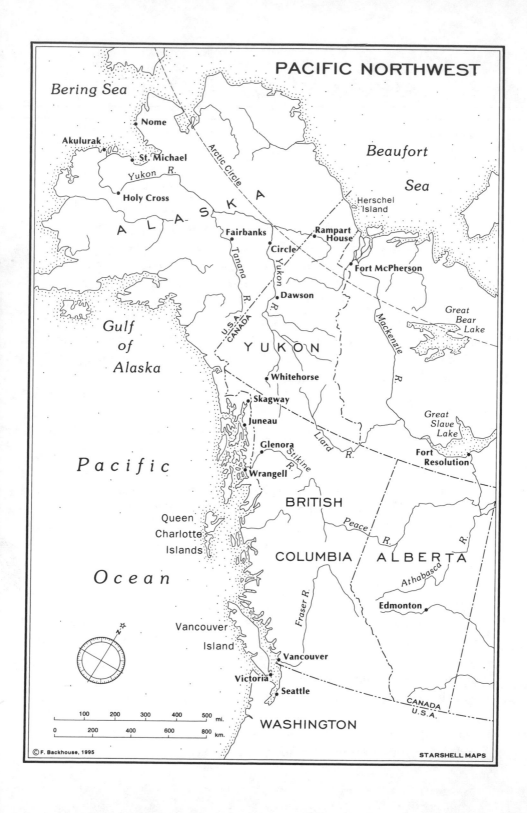

PACIFIC NORTHWEST

Bering Sea

Nome

Akulurak

St. Michael

Yukon R.

Holy Cross

A L A S K A

Arctic Circle

Beaufort

Sea

Herschel
Island

Fairbanks

Circle

Rampart
House

Fort McPherson

Tanana R.

Yukon R.

Dawson

U.S.A.
CANADA

Mackenzie R.

*Great
Bear
Lake*

Gulf
of
Alaska

Y U K O N

Whitehorse

Skagway

Juneau

Glenora

Stikine R.

Wrangell

Liard R.

*Great
Slave
Lake*

Fort
Resolution

Pacific

BRITISH

Peace R.

Queen
Charlotte
Islands

COLUMBIA

A L B E R T A

R.

Ocean

Fraser R.

Athabasca R.

Edmonton

Vancouver
Island

Vancouver

Victoria

Seattle

CANADA
U.S.A.

100   200   300   400   500 mi.

0   200   400   600   800 km.

WASHINGTON

© F. Backhouse, 1995

STARSHELL MAPS

1

FIRST WOMAN
—of the—
KLONDIKE

On August 16, 1896, in the far northwestern corner of the continent, three men made a discovery that altered the course of North American history. Halfway down a small tributary of the Klondike River known as Rabbit Creek, they came across an accumulation of gold that outshone anything they had ever laid eyes on. From the moment they saw the shiny, yellow metal lying thick between the slabs of bedrock—like cheese in a sandwich, one said later—they knew they would be rich. But the enormity of the events they were about to set in motion was beyond their wildest imaginings.

Two of the men—Keish, known to whites as Skookum Jim, and K̲áa Goox̲, or Dawson Charlie—were Tagish Indians. The third was an American prospector, George Carmack, who had spent years doggedly searching for gold along the rivers and creeks of Alaska and the Yukon with little success until that moment.

As soon as they had marked their claims, the three men hurried to the nearby town of Forty Mile on the Yukon River to register them. Word of their find spread like wildfire throughout the Yukon River valley and people immediately began converging on the area from all directions. By the end of August, every inch of Rabbit Creek, already renamed Bonanza Creek, was staked. A few days later, the riches of neighbouring Eldorado Creek were revealed, feeding the frenzy of incoming fortune-hunters. The district's two established gold-mining settlements—Forty Mile and Circle City—emptied almost overnight as prospectors and entrepreneurs flocked upriver to the new town of Dawson that was rising on the floodplain at the junction of the Yukon and Klondike rivers.

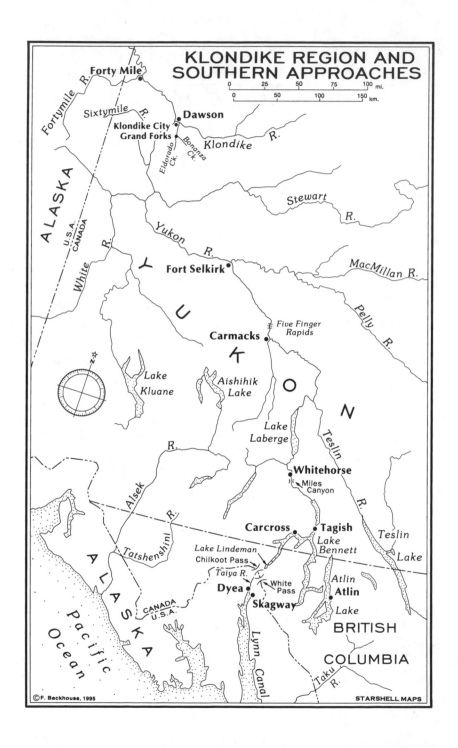

KLONDIKE REGION AND SOUTHERN APPROACHES

Forty Mile

Fortymile R.

Sixtymile R.

Dawson

Klondike City
Grand Forks

Eldorado Ck.

Bonanza Ck.

Klondike R.

ALASKA

U.S.A.
CANADA

White R.

Yukon R.

Stewart R.

Fort Selkirk

MacMillan R.

Y U K O N

Five Finger Rapids

Carmacks

Pelly R.

Lake Kluane

Aishihik Lake

Lake Laberge

Teslin R.

Whitehorse

Miles Canyon

Alsek R.

Tatshenshini R.

Carcross

Tagish

Lake Bennett

Teslin Lake

Lake Lindeman
Chilkoot Pass

Taiya R.

Dyea

White Pass

Skagway

Atlin

Atlin Lake

ALASKA

CANADA
U.S.A.

Pacific Ocean

Lynn Canal

Taku R.

BRITISH

COLUMBIA

© F. Backhouse, 1995

STARSHELL MAPS

The Klondike gold rush was under way, but for nearly a year the excitement was restricted to people already in the north. There were no telephones or telegraph lines to carry the news and letters took many months to reach destinations in the south.

All through the fall and winter of 1896–97, the Klondike miners worked their claims. They tended fires to thaw the frozen ground and scraped away the layers of softened muck. Slowly they sank shafts down towards the solid bedrock, using buckets and hand-powered windlasses to haul the excavated material to the surface. When they could dig no deeper, they tunnelled horizontally. They built sluice boxes beside the ever-growing piles of dirt and waited impatiently for spring to arrive and release the water required to wash out the gold.

Many were rewarded handsomely for their months of labour. As soon as the rivers were clear of ice, they loaded their hard-earned gold onto outbound paddle-wheelers and headed down the Yukon. When they reached the port of St. Michael on Alaska's north coast they transferred to larger steamers and continued south.

On July 14, 1897, the steamship *Excelsior* pulled into San Francisco harbour and a band of scruffy individuals, fresh from their Klondike claims, walked down the gangplank dragging suitcases and sacks that collectively held half a million dollars' worth of gold. Three days later, sixty-eight miners who had come south on the *Portland* arrived in Seattle carrying more than a ton of gold dust and nuggets. Word of their coming had preceded them. Although it was barely past dawn when they tied up at the dock, more than five thousand people were on hand to watch them disembark.

The passengers of the two boats were an unlikely-looking lot of millionaires. Most had not seen civilization for several years and were dressed in rough, northern garb. The dresses of the few women in their midst were hopelessly out of fashion. Nevertheless, they were instant celebrities. Within days, newspapers around the world were filled with stories of their fabulous wealth and good fortune.

The arrival of the *Excelsior* and the *Portland* marked the beginning of the second phase of the Klondike stampede, when the trickle of gold-seekers became a torrent. Over the next few years, some 100,000 people set off for the Klondike. Although not all reached their destination, Dawson soon became the largest community north of Seattle and west of Winnipeg, with an estimated population of between sixteen and thirty thousand. The height of the stampede occurred in 1898. After that the flood of new arrivals began to subside and the number of people leaving the Klondike to try other gold fields or to return home increased.

Prior to the 1896 discovery of gold on Bonanza Creek, the Yukon River valley was home to a thousand or so non-native men. Most were prospectors who had given up the comforts of civilization to pursue their elusive dream; the remainder, an odd assortment of traders, missionaries, and government officials. The number of non-native women—wives, prostitutes, entertainers, and businesswomen—probably did not exceed one hundred. When word got out that gold had been discovered in the Klondike River district in quantities that rivalled anything yet found in the north, almost every one of these men and women made a beeline for Dawson.

Various women claimed to have been the first to reach the Klondike gold fields in August 1896, but the title of first woman of the Klondike rightly belongs to Kate Carmack. Although not present when her husband, George, her brother Keish, and her nephew, Káa Goox, discovered the rich deposits of gold that started the stampede, she was the first person to share their good news.

Kate Carmack was not typical of the women who participated in this famous historical event. The biggest difference was that she became involved through circumstance, not by choice. Born Shaaw Tláa, she was the daugh-

Kate, Graphie and George Carmack in front of their Bonanza Creek cabin, 1897.

ter of a Tagish woman and a Tlingit man. Her childhood in the south-central Yukon was grounded in traditions that had been passed from generation to generation. Her adult years, however, were fraught with the turmoil of radically changing times. When the gold rush began she was in her late thirties. She had been married to George, who had given her the name Kate, for about ten years and they had a three-year-old daughter, Graphie Grace. Her first husband, a Tlingit man, and their infant daughter had died during an influenza epidemic that ravaged the native population of Alaska and the Yukon.

In the late 1880s, when George and Kate first began living together as husband and wife, marriages between native women and white prospectors or traders were rare, although temporary liaisons were common. George was less disdainful of natives than most of his peers. Soon after his arrival in the north he had become friends with Kate's brother, Skookum Jim. That friendship led him to marry one of Kate's older sisters, who died shortly afterwards of influenza, and then Kate herself. "Squaw men" like George were looked down upon by other whites, but he recognized the value of having a wife who was at home in the wilderness and knew how to live off the land.

For the first year after George, Jim, and Charlie made their big discovery, there was little change in Kate's life. The men built a cabin on Bonanza Creek and worked together on their claims. Kate kept house, cared for Graphie, and took in laundry to make some money to see them through until spring when they could wash the gold out of their diggings. She also put to good use skills learned as a girl and perfected as a young woman: she sewed moccasins and warm winter clothing to sell to the other miners, and helped provide for her family by picking berries and snaring rabbits and ptarmigan.

When the gold-laden steamers *Excelsior* and *Portland* headed south in the spring of 1897, the discoverers of the Klondike were not on board. Their mines were doing well enough that they could now afford to buy luxuries like tinned peaches and hire men to help with the heavy labour, but they were content to remain on Bonanza Creek. By 1898, however, George was entertaining thoughts of a trip "outside." When spring clean-up that year yielded $150,000 to be shared between the three partners, they all agreed it was time for a holiday.

George was particularly looking forward to seeing his sister, Rose

Watson, in California, although he was apprehensive about introducing his Tagish family to her. Throughout his years in the north he had corresponded regularly with Rose, but not until June 1897 did he reveal to her that he was married. Even then he did not confess Kate's true origins. "My wife is Irish," he wrote, "and talks very broad English, but I have the prettiest little daughter you ever saw."[1]

Although he may have had misgivings about how his sister would view Kate, George made no attempt to hide his association with her or her relatives during their first trip south. In Seattle, he told newspaper reporters he planned to take his family to the Paris Exposition in 1900 and said he would be glad to have Jim and Charlie along. "They're good company," he explained, "and [I] would not care to go to Paris and see all the sights knowing that they were missing it all."[2] Before long, George would be denying that he and Kate had ever been legally married, but in 1898, he signed her into hotels as Mrs. Carmack and proudly draped gold-nugget necklaces around her neck to show off his wealth.

Unfortunately, adapting to life in the big city was not easy for the Tagish. The crush of people and the fast-moving traffic made them nervous, and they easily became disoriented amongst the tall buildings. All three drank too much, perhaps because they were unaccustomed to the ready supply of liquor, or maybe in an attempt to numb their feelings of bewilderment.

Much to George's chagrin, the newspapers took great delight in reporting their misadventures and portraying them as wild and ignorant savages. Editors cared little whether the stories were true, as long as they were colourful.

After a few weeks in Seattle, the Carmacks went on to California to stay with George's sister—a strict Baptist teetotaller—and her husband on their ranch. Rose was delighted to see her brother, but gave his family only grudging welcome. Kate spent the winter trying to conform to her sister-in-law's notions of proper comport-

Kate Carmack in California, 1898.

ment and watching her daughter be seduced by a foreign culture. In the spring of 1899, Kate, George, Jim, and Charlie returned to Bonanza Creek, leaving Graphie to spend the summer being "civilized" by her aunt.

The pressures endured by Kate and her relatives in Seattle and California were extreme examples of the culture shock experienced by all the native inhabitants of the Yukon and Alaska as the Klondike gold rush swept over their land. Sooner or later even those who remained far from the gold fields and the major transportation routes felt its impact. The ones who were closest to the action saw their familiar world turned upside down and their lives permanently transformed.

For the Han, whose fishing camp at the junction of the Yukon and Klondike rivers was supplanted by Dawson and Klondike City and whose hunting grounds were overrun by stampeders, the gold rush brought massive social disruption. Retreating to the village of Moosehide, just downstream from Dawson, they watched the white invasion with amazement and dismay. "My people knew all the Klondike, but they never know nothing about gold," recalled a Han woman whose father was chief at the time of the gold rush.

> Lots of big nuggets along the creeks. But what do they know about gold? Nothing. So the white people come to the country and they found

Yukon natives, such as this group camped at Champagne, saw a flood of gold-seekers arrive in 1898.

nuggets all around the place. Very strange, very strange to my father that all those people come for gold. Too much money. The way my dad used to say, "They throw the money around; they throw the gold around. There's too much of it."[3]

Some natives, like the Tlingit who lived near what would become Skagway, saw that there was something to be gained from these whites who threw their money around so freely. While they may have deplored the chaos created by the stampede, they were shrewd enough to take advantage of the opportunity to earn large sums packing stampeders' supplies over the Chilkoot Pass. They were intimately familiar with this long-established trade route between themselves and the inland Tagish. Women often worked alongside their men, shouldering loads of fifty to seventy-five pounds—at up to a dollar a pound—and occasionally carrying their babies with them too. White observers marvelled at their strength and stamina, but the work was nothing new to the women. Traditionally they had transported most of the food and supplies, leaving the men free to break trail and keep watch for game.

Native women also sewed moccasins and parkas to sell to ill-equipped southerners, did laundry and mending, and worked as cooks and housekeepers. Some married white men, but these unions were seldom formalized by church or state. And as Kate Carmack was to learn, native wives were frequently discarded by their prospector husbands when the men tired of living in the north.

Cracks began appearing in the Carmacks' marriage during their second trip south in the summer of 1899. With Klondike fever be-

Two native women display their birchbark baskets.

ginning to wane, Kate may have hoped to escape the glare of publicity this time, but she and Skookum Jim were still too exotic for the press to ignore. On July 26, while George was out of town checking some investments, the *Seattle Post-Intelligencer* reported that "Mrs. George W. Carmack, the Indian wife of the discoverer of the Klondike, slept last night in the city jail, charged with being drunk and disorderly and disturbing the peace." She was arrested, the newspaper claimed, "while executing an aboriginal Yukon war dance in the second floor corridor of the Seattle Hotel."

This was followed by a highly imaginative and thoroughly bigoted account of a fight between Kate and Skookum Jim's wife. After the fight Kate was alleged to have started breaking down hotel room doors in a misdirected search for her husband, all the while "crooning a wild and warlike melody and punctuating the pauses in the tempo with bits of Indian profanity."

When he read the story in the *Post-Intelligencer*, what little sympathy or patience George had once had for Kate and her relatives vanished. "I am disgusted by the whole outfit," he wrote angrily to his sister. "I feel like taking an axe and smashing something. . . . If Kate's trunks were here I would ship her back to Dyea mighty quick. She is getting so unreasonable. I am simply boiling mad now."[4] Yet rather than sending Kate back to the Yukon, George left her with Graphie at Rose's ranch and returned alone to the Klondike.

Free from matrimonial encumbrances, George joined the other gold barons living the high life in Dawson over the winter of 1899–1900. At one of the many parties he attended he was introduced to Marguerite Laimee, an American businesswoman with a somewhat dubious reputation. Instantly smitten, he asked her to marry him the evening they met. At twenty-six, Marguerite was already a veteran of the gold camps in South Africa and Australia and had two or three marriages behind her. She knew a good offer when she saw one and accepted George's proposal on the spot.

George and his bride-to-be left almost immediately for Seattle, where he met with Skookum Jim and Dawson Charlie to terminate all their business partnerships. Severing his ties with Kate was less simple. Hurt and furious when she heard the man she had considered to be her husband for thirteen years was leaving her for another woman, her first response was to charge George with adultery and file for divorce. Unfortunately, she could produce no legal papers to prove she and George had been legally married.

This lack of documentary evidence, along with the suggestion from friends that there was hope of a reconciliation if she quit the legal proceedings, convinced her to withdraw the suit. It was a futile attempt. George married Marguerite on October 30, 1900, and began his new life in the south. Although he proudly wore the title of Discoverer of the Klondike until the day he died, he never returned to the Yukon.

In January 1901, Kate launched another lawsuit against George, this time seeking maintenance money for herself and Graphie. Seven months later, seeing no sign that justice would be served, she gave up hope of receiving any money from him. She had been gone from the north for two years and decided it was long past time to go home.

Upon her return, Skookum Jim built Kate a cabin in Carcross, where most of their family had settled. He also paid Graphie's school fees. Kate earned a small income from selling her needlework to tourists and sometimes those who knew her story paid her to pose for photographs.

Meanwhile, George steadfastly refused to send a single dollar to support either his daughter or his former wife. Instead, when Graphie was sixteen, he secretly arranged for her to leave the mission school in Whitehorse where she was studying and join him in Seattle. For Kate, who held firmly to the Tagish belief that children belong with their mother's clan, this was a serious breach of trust. It was also a devastating loss. A year later Graphie married her step-mother's thirty-two-year-old brother and turned her back on her northern roots. She never saw her mother again. Kate died of influenza on March 29, 1920, and was buried without fanfare in the Carcross cemetery.

For the first woman of the Klondike, the gold rush was more tragic than glorious. She was not, of course, the only person who lost more than she gained. In every gold rush there are more losers than winners. But most non-natives who joined the stampede to Dawson did so by choice. Kate and her people, on the other hand, were simply caught up in the dramatic events that unfolded on their doorstep. They coped as well as they could with the sudden influx of gold-seekers, and a few even prospered. But it is unlikely any of them truly comprehended the potent Midas dream that enticed tens of thousands of men and women to leave their homes and risk everything in a foreign land.

2

WOMEN
—on the—
GOLD RUSH TRAIL

The Klondike gold rush was as much an accident of history as of geology. Other stampedes, such as those in California, South Africa, and Australia, yielded more gold, but none ever matched the frenzy of the Klondike. In 1897, the United States and much of the rest of the world were in an economic slump. Countless unemployed men and women were desperate for a chance to break the chains of poverty, while those who had jobs were looking for something to lighten the grim mood of restraint and worry. At a time when it seemed there were few new frontiers to explore, the romance of the northern wilderness held great appeal, and with travel by train and steamship becoming increasingly efficient and affordable, the gold fields were not an impossible distance away.

Conditions were ripe for an epidemic of Klondike fever, an affliction that was highly contagious and struck indiscriminately. Rich and poor, young and old, factory workers and educated professionals—there was no predicting who might succumb. Even women, normally constrained by nineteenth-century standards of propriety, could join the quest. Their own families might look at them askance, but many people admired and envied them because they dared to do what others only fantasized about.

Lillian Oliver was one of the thousands who were lured north by the promise of gold and the better life it would bring. For her the Klondike seemed to offer the perfect opportunity to make enough money to allow her chronically ill husband to quit his job and regain his health. Lillian's gold fever was precipitated by the visit of a friend who was planning to go to Dawson.

That night I got no sleep—thinking, thinking—until I formed a plan to accompany these people . . . I fancied I saw how I could save a precious life. I dreamed of rich finds; and bags of gold haunted me all day and at night troubled my rest. I saw in my mind's eye the vision of a proud wife bearing home to a long-suffering man the wherewithal to take him away from dreary toil and give his tired brain a rest. In fancy we were taking a trip around the world; I was watching for the colour to come back to cheeks that had long been a stranger to it; I saw fire come to the eye grown dim; elasticity to steps grown weak; and happiness to both of us.[1]

At first Lillian's husband was reluctant to let her go, but her determination won him over. Then, when the rest of the party dropped out a fortnight before the departure date, she had to fight another battle to carry on alone. She refused to give up what she called "the dream of my life" and so the moment of parting came.

My husband is the last to bid and kiss me good-bye. Holding me in his arms, he calls the blessings of heaven down on his wife, asking God to send her safely back again, and making me promise that, successful or not, I would return in two years, for that was the limit. One more kiss, one more "God bless you," . . . and the train slowly pulled out of the depôt.

I never fully realized until then the herculean task I had undertaken. In the feverish time of preparation, I had no time for thought, and I made a mental resolve that, with God's blessing, I would come back a successful woman. . . . I was going into this terrible country without sufficient means, and I knew it; but a brave heart can accomplish much.[2]

Unfortunately, Lillian ended up with another sick man on her hands when the guide she had hired in Seattle came down with a severe case of pneumonia almost as soon as they reached Dawson. For seven weeks he lay in his tent coughing up blood, while she nursed him with little hope for his recovery. Finally, acquaintances offered to send the invalid home and to pay Lillian's fare if she would accompany him. At this point, visions of prosperity took second place to the debt she felt she owed this man who had brought her safely through the hazards of the trail. Furthermore, her seemingly endless store of confidence had finally run out and she feared remaining in the north without her trusted friend.

Lillian left the north penniless, but still burning with gold fever. As her boat steamed out of Dawson, two months after her arrival, she wrote: "How glad and grateful I am to leave this place, where I have gone through so much trouble. I want to, and will, come back to this country though—for there is gold dust for all, and I will yet get some of it."[3] There is, however, no record of her making a second trip to the Klondike.

While Lillian Oliver was motivated by the promise of riches, others sought adventure. Frances Dorley had always considered herself a bit of a dare-devil, but as a strictly reared young woman, she had found no opportunities for expressing her true nature. The twenty-six-year-old dressmaker and milliner was living quietly with her parents in Seattle when gold rush hysteria inundated her home town. From the moment the news hit the streets she began pestering her parents to let her go and see for herself what all the fuss was about. They finally gave in and allowed her to make a three-week trip to Skagway.

If they thought their headstrong daughter would then come home and settle down, the Dorleys were in for a surprise. Frances returned wide-eyed with all she had seen and declared that she was going back, this time all the way to Dawson. Her announcement was not well received. "My parents were bitterly and justifiably opposed to my plans," she later recollected, "but after three weeks of insistent pleading I finally won my mother's tearful consent and my father's reluctant blessing."[4] In April 1898, she sailed once more for Alaska.

Gold fever prompted even the most sober-minded citizens to make impetuous decisions. Emily and A.C. Craig, for example, had been married ten years and were leading a comfortable and staid life in Chicago when the "electrifying news" of the Klondike gold strike began appearing in all the papers.

> My husband read every word about the gold fields and at night would talk about the reports. . . . when he was at work I would read the same pages and thrill at the stories. Once he told me of seeing some nuggets . . . in a jeweller's window . . . and his eyes had a long and far-away look in them. The next day I hunted up the store, and there, sure

enough was the gold. . . . From then on I could believe any story—we both caught the gold fever—and that is no childhood disease either.[5]

Before the summer was over the couple had put down one thousand dollars to join a guided expedition to the Klondike. It was their Viking blood, Emily later claimed, that made them drop everything and go.

On the whole, there was little difference between women's and men's motivations for joining the stampede—they were seeking gold or adventure or both. But the Klondike also held a special attraction for women who believed it was time for the two sexes to stand on a more equal footing. In the chaos and single-mindedness of gold rush society, normal standards were, to some degree, suspended. Mrs. Slaughter, a Tacoma society matron and women's rights activist, argued that the Klondike was "the place for a display of women's courage and powers of assistance." It was time, she believed, for women to "exert themselves gently but persistently in compelling recognition of their ability to stand side by side with their fathers and brothers [and presumably their husbands] in the material struggles of life."[6] In February 1898, she and a number of like-minded women, all prominent in Tacoma society, decided to put their principles into practice and mount their own expedition to the gold fields. Unfortunately, no record of their trip exists.

Whatever their reasons, many women made their way north to the Klondike alongside the tens of thousands of stampeding men. The exact number of women is not known, however, since official censuses of the Yukon's turn-of-the-century population, conducted in 1891 and 1901, completely missed the gold rush peak. Some of the best clues as to the sex ratio in the Klondike come from passenger lists for the steamers that plied the upper Yukon River and North-West Mounted Police records of those who went down the river in small craft. (Although this only accounts for stampeders who went in via the Chilkoot or White Pass trails that led to the headwaters of the Yukon River, these were the most popular routes.) Between December 1898 and September 1900, the names of about 1,500 women were entered on these lists, representing about seven percent of the total number of travellers.[7] Anecdotal evidence suggests that in the early days of the stampede, men formed an even greater majority, with perhaps no more than a few hundred non-native women in the Klondike region before the summer of 1898.

The short but gruelling Chilkoot trail was one of the most popular routes to Dawson.

Despite being greatly outnumbered by male stampeders, or perhaps because they were such a novelty, women on their way to the Klondike received a great deal of attention in the press. In particular, much ink was devoted to the question of how they should dress for the journey.

Women's clothing of the day was not well suited to fording streams, climbing mountains, clambering in and out of boats, and hiking over rough terrain. The wide, full skirts that had gained popularity in the mid-1890s were typically made of five to ten yards of material and weighed many pounds. Hems trailed on the ground and elaborate petticoats hindered movement of the legs. Corsets were worn whenever women appeared in public and, despite increasing criticism of the way tight lacing restricted breathing and activity, fashion dictated that waists were smaller than ever in this era. Stand-up collars stiffened with interlining or boning forced wearers to hold their chins unnaturally high and, in extreme cases, even tilted their heads backwards.

Martha Purdy, the daughter of a prominent Chicago family, prepared for her Klondike journey by purchasing the most fashionable "outing costume" she could find.

> [It] was made of heavily ribbed tobacco-brown corduroy velvet with a skirt of shockingly immodest length (it actually showed my ankles),

five yards around the bottom, edged with brush braid, and lined with brown silk and interlined with a foot of buckram, which gave it a fetching swing as I walked. It had a Norfolk jacket with many pleats, a blouse with a high stiff collar almost to my ears, and a pair of voluminous brown silk bloomers, which came below the knee.[8]

Martha later had plenty of time to contemplate the absurdity of her outfit as she toiled up to the summit of the Chilkoot Pass.

As the day advanced the trail became steeper, the air warmer and footholds without support impossible. I shed my sealskin jacket. I cursed my hot, high buckram collar, my tight heavily boned corsets, my long corduroy skirt, my full bloomers which I had to hitch up with every step.[9]

Fashionable clothing was equally impractical in winter. In the San Francisco *Examiner* of September 18, 1897, reporter Helen Dare described the plight of one woman she met whose husband had forbidden her to shorten her hems for walking the Chilkoot trail. Her long skirts were "a disadvantage and discomfort to her, freezing stiff and standing out like hoops when she walked."

Despite the restrictiveness of contemporary styles, it was also the era of the New Woman and opinions about acceptable dress were changing. Since the 1870s, farsighted reformers had been calling for softer, looser women's

Many female stampeders boldly shortened their hems. Dawson City, 1898.

clothing. While few of the ideas of this "rational dress" movement had gained wide acceptance, a number of women wore flannel dresses on the trail. Some even went so far as to abandon their corsets. An increase in women's participation in sports had also begun to influence fashion. The newly invented bicycle was all the rage, and bloomers, which had been introduced and rejected in the 1850s, had reemerged as the costume of choice for female cycling enthusiasts.

Bloomers, or knickers as they were also called, were baggy pants that were gathered below the knees, or sometimes at the ankles. They were often worn under a knee-length or calf-length skirt, since many people were still scandalized by clothing that revealed women's lower limbs. One woman wrote to the San Francisco *Examiner* to tell prospective stampeders that no woman should attempt the Chilkoot Pass unless she wore bloomers, as she herself had done. Long dresses were dangerous, she advised, although she thought a short skirt worn over the bloomers would not be an impediment.

A number of newspapers and guidebooks offered women guidance in preparing for an expedition to the gold fields. Annie Hall Strong, writing in the *Skaguay News* on December 31, 1897, provided a detailed packing list for Klondike-bound women. "First and most important of all," she admonished, "is the selection of proper footwear." She recommended including one pair each of the following: house slippers; knitted slippers; heavy-soled walking shoes (a "tall bicycle shoe with extra sole" was her suggestion); rubbers to fit over the walking shoes; arctics (presumably a type of boot); felt boots; heavy gum boots; ice creepers; and moccasins, which she noted could be purchased from local Indians. In terms of clothing, she considered the minimum requirements to be:

1 good dress
1 suit heavy mackinaw, waist (similar to a blouse) and bloomers
1 summer suit, waist and bloomers
3 short skirts of heavy duck or denim, to wear over bloomers
3 suits winter underwear
3 suits summer underwear
1 chamois undervest
1 long sack nightdress, made of eiderdown or flannel
1 cotton nightdress
2 pair Arctic mittens

1 pair heavy wool gloves
1 cap
1 Arctic hood
1 hat with brim broad enough to hold the mosquito netting away
   from the face
1 summer dress
3 aprons
2 wrappers
2 shirt waists
Some sort of gloves for summer wear to protect the hands from
   mosquitoes
1 pair German socks
3 pair heavy all-wool stockings
3 pair summer stockings

The San Francisco *Examiner* also published a list of necessities for women on their way north, drawn up by an anonymous "woman who has roughed it on the Klondyke." The inventory of garments included "three warm, woollen dresses, with comfortable bodices and skirts knee length— flannel-lined preferable" and "three pairs of knickers or bloomers to match the dresses."[10]

Although, as Martha Purdy discovered, voluminous bloomers could be almost as troublesome as long skirts, very few women were so bold as to wear trousers. In March 1898, a few women dressed like men in the typical miner's outfits were seen boarding a Klondike-bound steamer in Victoria. These brave souls may have regretted their decision to choose comfort over convention when faced with the vituperative comments of some of the men they encountered en route. One man, appalled to see members of "the fair sex" donning men's shirts and pants, was of the opinion that the "horrid bloomer girls of the West are as modestly attired as a discreet Boston maiden in comparison with the female argonauts."[11]

The debate over what was appropriate apparel for female stampeders was a lively one, but ultimately women, like men, had a more important question to consider: which route they should take to the Klondike. The three main choices were the all-water route up the Pacific coast to St. Michael, Alaska, and then up the Yukon River to Dawson; the all-Canadian overland routes that began in northern British Columbia and in Edmonton, Alberta; and the parallel Chilkoot and White Pass trails leading from Skagway, Alaska, to the headwaters of the Yukon River. Each had advantages and disadvantages.

By far the easiest way to reach the Klondike was the all-water route. It was also the most costly. Another major drawback was that the last third of the trip—seventeen hundred miles up the Yukon—could only be completed during the two or three summer months when the river was ice-free and still had enough water for steamships to operate. Most of the stampeders who tried to get to Dawson by this route in 1897 got no farther than St. Michael before the navigation season came to a close. Twenty-five hundred unfortunate souls spent a bitter winter at various points along the river. In subsequent years, this kind of miscalculation rarely occurred and travellers were assured of a comfortable journey.

Among the most gruelling avenues to the Klondike were the various all-Canadian routes, enthusiastically promoted by businessmen who wanted to capture a share of the lucrative outfitting market. These routes were also championed by patriots concerned that the majority of Klondikers were from the United States. With Canada's sovereignty not yet firmly established in the North, this influx of Americans was a sensitive issue. Accurate information about these trails was almost impossible to come by, although the exaggerations and lies of those touting the all-Canadian routes were no worse than those of the other routes' advocates.

One of the all-Canadian routes actually began in Wrangell, Alaska, but earned its designation because the 1871 Treaty of Washington had given Canada the right of free navigation on the Stikine River. When the Canadian government decided to send a military contingent into the Yukon as a symbol of Canadian sovereignty in 1898, the Stikine trail was the chosen route. The two-hundred-man Yukon Field Force was accompanied by six women: Toronto *Globe* correspondent Faith Fenton; Mrs. Starnes, the wife of a North-West Mounted Police officer stationed in Dawson; and four members of the newly formed Victorian Order of Nurses.

The four-day trip up the Stikine River to Glenora, B.C. was a mixture of breath-taking scenery, heart-stopping moments, and stretches of pure tedium. Shallow sections, where the paddle-wheelers that carried the Yukon Field Force grounded on sand bars every few hours, alternated with narrow canyons, where the captains ordered the boilers stoked to the limit and they inched their way upstream, gingerly making their way past boulders that lurked beneath the seething waters. Most travellers found the latter part of the journey—down the Teslin River to Fort Selkirk, and then on down the Yukon River to Dawson—easy in comparison. But in between the two river sections was a punishing 150-mile trek from Glenora to Teslin Lake.

"The trail is bad," wrote nurse Georgia Powell after the month-long ordeal was over,

> bad for people and very bad for packed animals. . . . From mountain to swamp and bog—bogs into whose cold, damp, mossy depths we would sink to our knees . . . swamps where we trampled down bushes and shrubs to make footing for ourselves . . . and where the mosquitoes held high revelry. Let me say right here, for number, size and ferocity these mosquitoes cannot be exaggerated, and despite leggings, gloves and the inevitable veil we were badly bitten. Through deep forest we went, where the trail was narrow and the branches of trees threatened our eyes or tore our veils disastrously, through tracts of burnt and blackened country, in some places the ashes still hot from recent burnings, and the dust rising in choking clouds after our feet; through forests of wind-fallen, upturned trees, whose gnarled roots and tangled branches made insecure and often painful footing; over sharp and jagged rocks where slipping would be dangerous, we went trampling, leaping, springing and climbing, a strain that only the strongest and most sinewy women could bear.[12]

A defeated Klondiker pauses on her return journey up the Athabasca River to Edmonton in 1899.

The trail conditions that Georgia described were similar to those on the overland routes beginning in Edmonton. The difference was that the various ill-defined routes that wound their way across northern Alberta and British Columbia and into the Yukon were between fifteen and twenty-five hundred miles long. Stampeders setting off from Edmonton typically took up to two years to achieve their goal, if they made it at all. Of the sixteen hundred people who departed from Edmonton, bound for the Klondike, only about half succeeded, the others either turning back or perishing along the way. Many of those who managed to complete the journey found that by the time they reached Dawson the gold rush excitement was over.

The first woman to depart from Edmonton for the Klondike was Nellie Garner from Fresno, California. On August 24, 1897, Nellie, her husband, and three friends set off on horseback, aiming for the Peace River district and the Liard and Pelly rivers beyond. It appeared to be the most direct way to get to Dawson from Edmonton, but the trail was appallingly bad. The Garner party barely made six hundred miles before the snow began to pile up, forcing them to stop and spend the winter just across the Alberta-B.C. border.

The following spring they continued on their way up the Peace River towards the Rocky Mountains, only to turn back in late July because several members of their party were too sick with scurvy to continue. They hob-

In August 1897, Nellie Garner became the first woman to attempt any of the Edmonton routes to the Klondike.

bled back into Edmonton on September 5, 1898, and regretfully returned to California, never having even come close to reaching their destination.

The longer routes out of Edmonton followed the Peace and Athabasca rivers north to the mighty Mackenzie and then branched off to the west at various points along the way. More people managed to reach the Klondike by these routes than by the other Edmonton trails, but few realized beforehand what an epic journey they were about to embark upon. Emily and A.C. Craig, the Chicago couple with Viking blood in their veins, chose the Mackenzie River route on the advice of a guide who claimed to be experienced but turned out to have never previously been beyond the Chicago city limits. Since this revelation came after he had already spent their money on supplies, they decided there was nothing to do but carry on. The Craigs left Chicago on August 25, 1897, and finally reached the Klondike on August 30, 1899, with no thanks to the leader of their party, who had abandoned them two months into the trip.

Like many female stampeders, Emily soon discovered she was entirely responsible for cooking for her party and would not be paid for her services. It was not a question of fair division of labour since there were thirteen men in the group to share the heavy work, while she carried the domestic burden alone. Furthermore, she was just as tired at the end of the day from walking as they were.

Emily had only ever cooked for herself and her husband, and always in a well-equipped kitchen with a grocery store around the corner. Now she was faced with trying to make appetizing meals for fourteen people, three times a day, from flour, corn meal, salt pork, beans, dried potatoes, dried onions, and dried eggs. As if that was not enough of a test, one of the men in the party was a ventriloquist and thought it amusing to make the stove talk while she was cooking. Emily did not share his sense of humour.

It was a common complaint among women on the trail that men did not recognize that temperamental portable stoves, lack of ingredients, rain, and mosquitoes all made even simple meal preparation an onerous task. Emily met one woman who quit cooking for the men in her party after they threw dishes at her because they did not appreciate her culinary efforts. As Rebecca Ellery of the Salvation Army Klondike contingent noted, her greatest challenge was trying to keep enough good food cooked for the men. "Some of them want it like they would get it at home," she complained secretly to her diary. "They don't seem to have got into the way of putting up with things as they come."[13]

Fortunately for Emily, her party split up after their guide left them. She cheerfully bid adieu to the annoying ventriloquist and the eleven other hungry men, and she and her husband proceeded alone. By the time the Craigs saw the lights of Dawson, they had been on the trail for twenty-four months, clambering over deadfalls in dense spruce forests, slogging through muskeg, and braving wind-swept lakes and wild rivers in hand-built boats. They had spent one winter living in the Hudson's Bay Company carpentry shop at Fort Resolution, and another north of the Arctic Circle in a small cabin on the Rat River near Fort McPherson. Yet despite the hardships, Emily looked fondly back on their adventure as a time when they were "alone and free—alone where nature's scenery was grand and the very solitude drew us close together."[14]

Meanwhile, there was little solitude for stampeders who had chosen to approach the Klondike by the Chilkoot or White Pass routes. Although parts of the trip over the coastal mountains from Skagway and down the Yukon River could be as difficult and hazardous as the all-Canadian routes, this was the most direct and least expensive way to reach the gold fields, and therefore, the most popular.

Most Klondike-bound steamers departed from Seattle, Victoria, Vancouver, or San Francisco. The trip from Seattle to Skagway took from five to seven days. For some it was like a luxury cruise; for others a week in hell.

On board the *Athenian*, Lillian Oliver wrote to her "Dear Hub" that the scenery was grand. "Mountains on the right, and open sea on the left. Sun shines brightly, and porpoises and whales are playing around us on all sides." Lillian's enjoyment of the sights was not impaired by seasickness, but she noted that half her fellow passengers were "laid up for repairs, and the rest look[ed] green around the mouth."[15]

Lulu Craig, a teacher who had taken a year's leave of absence from her job to accompany her brother and his family to Dawson, also waxed poetic as she sailed north in February 1898.

What a fascinating picture to stand on deck and watch the dashing, foamy waves sparkle and gleam in the bright sunshine, the flying of graceful sea gulls and the ducking of little water-quails ever and anon, as they skim over the water; the mountains dimly visible in the distance through the low overhanging clouds. To these pleasures of sight are added that charmingly delightful feeling which steals over one's senses as the steamship is propelled so smoothly over the quiet waters.[16]

The latter part of Lulu's trip was less pleasant, as the views were obscured by dense fog. When a snowstorm restricted visibility even further, the ship ran aground and was stranded for seven hours. A fire in the linen room added to the tension during the long night as they waited for the tide to rise and lift them off the rocks.

Unperturbed as Lulu was by this episode, she and other steamship passengers had good reason to fear for their safety. Within days of the arrival of the gold-laden *Portland* in Seattle on July 17, 1897, thousands of people had begun trying to book passage to Alaska. Soon every vessel along the Pacific coast—seaworthy or not—was pressed into service. A shortage of competent men to run the boats often left passengers at the mercy of alcoholic captains and inexperienced crews. Since little effort was made to clean the ships and make them fit for human use, even some first-class passengers found themselves covered in coal dust or sleeping in compartments that still looked and smelled like cattle pens.

Unscrupulous owners filled boats beyond capacity, knowing that the desperate stampeders would put up with almost anything to reach Alaska. The crowding was particularly disturbing for women because they were not used to being in such close proximity to hordes of men. A proper Victorian woman would normally never dream of sleeping in a room with a man to whom she was not married, yet some had no choice.

The fashionably attired Martha Purdy, travelling with her brother and family friends, had paid the extravagant sum of $120 to reserve an entire cabin for herself to ensure privacy. When she boarded the *Utopia* she was dismayed to discover that she would have to share her quarters. The double berth below hers had been assigned to a gambler and his female companion. Above her was a woman of doubtful morals named Birdie. Unable to convince the purser to alter the arrangements, she resigned herself to the situation. Once she got over her initial indignation at being thrown together with such people, she realized they were not as bad as she had expected.

I became accustomed to my stateroom companions; their kindness soothed my outraged feelings. Every morning the gambler brought me coffee, and I heard his bedfellow tell him, "You see that her toast is thin, you know she has a delikat stummick." Birdie, too, often gave me an orange or apple from her supplies. No longer did I weep in secret at our strange sleeping arrangements.[17]

The ocean voyage ended at the head of the Lynn Canal. Travellers disembarked at Skagway if they had chosen the White Pass trail, or continued ten miles farther up the waterway to Dyea if they were going in over the Chilkoot Pass. The two routes converged at lakes Lindeman and Bennett, the beginning of navigable waters on the Yukon River system.

Skagway was the larger of the two towns and the most notorious. Northbound travellers heard many alarming stories of the perils that would greet them there. One woman was so upset by accounts she heard along the way that she almost turned back at Juneau. "Judging from the terrible tales told by returning and disheartened gold-seekers I was to fall among the riff-raff of the whole country. . . . Cut-throats and mobs of evil-doers were said to form the population, and it was alleged they lay in wait for the arrival of 'tenderfeet.'"[18] What she actually found when she got up the nerve to venture ashore was surging crowds but a general air of order and calm, with "no evidence of violence or crime—nothing but kindness." Similarly, Lillian Oliver found the town much quieter than she expected after having heard it was run by gamblers and "toughs."

The majority of contemporary observers described Skagway as a wild and dangerous place, overrun with criminals who specialized in conning naive stampeders out of their money or luring them into vulnerable situations and robbing them. Nevertheless, there are few accounts of women travellers being preyed upon, perhaps because of chivalry on the part of the thugs and con artists, or maybe because women were more accustomed to being cautious. To Clare Boyntan, a forty-year-old divorcée travelling with three other women, Skagway seemed a lawless, desperately wicked town, with shooting day and night. Yet she gave no indication that she or her friends felt threatened during the few days they spent there making final preparations for their journey.

In the early days of the gold rush, neither Skagway nor Dyea had wharves for the steamers. The ships dropped anchor, and passengers were ferried to shore in small boats, while their cargo was loaded onto barges towed by tugs. Because Canadian officials had decreed that no stampeder could enter Canada without a year's worth of food and supplies, each person arrived with approximately fifteen hundred pounds of provisions. Landing at low tide meant a frantic scramble to move the tons of freight off the mud flats before the sea rose again. Then began the task of transporting everything across the mountains to the point where boat travel could be resumed.

Although the forty-two-mile White Pass trail was longer than the Chilkoot trail, it had the advantage of more gradual grades. Theoretically, this meant it was negotiable by pack animals, but many of the pathetic creatures that were pressed into service were completely unfit for the work and perished along the way. Even healthy animals broke their legs in crevices, lost their footing on the narrow paths that snaked along precipitous ledges, and drowned under the weight of their loads during river crossings. No one who travelled this route at the height of the gold rush could ever forget the misery and carnage.

Alice Rollins Crane, a California ethnologist on a scientific mission, observed many instances of pack animals being treated cruelly on the White Pass trail during the winter of 1898. She was shocked that

> with few exceptions, men and women seemed to have lost common decency, showing no feeling for . . . the poor, unfortunate brutes which fell into their keeping. . . . The air rang constantly, night and day, with curses, oaths, screams, the braying of asses and cries of tortured dogs, which were beaten, yelping in agony and crying for mercy, but seldom receiving it. What I saw and heard on the [White Pass trail] will never be effaced from my mind. It is an awful nightmare; purgatory itself could be no worse.[19]

Clare Boyntan recorded similar impressions. Like Alice, she was spared the stench of rotting carcasses that sickened summer travellers, but not the sights and sounds.

> We camped at the foot of a huge boulder, an awful canyon. The boulder, named I believe, for its resemblance to a porcupine. The quills represented by sharp needle like rocks over which were great awful rocks, steep and extremely dangerous. There was a dreadful suffering of the poor men and animals trying to get their outfits over the hill. My heart just ached for . . . the poor patient horses, burros, oxen and dogs that

Clare Boyntan's heart ached for the bruised and bleeding pack animals along the trail.

were bruised and bleeding till the trail was simply a trail of blood. . . . The strain and hardships told on the men and many of them were cruel almost beyond description. Numbers of poor beasts gave up the struggle and on both sides of the trail we could count their bodies by the dozens.

This is one of the most heartrending scenes I witnessed: A man was trying to drive up this awful hill with a young spirited horse, with a four foot loaded sled hitched behind. This brute (I cannot call him a man) cursed at and beat this poor horse with an axe handle with all his might for half an hour. Then he took a long rope and fastened it around the horse's neck and pulled the rope up over the limb of a tree, pulling the horses two hind legs together, and then cut an ear off, leaving the horse to die! The man went on up the trail, and has never been seen since. The horse died before morning, even though he was cut down from his strangling condition.[20]

Aside from her distress about the mistreatment of animals on the trail, Clare generally enjoyed the trek. When her party camped at the barren White

Pass summit she was entranced by the way "the stars snapped and sparkled, and the pure white snow glistened like a myriad of diamonds."[21] Although it was sixty degrees below zero, she slept comfortably in her fur coat, hood, and mittens. No doubt the privacy of her own tent was a relief after staying at the White Pass Hotel on the previous night. It had been Clare's first experience in a Klondike roadhouse, and not at all what she was used to.

Clare and another of the women who preferred to walk rather than add their own weight to the already overburdened sled dogs had gone ahead of the group. The others were to join them the next day.

> The day was perfect. A long winding hill, not steep, with rocks and great trees on each side, made the walking easy. We walked the nine miles, but were so tired we sat down on a snowbank to rest. I saw no sign of the hotel, so asked a man whom we met how far it was to the White Pass Hotel. He said, "Why bless your blue eyes! There it is a hundred feet ahead." I said, "Oh, is that it? I thought that was a horse stable or pig sty!" Well, I was glad our tramp for that day was over and thought I would rest and have dinner. I went in and asked the landlord if he would please show me to my room, as I was very tired. He looked at me a moment, then roared with several other men who were sitting there. Then he said, "Well, Miss, I've only these two rooms. One is a kitchen, the other is a barroom, dining room and settin' room. You'll have to sleep here if you stay." My heart sank, but soon other women came and at 10:30 PM the landlord spread some blankets on the floor, with the others to be used as covering, and we all slept side by side—five women with our heads under the bar.[22]

It seemed they had hardly closed their eyes before it was four o'clock and the landlord was rousing them so he could serve breakfast and whiskey to his early morning customers.

Crude as the White Pass Hotel seemed to a New York City woman like Clare, it was no worse than most accommodation along the trails. Della Banks described one White Pass roadhouse she stayed in as nothing more than

> a large tent divided through the center into two long, narrow rooms; one the kitchen and dining room, the other a bunk room. The bunk room had a tier of three single bunks at one end, a large stove in the

middle, and a tier of three double bunks at the other. A blanket in front of the double bunks closed them off as a "ladies' annex"....

As first-comers, Mrs. Brand and I chose the lower bunk. Very crude they were, each made of four poles built in a square, with a fifth pole in the center to divide it into two beds. A canvas bottom was nailed to the four poles, but not to the fifth. Whoever got into bed first sank down into a long hole, to be brought up level when her partner got in on the other side. Luckily Mrs. Brand and I were about equal in weight.[23]

Lillian Oliver, on the other hand, had the rare pleasure of sleeping on a feather bed at the Wisconsin House hotel on the Chilkoot Pass trail.

<hr/>

Much of the thirty-three-mile Chilkoot trail was no more arduous than the White Pass route, but the final half-mile ascent to the summit of the pass was extremely demanding. Most of the women who struggled up it had led sedentary lives prior to embarking on this adventure, as had many of the men. What they lacked in physical fitness, however, they generally made up for in perseverance. The women often proved tougher than others expected and sometimes even surprised themselves.

Lillian Oliver had several harrowing experiences on the Chilkoot trail, which she described in a series of letters to her ailing husband back in Chicago. On June 11 she wrote home from Canyon City, one of several bustling, makeshift settlements that had sprung up along the trail.

I am not gifted enough to tell you of the awful grandeur of my first day's walk on the bed of the river, between Dyea and this place. The river crossed our path fourteen times. I crossed on a fallen tree once, waded four times, and was carried across nine times. We walked on and on, and did not see anything of [Canyon City], so I had to call a halt. I had started with the determination of keeping my troubles to myself, but ... my feet were too blistered to go further. We had had a terrible walk four miles over sharp rocks, and I was in great pain every step I took. I wanted to lie down and rest, but was afraid of bears; for they had been seen on this part of the trail. At length, becoming too tired to resist, I lay down by the side of the trail.... After a while tired nature got the better of me and I fell asleep. Don't know how long I had slept, when I was startled by a noise near by, and, hearing the guide jump up, concluded the bears had come. Without waiting to ascertain,

I set up a yell that would have wakened the dead; and on jumping up was in time to see a horse shying and trying to throw its rider. No wonder; I had tied a large towel round my head to keep those dreadful mosquitoes from eating me up, and it was this white thing popping up out of the bush, accompanied by the scream, that had startled the poor horse.[24]

Once Lillian regained her composure, she discovered they had stopped just short of Canyon City, which was about eight miles from Dyea. After finding a restaurant in the town and eating, she and her guide rested until the heat of the day had abated. Then they pushed on. The final five miles to Sheep Camp, the last staging area before the gruelling climb to the pass, was

over a terrible trail—through heavy woods, along steep, rocky, and often boggy hillsides, broken by several deep gullies. The ascent was abrupt in places, and over huge masses of fallen rock, or steep, slippery surfaces of rock. . . . At our feet was flowing a fearful river, boiling and bubbling over huge boulders. . . . We crossed this on three logs thrown over for a bridge, and it trembled as we touched it.[25]

Fear and exhaustion did not prevent Lillian from appreciating the scenery, especially once she reached Sheep Camp and the Wisconsin House hotel with its cozy feather beds. Having checked in and eaten her "first decent meal since leaving the ship," she continued her correspondence.

In front of the window where I am writing is a waterfall, tumbling down in a huge white mass from a glacier . . . 5,000 ft. above. . . . Oh! who would live in civilization when they can surround themselves with such pictures? I step out and breathe this pure, fresh air, fill my lungs, and it makes me stronger, braver, to do and dare.[26]

Lillian would need all her strength and courage for the next day. Only after she was "safe and sound over the much-dreaded Pass" and relaxing on the shores of Lake Lindeman did she take up her pen again.

We crossed [the Chilkoot Pass] at 1:30 a.m. Monday, and it was as light as day—our party being the only one in sight. I must plead guilty to being nervous, and was afraid to look back for fear I would fall to the bottom. Imagine a mountain near 4,000ft. high at an angle of 45deg., covered with snow to a depth of about 40ft., and which during the day, gets soft, making climbing easier—but at night freezes over, making walking not only hard but fearfully dangerous. I could not get a foothold. My rubber boots caused me to slip backwards. The guide went ahead and dug holes with his heels in the ice for me to put my feet into; I taking hold of his hand and with my other carrying a stick, which I drove down into the snow and held on to. Every now and then I got so nervous, that I had to sit down on the snow. In this way, after hard work, I finally reached the top, and though it was intensely cold, I was in a profuse perspiration. . . .

The Chilkoot Pass is difficult and dangerous to those not possessed of steady nerves, for towards the summit there is a sheer ascent of 1,000ft., where a slip would certainly be fatal. At the actual summit, which for seven or eight miles is bare of trees or bushes, the trail leads through a narrow, rocky gap, and the whole scene is one of the most

The sheer ascent to the summit of the Chilkoot Pass was an intimidating sight.

complete desolation. Naked granite rocks rise steeply to snow-clad mountains on either side. Descending [on the inland side of the summit] is equally bad travelling, largely over areas of shattered rocks, where the trail may easily be lost.[27]

Georgia White, a widow from California who had left her children in the care of friends while she went north to seek her fortune, also found her nerves needed steadying as she climbed the Chilkoot Pass. During the ascent, she and her friend, Minna, stopped every few minutes to rest and sip from a bottle of spirits they carried. By the time they reached the summit the liquor had gone a little to Georgia's head, but she carried on and reached Lake Lindeman eleven hours after leaving Sheep Camp. Too tired for supper, she drank a glass of hot lemonade, had an arnica bath, and fell into bed. Her bones, she said, ached all night.

Not all women found the pass so daunting. When Edna Bush made the crossing she got to the top with energy to spare. Her sister and brother-in-law, Ethel and Clarence Berry, who were on their second trip in to the Klondike, wanted to rest before starting down. "But not I!" decided the exuberant young Edna. "I picked up a small piece of board and, using it as a sled, I tucked my feet up, held my skirts between my knees, and with one big 'whoopee' I was on my way."[28]

Although weather made a great deal of difference in how difficult the crossing was, there was no ideal season for tackling the Chilkoot Pass. While pleasant for travelling, the warm, sunny days of spring and summer were the most dangerous time for avalanches which thundered down without warning, burying supplies and sometimes taking lives. The worst such incident was the April 3, 1898, snow slide at Sheep Camp which killed sixty-three men and one woman. In winter, snow smoothed the edges of the jagged rocks and made climbing easier, but the constant cold sapped people's energy and storms often impeded progress.

When Emma Kelly, a correspondent for the Kansas City *Star,* arrived at Dyea late in the fall of 1897, blizzards had set in on the pass and she could find no experienced packers willing to attempt a crossing. Anxious to reach Lake Lindeman before freeze-up, she approached deck-hands from the steamships and managed to assemble a team of ten men, none of whom had ever packed on the trail.

After securing my packers I waited a day in Dyea for the subsidence of the storm, keeping my men herded away from the old packers, who were full of fearful accounts of the dangers of the storm on the pass.

On the following day I secured Healy and Wilson's pack train to take my goods to Sheep Camp . . . with my packers I fell in immediately behind the horses, and after plodding all day through slush and muck, in the face of a terrific storm of sleet which drove into our faces like tacks, we reached Sheep Camp at five o'clock in the evening. As the storm was still raging I had to lay over a day waiting for it to subside, having again to herd my packers from those in camp.

The trail from Dyea to Sheep Camp, always terrible, was in wretched condition, the entire distance being through snow, slush, and muck, up sharp elevations, down precipitous cañons, and over rocks and bowlders covered with snow and ice. Up to the winding cañon the trail crosses one stream sixty-one times, and when the water was too deep for me to wade, I would have a packer carry me over on his back.[29]

At Sheep Camp, some of Emma's men wanted to turn back, but she refused to release them from their contracts, telling them that if she could make the trip they could also. Fortunately, the weather cleared. The next day they made it over the pass and to Lake Lindeman without incident. Although she had been up at 5:00 A.M. to cook breakfast, and on the trail for fourteen and a half hours, Emma ate only a few mouthfuls of dinner before setting out to try to arrange boat transportation to Dawson for herself, her Newfoundland dog, and her thousand pounds of supplies. This done, she finally retired to her tent for a well-earned rest. She woke up the following morning barely able to move.

I was lying on the ground, rolled up in my blanket, and was so sore and stiff and ached so from the long climb and walk in the water, mud, and snow of the previous day, that I was unable to get up without help. One of the men helped me, and I had almost to crawl about that day, but I made no complaint that I felt badly and said nothing of my condition for fear I would be thought a nuisance from the start.[30]

Having survived the rigours of the trail from Skagway or Dyea, most stampeders believed the worst of the journey was behind them. There were, however, a number of potential hazards to be faced during the five-hundred-mile boat trip to Dawson. The journey began with a series of lake crossings, often made risky by strong winds. Once onto the river, there were several sets of rapids to be negotiated. Overloading, poor boat construction, and lack of navigational skills greatly increased the accident rate. The lucky ones were merely delayed for a few days while they dried their outfits; those not favoured by fate lost everything they owned, and sometimes their lives. Lillian Oliver noted that scarcely a day passed during the trip downriver when she did not see a cairn or wooden cross marking the final resting place of a fellow traveller.

In June 1898, Superintendent Sam Steele of the North-West Mounted Police decreed that the swift waters of Miles Canyon and Whitehorse Rapids were too hazardous to be attempted by women or children. Prior to the issuing of this protective edict, 150 boats had been wrecked in this stretch of water, resulting in the deaths of ten men. It was, however, already common practice for members of "the weaker sex" to walk around the dangerous sections. Only the most daring braved the boiling waters and treacherous rocks, almost invariably against the wishes of their male travelling companions.

Ethnologist Alice Crane, who was travelling solo, claimed the distinction of being the first white woman to run the Whitehorse Rapids. Never

The wild waters of Miles Canyon thrilled women like Emma Kelly.

had she felt "lighter-hearted or more like singing,"[31] she said, than during her exhilarating seven-and-a-half-minute whitewater ride.

Another female thrill-seeker was Emma Kelly of the Kansas City *Star*, who "wanted to see and experience this so-called danger, which men freely court, but which women may only read or hear of." She enjoyed her first time through Miles Canyon so much that she decided to do it again. While walking back to the top of the rapids, she fell fifteen feet down a cliff and lay there unconscious until her dog's barking alerted a passerby. Although she felt "pretty badly shaken up," her tumble did nothing to dampen her enthusiasm. After her second run through the narrow, high-walled canyon, she continued on to the treacherous Whitehorse Rapids, a few miles downstream.

> [These] rapids looked much more dangerous than those at the cañon. The foaming, angry waters, piled high in the channel, looked as if some immense stern-wheel boat were running, bottom up, beneath them, churning and lashing them into a fury. As for the ride through, I do not know when I ever enjoyed anything so much in my life. I snugly stowed myself away in the prow of the boat, the men got ready . . . and we were off. The boat gave a screech, a groan, seemed to stretch itself and reach its nose to every bounding billow. . . . On we went, faster and faster yet. . . . Wild waves rocked and rolled our boat and occasionally broke over us. The spray rose so thick and high we could not see the shore, the very air seeming a sea of misty spray. It was simply glorious. All too soon we rowed into comparatively smooth yet rapid water. A few more strokes of the oars sent us to the shore and the ride was over, leaving a sensation never to be forgotten.[32]

Again she could not resist a second trip. This time she worked one of the oars, which prompted wild cheering from the men watching on the riverbanks, though Emma herself did not feel she had done anything particularly remarkable.

The second most feared navigational hazard was Five Finger Rapids. Frances Dorley, the Seattle dressmaker who had gone north with her parents' reluctant blessings, nearly became one of its many victims because of the stubbornness of her travelling companions. Frances had joined a party of three men in Skagway, working as their cook in exchange for travelling with them to Dawson. As long as she kept to her domestic role, all was well, but the men did not take kindly to her offering counsel on matters they considered outside her feminine sphere.

> I had bought a book in Skagway which told of the great dangers hidden in the foaming water that churned violently between the menacing rock spires from which the rapids derived their name. I suggested we follow the advice given in my book, and take the channel furthest to the west— supposedly the only safe course. The little Scot, McChord, hooted at my "book-learned knowledge," and shouted that I, being a woman, could know nothing about navigation. With true masculine loyalty, the other men sided with him.
>
> The argument continued until we were almost upon the rapids. As our shallow boat floundered helplessly in the churning water, the three men grudgingly conceded that I was probably right and that we'd better try to row across to the safer channel.
>
> We all grabbed oars and began rowing frantically with all our strength. We managed to force our way through the turbulent white foam until we were in midstream before we realized that we couldn't possibly reach the far side of the river. We were being drawn into the thundering rapids. We were all thoroughly frightened by this time, and it was a relief when Britton took command and told us to try to shoot through the center.
>
> I closed my eyes, said a little prayer, and tried to hold fast to my ebbing courage. Then we were shooting with brutal speed through the giant finger. Miraculously we passed through with our boat and our lives intact, albeit the former was cruelly battered and the latter sorely threatened.[33]

Beyond Rink Rapids, about six miles downstream from Five Finger Rapids, the only hazards were sand bars. If the weather and mosquitoes cooperated, the rest of the journey could be pleasant and peaceful.

Toronto *Globe* correspondent Faith Fenton, travelling with the Victoria Order of Nurses and the Yukon Field Force, described the scene one September night as they camped along the shores of Teslin Lake. Although they had not yet joined the Yukon River system or braved Five Finger Rapids, it was the type of scene many other stampeders enjoyed as they drifted north to Dawson. After a day of "splendid warmth and sunshine,"

Beyond Rink Rapids, floating down the Yukon River towards Dawson was often peaceful and pleasant.

tents were pitched, and the evening meal served, the men moving about in a glory of sunset color, not glowing with crimson, as in the east, but full of exquisite purples and browns. From deepest velvety purple, through shades of violet and heliotrope, to delicate pearly grey, the higher mountains stood like richly mantled kings, while the lower hills, pine green to the timber line, caught the sun upon their bald, moss-covered brows in a harmony of browns. The lake stretched its half-mile of blue from bank to bank, while far off between the lower heights three snow-capped peaks caught the one touch of scarlet.... a gentle warmth was in the air, and a cobweb breeze toned to delicate softness. Only a Canadian northland sunset—but the most perfect and richest bit of color ever seen.[34]

Emma Kelly, on the other hand, raced the impending winter late in October and endured the worst possible conditions.

We travelled from about eight o'clock in the morning until nearly dark. ... Each day as we proceeded farther north, with the season growing later and the days shorter, the drift ice thicker, the temperature lower, it was, oh! so much colder. ... Finally we could do no more than drift with the ice, which was forming in large cakes ten to twenty feet in size, the blocks wedging around our boat so close that it was impossible to use the oars. . . .

Sitting all day cramped in the little boat, with continuous rain, sleet, and snow, and to save time making no stop for warm noon lunch, but eating frozen bacon and beans left over from breakfast, with the temperature at twenty degrees below zero, and as evening approached working our boat from the middle of the Yukon, through the drift ice, to reach the shore at dark, camping and sitting on the snow while eating our supper, then rolled in wet and frozen blankets for the night, with occasional cuttings of spruce boughs for bedding, was my experience of camp life in the Yukon. . . .

Never a day passed that I did not sit, singing at the top of my voice . . . partly to brace myself up and also because I thought it would help the rowers a little and cheer them as well. Always as a child when alone in the dark I would sing or talk to myself. And though the dangers through which I passed were different from any I had experienced, singing seemed to lessen my fear and give me more heart.[35]

When they reached Fort Selkirk, the twenty-two men with whom Emma was travelling wanted to abandon the river and camp until there was enough snow to continue by dogsled. Just as she had refused to let her reluctant packers quit at the base of the Chilkoot Pass, she now insisted that she had paid for passage to Dawson by boat and would be satisfied with nothing else. Reluctantly they agreed to continue, and on November 1, with the river nearly impassable, they landed at Dawson.

To celebrate their arrival, and to discourage the men from going to the saloons and leaving her alone, Emma put up the money to purchase a couple of bottles of whiskey. While the men drank to their successful journey, Emma played her guitar and led them in singing songs of home.

3

LOYAL WIVES
—and—
HOPEFUL SPINSTERS

When the gold-laden *Portland* steamed into the Seattle harbour on July 17, 1897, thousands of people crowded the waterfront, hoping to catch a glimpse of the new millionaires. Those who saw Ethel Berry walk down the gangplank were astounded to learn that this woman wearing an old wrapper with a necktie as a belt, her laceless shoes flopping with every step, was the wife of one of the most successful Klondike Kings.

From the moment Ethel Berry disembarked on that historic July morning, she was besieged by newspaper reporters and curious strangers. Over and over she was asked why she had gone to the Yukon. "I went," she replied, "because my husband went, and I wanted to be with him."[1] Ethel was but one of the many loyal wives who followed their men to the gold fields, but she was the one proclaimed as "the Bride of the Klondike." Hers was a romantic, rags-to-riches story that had universal appeal: her husband, unable even to afford a diamond ring for their wedding, had taken her to the frozen north for their honeymoon and brought her home sixteen months later, wealthy beyond her wildest dreams.

Clarence Berry, the man Ethel Bush would marry, was one of the early gold-seekers in the Yukon River valley. In the fall of 1895, having been away for two long years, he made a trip outside to visit his family and fiancée in California. Over the winter, Ethel convinced her parents and Clarence himself that the wedding should not be put off any longer. Rather than letting him return to face the trials of the prospecting life alone, she wanted to go with him. Once she had overcome all their objections she began preparing her trousseau, not one "composed of the dainty laces and frills brides

— 39 —

usually have, but good, strong, warm, substantial material that could stand the wear and tear of a year, and maybe more, of that bitter cold country."[2]

After exchanging their vows on March 10, 1896, the newlyweds immediately boarded a steamer in San Francisco and began their "wedding tour," accompanied by five friends who were also going north to search for gold. It took about nine weeks to make their way from Juneau to Forty Mile, by way of the Lynn Canal and the not-yet-famous Chilkoot Pass trail. Ethel, the only woman in the party, was pampered by all the members of the entourage and found it a rather agreeable journey.

> We put on our warm clothes, heavy flannels, fur coats, moccasins, fur cape and gloves. I was rolled snugly in a fur rug and bound securely to a sled, so wherever that sled went I was sure to go whether I wished to or not. We travelled slowly, on account of the dogs. . . .
>
> It was not hard work for me, though. The men pitched the tents at night, cooked the meals and washed the dishes. I had only to hold my hands and play lady. It was an interesting trip; so different from anything I had ever thought or dreamed of before. I was prepared for the hardships, having known perfectly well before I decided to go that it would be no bed of roses, so I did not waste time worrying or fretting, but enjoyed whatever there was to enjoy.[3]

But when they reached Forty Mile, a rough mining town that sprawled across the flats at the junction of the Fortymile and Yukon rivers, the fun was over. No sooner had they arrived than Clarence left on a prospecting jaunt. The five weeks he was gone seemed like an eternity to Ethel, who quickly ran out of activities to fill the days and evenings and distract her from the isolation of her new home.

> There was nothing, absolutely nothing to do. No one who has not had a like experience could appreciate even half the misery contained in those words—nothing to do. Just imagine sitting for hours in one's home doing nothing, looking out a scrap of a window and seeing nothing, searching for work and finding nothing. There were a few people at Forty-mile, but I was not acquainted with them, and at times when I felt I could not bear another minute the utter blankness of such an existence I would walk to a little cemetery near by for consolation. Even a cemetery can be pleasant under such circumstances, if only as a break in the landscape.[4]

The enforced idleness of Ethel's first weeks in the Yukon were in marked contrast to those of Emilie Tremblay, another young bride who ventured north with her miner husband in the pre-Klondike years. Emilie, a twenty-one-year-old French Canadian, arrived in the Fortymile district in 1894. She had just married Pierre-Nolasque Tremblay, better known among his peers as Jack, a thirty-two-year-old veteran prospector whom she had met less than a year before. Jack had been searching for gold in Alaska and the Yukon for seven years and had developed a few rough edges that may not have been obvious to Emilie during their whirlwind courtship.

Emilie was an intrepid soul who, in her old age, thanked God that "the profession of explorer has not been—even in the north—the lot of men alone."[5] She also took pride in being the first white woman to brave the Chilkoot Pass (although that distinction probably belonged to a prostitute known as Dutch Kate who crossed it with a group of miners in 1888). Emilie could not, however, hide her dismay when she first stepped over the threshold of her new home on Miller Creek, which Jack had previously shared with a number of other miners.

The building was a one-room log cabin with a sod roof, half its floor covered with packed dirt and half with split poles laid flat side up. The sole window was made from glass bottles. Emilie was not troubled by the austerity of the cabin. It was the supreme filthiness that stopped her in her tracks. When she enquired about the particularly disgusting mess at the base of a pole in the centre of the room, her husband matter-of-factly told her it was spit. Often when the men lay in their bunks, passing time reading or talking, they chewed tobacco, and in order to avoid hitting each other when they spit, they

Emilie Tremblay before going north with her new husband in 1894.

agreed to aim at the pole. Apparently, none of them had ever bothered cleaning up the brown sludge that had accumulated over the years. This explanation only confirmed Emilie's conviction that her husband was in dire need of a wife's saving graces. To Jack's credit, he did help with the clean-up, which began with a shovel.

During the winter of 1894–95, there were only an estimated twenty-eight non-native women residing in the Yukon, none of them on Miller Creek. The lack of female company was difficult for all the women, but Emilie had a greater social barrier to overcome as she spoke only French. She had, however, brought an English grammar book with her and once the cabin was made liveable, she applied herself to learning the language. Where words failed her, gestures such as preparing an elaborate Christmas dinner for her neighbours did much to endear her to them.

Jack's claims in the Fortymile district were decent ones, but the Klondike strike was the kind of chance he, and every other prospector in the north, had been awaiting for years. Unfortunately, when the discovery was made the Tremblays were in New York visiting relatives. Not until 1898 were they able to return to the Yukon. Although they managed to buy into some good mining properties and prospered from their work in the gold fields over the next sixteen years, they had missed the moment that might have made them millionaires.

The Berrys, on the other hand, were in the right place at the right time. After returning from his five-week prospecting trip, Clarence decided to stay closer to home. It was a fortuitous decision because the day George Carmack swaggered into Forty Mile boasting of his incredible find on the creek he called Bonanza, Clarence was tending bar at McPhee's saloon and was among the first to hear the news. Like every other male in Forty Mile, Clarence immediately dashed up the river and staked a claim. He then returned for his wife and enough provisions to see them through the winter. With his rowboat loaded to the gunnels, he started back for Dawson. Ethel would follow with the rest of the cargo on the next passing paddle-wheeler.

When the *Arctic* steamed into Forty Mile a few days later at six o'clock in the evening, Ethel was informed that she would have to be ready to depart at six the next morning. It was no easy matter to organize five tons of supplies in twelve hours, but with a little help, she managed to meet the deadline.

When the Berrys arrived in Dawson it was bustling with activity. Ethel and Clarence pitched their canvas tent among the hundreds of others scattered across the floodplain at the mouth of the Klondike River and spent several weeks in the new boom town waiting for more permanent lodgings to be constructed on Eldorado Creek. Winter weather was already setting in and Ethel felt constantly chilled by the icy wind. Their hastily built log cabin, once it was finally completed, proved only marginally better than the tent. According to one report, the Berrys "kept warm by cuddling—a thing somewhat unknown in civilized communities, but absolutely necessary with the mercury disappearing in the bulb, and wood worth its weight in gold."[6]

One of Ethel's few female neighbours on Eldorado Creek was a lithe, little woman named Salome Lippy. The two had first met on board the *Arctic* en route to Dawson from Forty Mile. Salome and her husband, Thomas, a brawny former iron worker and YMCA physical-training instructor, were recent arrivals in the Yukon River valley. They had gone north on borrowed money, but staked one of the highest-yielding Klondike claims, eventually taking out more than 1.5 million dollars' worth of gold.

Both Ethel and Salome worked hard their first year in the Klondike. According to Ethel, housekeeping in the north was "no child's play," especially in winter.

> We could not get one drop of water without first melting the ice, which necessitated keeping a fire all day. Keeping the fire is enough to occupy the whole of one person's time. The wood is full of pitch and blazes up and is out again almost before one can walk across the room and back. . . . All our supplies, which we kept in the cache, had to go through the same process of thawing before being cooked.[7]

Since visitors were frequent and could never be refused hospitality, Ethel rarely cooked only for Clarence and herself. On one occasion, ten men arrived at their door just as the Berrys were sitting down to eat. They were welcomed without hesitation, but since the meal she had prepared could not be stretched to serve twelve, Ethel had to cook another entire dinner. She never resented this spontaneous entertaining, however, because the men usually helped her in the kitchen, something she was quite unaccustomed to back home.

Aside from sharing meals, there was little time for diversions. "We never felt like playing games or going in for any kind of amusements after the day's hard work was done," Ethel told journalists who assailed her upon her return to the United States. "We did not think of anything but sleep and rest. That was the main reason we did not die of homesickness. We had no time to think. Good, hard work is the most effectual remedy for discontent."[8] Salome echoed her neighbour's words: "Amusements? Well, nobody bothered much about amusements. Everyone was busy and kept busy all the time. I did my work. Mining is . . . genuine toil, and when Mr. Lippy finished he wanted to rest."[9]

After the first demanding winter, homes were improved and mining operations better established. Once there was more time for relaxation, cabins where wives and sisters resided became social centres. These warm havens of home-cooking, female laughter, and domestic refinements were a respectable alternative to the saloons and dance halls.

By the time Edna Bush—the woman who hiked up her skirts and tobogganed down from the Chilkoot Pass on a board—joined her sister Ethel

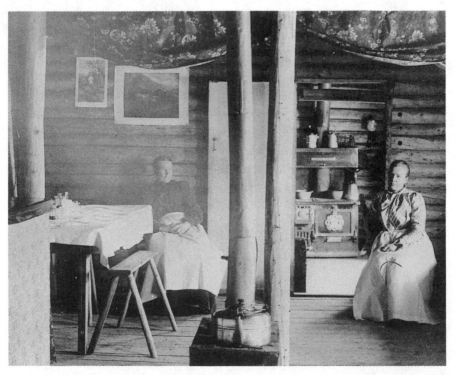

The presence of women usually meant home-cooking and cozy domesticity.

on Eldorado Creek in 1898, the Berry home was a much livelier place. Friends often gathered for card games that went well into the night, and although the women never played, they watched and bantered with the men and sat up talking until morning after the games were over. They also made sure the guests were well fed. In summer, when it barely got dark at night, Edna and Ethel thought nothing of preparing a full meal at two or three in the morning, complete with hot biscuits and all the trimmings.

Her sister's company and a more comfortable house may have altered Ethel's outlook, but when asked after her first year in the north what advice she would give women contemplating joining the stampede, her reply was a blunt "Don't go." She qualified this, however, by adding that, although the Klondike was no place for single women, wives were always a help to their husbands.

> It's much better for a man . . . if he has a wife along. Whatever stories of miserable living and excessive hardship there are, are about the poor fellows who had not sufficient outfit or suffered by their own poor cooking.
>
> The men are not much at cooking up there, and that is the reason they suffer with stomach troubles, and . . . scurvy. After a man has worked hard all day in the diggings he doesn't much feel like cooking a nice meal when he goes to his cabin, cold, tired and hungry, and finds no fire in the stove and all the food frozen.[10]

Cooking nutritious meals was not the only contribution women made to the welfare of their men. Although the feminine ideal in the late nineteenth century was still one of modesty, fragility, and helplessness, some women were better equipped to cope with the Klondike experience than their men. Mrs. Adler, for instance, was clearly the strong one in her family.

When the Adlers discovered at the end of their voyage from San Francisco that they were to be offloaded on a rocky point five miles from Dyea, Mrs. Adler was the one who confronted the purser and demanded they be taken all the way to town. Her objections fell on deaf ears, however, and the Adlers and their fellow passengers were soon standing on the shore, surrounded by their tons of provisions, while the *Noyo* and its uncooperative crew steamed south for another load of gullible stampeders. "It was then," a returning stampeder explained in the San Francisco *Examiner* of August 24, 1897, that Mrs. Adler and her niece gave evidence of true grit and pluck. Mr. Adler is a weakly sort of man and his sons seem helpless. Mrs. Adler and her niece had donned short skirts and knickerbockers just before they went ashore, and the moment they landed they went to work and soon had their supplies in a pile ready to transport up the river. Mrs. Adler was rolling bundles and boxes about with the assistance of her niece. She hired boats, stowed freight on board and soon had the supplies well on their way to Dyea.

Shortly after setting off down the trail, Mr. Adler fell while crossing a stream and knocked himself out. His wife and niece quickly pulled him from the water and revived him by vigorously rubbing him with alcohol.

Solomon Schuldenfrei may not have been as hapless as Mr. Adler, but his wife knew he was no hardy outdoorsman and refused to let him go to the Klondike alone. Described by one woman who met her in Seattle as "the Lady who goes to the Klondike in a silk skirt,"[11] Rebecca Schuldenfrei was no more accustomed to roughing it than her husband. Nevertheless, she felt she would worry less if she were at his side.

Beckie and Sol had both immigrated to the United States when very young. Born in Cracow in the Austro-Hungarian empire and raised in New York City, they were urbanites to the core. Until 1897 they had never seen any reason for leaving the comfortable familiarity of their adopted city. Their small necktie and shirtwaist manufacturing business was moderately profitable and they were happy bringing up their children—Herbert, Ludwig and Nellie—in the middle of New York's thriving Jewish community.

Much to everyone's surprise, however, the normally mild-mannered Sol became consumed with Klondike fever as soon as he read the first headlines. Almost at once, he and an associate began planning an expedition; when his partner could not leave soon enough, Sol elected to go alone. At that point, Beckie put her foot down and declared that if her husband insisted on facing the risks and hardships of the Klondike in order to provide for his family, she would go with him. Sol acquiesced and the children, who ranged in age from eleven to fifteen, were packed off to stay with Beckie's sister and brother-in-law in Pennsylvania. Then Beckie and Sol boarded a westbound train.

On September 8, 1897, as the Schuldenfreis sailed north from Seattle,

Beckie wrote to her sister Gussie that in the Klondike "we will have nothing else to do but pick nuggets and shovel gold, and we will not eat any snowballs either, as we have lots of nice things to eat." On the latter point she was correct, but if Beckie seriously believed that riches would be so easy to come by, she was in for a disappointment.

To finance their expedition, Beckie and Sol had thrown caution to the winds and sold their business. In addition, they had invested all of their savings and borrowed whatever they could from friends and relatives. By the time they got to Dawson, on October 15, they were down to their last dollar. Their food supply for the winter was more than ample, but they had nowhere to live. In desperation they resorted to selling a lynx fur robe they had bought in Seattle for Beckie. With the $250 they got for the robe, which had cost them only $70, they were able to rent a small, one-room log cabin.

Within days of their arrival, Beckie was sending home warnings to other Klondike hopefuls. Telling Gussie that "things do not look so bright as they are in the newspapers," she asked her sister to inform an acquaintance who was considering joining the stampede

> that she should rather try and struggle along as best she can, and if she only makes her daily bread, she shall be satisfied and thank Heaven that she did not come out here, as this beautiful Klondike is only good for very strong and hardworking miners, as any one, who is not brought up from childhood to the hardest kind of labor, is of no earthly use here or all along the trip; as for instance, if you are thirsty, you have to fetch water yourself from up the hill upon the ice; if you want to sit down, you must know how to pitch your tent and sit on one of your sacks; if you are cold, which is very natural for a person in this country, you must have wood. Now this is more easily said than had . . . and even if you have money to buy it, and it only costs about $3.00 a log, you must chop it yourself. . . . It costs $15 a day to hire a man to do it for you.[12]

Keeping the home fires burning soon emerged as their greatest challenge. Sol, who had never chopped wood in his life, was reduced to tears by the task more than once. Beckie lamented having to impose this chore on her husband, but she was even less capable of handling an axe, and their inefficient stove required stoking every ten minutes.

It did not take long for the Schuldenfreis to realize that Sol was not cut out for mining. As Beckie explained to Gussie, "you must know how to wield a shovel and a pick; and you must know how to carry your own provisions on your back as you go along, which means about one hundred pounds at a time." The Klondike was not a place, she continued,

> where a man or a woman, who is not the hardest kind of laborer, can make any money here, as education or penmanship or in fact any knowledge that is not mechanic is worth absolutely nothing here, because, if you can not work as a woodsman or a miner, a person is lost here except a man who has plenty of money, to bring in a big lot of things, can tenfold his money in less than a year.[13]

Lacking such assets, they decided instead to capitalize on their abundant food supplies and open a restaurant. There was a critical shortage of food in the Klondike that winter, and even simple meals were expensive. "Everybody tells us that in a restaurant, we might have a little mine of our own," Beckie wrote optimistically on October 20. Dinners were going for three dollars a plate, and an apple pie that would have sold for ten or fifteen cents in New York cost ten times as much in Dawson. With the fear of starvation on everybody's mind, the few stores that had groceries carefully rationed them in hopes of making them last through the winter. Customers were begging shopkeepers to sell provisions, Beckie reported, "and then they do not, except if you happen to arouse their sympathy because you are a woman; as a stranger (man) in town can not get any groceries for love nor money."[14]

Sol purchased the only cookstove he could find, which was in such bad condition Beckie figured it would have been rejected by a New York City junk shop. Then they curtained off the back half of their eighteen-by-sixteen-foot cabin for their living quarters and crammed a couple of tables and some benches into the front "dining room."

Beckie was not an experienced cook. In New York she had always spent much of her time helping Sol run their business and hired a servant to deal with domestic duties. Nevertheless, she managed to turn out acceptable meals and by December they were operating two small restaurants. Initially they were quite successful, bringing in a few hundred dollars in the first couple of weeks, but business was not consistent.

When the number of customers dwindled, Beckie hauled out her sewing machine and tried a new approach to earning money. "I am making a few neckties," she wrote on March 1, 1898, "and if we could sell . . . even a dozen a day we would make enough in one month to keep us well supplied with wood and water for almost a whole year." Unfortunately, it seemed that there was only a limited market for ties in the Klondike.

Far from being gloomy about their circumstances, Beckie and Sol were generally cheerful and content. Their mutual affection and respect seemed to carry them through whatever difficulties they encountered and they enjoyed the novelty of their adventure, which at times was almost like a holiday. In one letter, Beckie admitted

> we lead such a lazy life here. . . . We eat and drink and sleep all the time and do nothing, as business, and in fact all the town, is practically at a stand still . . . some evenings a couple of Jewish gentlemen . . . come to the cabin and we spend many a pleasant hour conversing and telling jokes . . . and having a little lunch . . . for having nothing else to do we exercise our jaw with mastication most of the time.[15]

Their only hardship, she felt, was being away from the children. In winter, letters from home could take up to six months to arrive. Beckie made no secret of how much she missed Bertie, Lew, and Puss. "My Sweet Darling Kidlets," she wrote three months after leaving New York,

> being parted from you . . . is the greatest trial I have to endure, and I try very hard to keep from thinking of home and sometimes a few days pass away and I do not look at [the photograph of] your sweet faces, because I know my courage and endurance give way, and it is hard for me to again resign myself to the thought and fact of not being able to see or hear you. Two gentlemen are going out on the ice tomorrow, they will take our letters along, and if I had the money it requires to go with them, I should, regardless of the consequences of actually risking my life only so I could hope to see you soon again, as I am sorely afraid that my strength or stock of forbearance is not equal to the task to only be able to think of my darlings and not once to feel their dear sweet lips on mine. I think I will not write very much more, as the tears blind me as I am sitting now and thinking that I must have been crazy to undertake it at all.[16]

Not all Beckie's letters to her children were so heart-wrenching. At other times she adopted a more practical tone, instructing them to obey their aunt and uncle, or reminding them to take a dose of cod liver oil three times a day through the winter.

In September 1898, Beckie went back to be with the children, while Sol stayed on to run the hotel they now owned. He had not yet given up his dream of making a fortune or at least recouping the money they had spent on their quest. Only when a fire burned down the hotel did he admit defeat. Although broke and in debt when he finally returned home in 1899, Beckie greeted her husband with open arms and they managed to continue making ends meet.

Beckie's anguish about leaving her children was shared by many wives who chose to go north with their husbands. Widows and other single mothers who saw hope for a better future in the Klondike and temporarily left their offspring in the care of relatives while they joined the stampede also felt torn. Almost from the beginning of her trip, Georgia White, the woman who nipped from her bottle to steady her nerves on the Chilkoot Pass, was despondent about leaving her children behind. "I think constantly of my little ones," she confided to her diary four months after leaving home, "and God knows at times it seems more than I can bear but I must—for Oh deliver me from becoming insane up here."[17] Georgia's prayers for sanity were answered, but she failed to find a well-paid job in Dawson and left before winter because she could not endure being apart from her family any longer.

In the early days of the gold rush, few dared to expose children to the hazards and hardships of the trail and the uncertainties of life in Dawson or on the creeks, but some gold seekers had no choice but to bring their young ones with them. Possibly the first white child to travel overland to the Yukon River valley was seven-year-old Vera Barnes, who accompanied her parents on a trip from Juneau to Circle City in March 1896.

On the day the Barnes family crossed the Chilkoot Pass, hardy little Vera walked almost the entire fifteen miles between camps. After the long climb to the summit she rode for a short distance in a dog sled, but could not keep warm sitting still. It was too cold to wait for the men, who were behind packing provisions over the summit, so Mrs. Barnes tried carrying her exhausted daughter on her back. After struggling along for about a mile through the deep snow she finally had to put her down again and coax her to walk the rest of the distance herself.

Few dared to expose children to the hazards and hardships of the Klondike.

Emma Anderson undertook an even more challenging trip than Mrs. Barnes, travelling from Seattle to Dawson with three children all under six years of age: five-year-old Ethel, four-year-old Dewey, and baby Clay, who was just past his first birthday. As a young woman Emma had immigrated to the United States from Sweden, learned English, and found a job and a husband. If she could do that, she concluded, she could pack up her children and go north to join their father in the Klondike.

She succeeded, but it was a wretched journey. Emma was terribly seasick, and lay feebly in her cabin all the way to Skagway, trusting that the crew and other passengers would keep her active youngsters—the only children on the ship—from getting into mischief or falling overboard. Weakened by the days at sea, she found the trek over the White Pass so traumatic that she would never talk about it in later years. The family barely reached Lake Bennett in time to book passage on the last steamer of the season. When they finally arrived at Dawson, the boat was unable to force its way through the thickening ice to the wharf. For three more days they were stuck on board, until the river froze and they could walk to shore.

The Andersons' reunion was a joyful one and the family was soon happily settled into their new home on Eldorado Creek. But not all men were pleased to see their wives. Some women followed their husbands north only to find they had become obsessed with gold and were changed men. Others showed up unexpectedly and discovered their husbands living with other women. Nor did marriages always survive when couples went to the Klondike together.

Eighteen-year-old Mabel Long had been married only six months when she and her husband—a man twenty years her senior who had been chosen for her by her parents—set off for the gold fields. What little affection she may have felt for Mr. Long completely vanished when their boat capsized on Lake Bennett and he watched helplessly while she floundered in the water. It was love at first sight, however, between Mabel and the man who did jump in and pull her to shore. The two soon managed to slip away from Mabel's husband and head downriver. Mr. Long pursued them, but gave up the contest when he realized his young bride was determined to get a divorce and marry her rescuer.

Martha Purdy, who was forced to share her steamship quarters with a gambler and two women of dubious virtue, also saw her marriage crumble en route to the Klondike. It was the last thing her strait-laced family would have expected.

Martha's upbringing had been typically upper-class Victorian. During her five years at St. Mary's finishing school she learned to dance, play music, sing, recite poetry, paint china and watercolour pictures, do fine needlework, and make lemon cream pies and angel food cakes. She received instruction in how to dress for receptions, dinner parties, musicales, and dances, and she practised proper comportment for these occasions. This training served Martha well when she made her social début in 1885, at the age of nineteen. Two years later she married her favourite beau, Will Purdy, a young man of good social standing.

Between extravagant wedding gifts from their families and Will's salary from his job with his father's railway company, the Purdys lived well from the beginning. The birth of two sons during the first five years of their marriage did not prevent them from sharing in the gaiety of the gay nineties. They formed a cycling club with nine other married couples, and rode out for picnics on their bicycle-built-for-two. In the evenings they invited friends in to play euchre or charades, held soirées for distinguished guests, and went to the theatre or music hall to see such entertainers as Lillian Russell and John Philip Sousa.

Martha's days were filled with caring for her children, attending to housekeeping duties (although most of the actual labour was done by their black maid), socializing with other young matrons, and doing charitable works, such as collecting food and clothing for the needy.

It was a pleasant, but rather empty existence, and both Will and Martha leapt at the opportunity for a diversion when news of the Klondike discovery broke. Their enthusiasm was no doubt fuelled by their close friends, Sophy and Eli Gage. Sophy's brother, Portus B. Weare, was president of the North American Transportation and Trading Company, which had its headquarters in St. Michael. By chance, the Gages had been in Alaska visiting Portus when the first load of Klondike millionaires came steaming down the river from Dawson. Eli promptly headed to the gold fields to investigate the situation, while Sophy sailed south on the *Portland*.

Upon Eli's return to Chicago, he and Will Purdy began conspiring to leave their tedious office jobs and join the stampede. Fired by her husband's endless talk of Klondike adventure, Martha campaigned to join the expedition and found unexpected allies in her parents, who offered to care for her sons on their Kansas ranch. She would not be the only woman in the party, as Sophy had made arrangements to leave her fifteen-month-old baby in Chicago and go along too. The Purdys planned to travel via Skagway, while the Gages would go back through St. Michael and meet them in Dawson. The party grew as Martha's younger brother, George Munger, and a cousin also became infected with gold fever.

Shortly before their departure date, Martha was entrusted with a special mission to carry out while in the Klondike. One of her father-in-law's employees was looking for someone to act as an agent for his family and claim a million-dollar legacy which they believed was being held for them in Dawson. It was agreed that this should be Martha's task and that she would receive a 50-percent commission for her efforts. In the end, it turned out to be a futile quest, but while it shimmered on the horizon, Martha's half million dollars' worth of gold was a powerful force in her life.

The Purdys kissed their little ones good-bye and began their journey in the spring of 1898. All went well until they reached Seattle and Will got cold feet. As he began to worry about conditions in the north, stories of great riches to be found in the Sandwich Islands caught his ear. Martha was furious when he suggested a change of plans: "Go to the Sandwich Islands? With my Klondyke ticket bought, my passage booked, my vision of a million dollars in gold dust? Even after ten years of married life how little Will Purdy knew me!"[18]

With neither partner willing to back down, the Purdys' marriage came to a sudden and dramatic end. Each perhaps believed the other would give in as they went their separate ways, but that was not to be.

At first when Martha told her brother about the split he insisted she should go straight home. Only after much pleading did he agree to let her continue on with him and promise to keep the news secret from their parents until they were well on their way. The full weight of what she had done did not really hit Martha until the vessel that carried them to Dyea dumped their provisions on the shore and turned south. Then she realized she had burned her bridges behind her. But she held fast to her conviction that she was following the right path.

When Martha's party reached Dawson they rented a cabin on the hillside overlooking the town. The men yielded to Martha's feminine instincts and allowed her a free hand in fixing up the place. Years later, she reminisced about her first Yukon home.

It contained one large room, a small corner "stateroom" for me, and the usual built-in bunks for the men. Instead of the dirt floor, we pounded into the earth small round poplar blocks, which not only made the place warmer, but was a convenience in cleaning, as I swept the dirt into the numerous cracks. The men made our furniture from tree-trunks and twigs, boards, and packing-cases. It included plain willow-withy chairs, with an armchair for me, a board bench, a table (two wide boards nailed to four slim poplar legs), and a packing-box cupboard and dressing table.

. . . although this was only a little northern cabin I tried to make it as pretty and homey as possible. Much against the will of the party I had brought two linen tablecloths with two dozen napkins, silver knives, forks, and spoons for company, and a bolt of cretonne. . . . I made this into curtains, packing-box covers, and, later, cushions which I filled with feathers of wild ducks. It was well worth the trouble of bringing as it did brighten the little cabin. I pinned our surplus blankets on the walls, put our fur robes on the bunks, laid the table with coloured oil-cloth which I scalloped with scissors, placed on it a bouquet of wild flowers in a tin can covered with birch bark, and arrayed my agate iron dishes and silver in the cupboard. When we were completely settled we were all proud of our little home.[19]

Martha then got busy trying to track down the missing inheritance. For a while she used her activity to stave off her growing suspicions that Will had left her with a parting gift, but eventually she could no longer deny that she was pregnant. By that time, however, winter had slammed the door on the Yukon. Martha felt alone and scared. When her other children were born she had received the best medical care available in Chicago. Now she did not even have a trusted female friend, since illness had forced Sophy and Eli Gage to abandon their Klondike plans. Fortunately, once they got over their shock, her brother and the other men proved supportive.

Martha's household, like many that winter, ran short of food. For six months they did without fresh fruit and vegetables, milk, butter, and sugar. Yet somehow Martha stayed healthy throughout her pregnancy. Candles were also rationed, but at night when she strained her eyes hand-sewing baby clothes from her precious linen tablecloths, the men relaxed their rules and allowed her to burn two candles.

As the end of her term drew near, Martha inquired about medical care and decided the cost of a hospital delivery with a doctor in attendance was more than she could afford. Instead she made up her mind to manage on her own at home. On January 31, 1899, attended by two old sea captains who were members of her party, she gave birth to a healthy, nine-pound baby boy.

Martha's son was not the only gold-rush baby, but infants were rare, and little Lyman was a hit. "What a welcome the camp gave my baby!" Martha recalled years later, still glowing with maternal pride.

> The men of our party, and my neighbours, all men, took full charge. They kept the fires going. They brought in foodstuffs—fresh-baked bread, cakes, chocolates, ptarmigan, moosemeat, every wild delicacy of the country. Miners, prospectors, strange uncouth men called to pay their respects. . . .
>
> With tears in their eyes my visitors told me of their own babies so far away. They wanted to hold mine, to see his toes, to feel his tiny

fingers curl in their rough hands, to see for themselves that his back was straight and strong. Later, his bath hour became a daily show.[20]

The summer after Lyman's birth, Martha's father came north to take mother and baby to the family home in Kansas. Martha left reluctantly and, although she was happy to be reunited with her older children, suffered acute homesickness for the north. Finally, seeing that her heart was in the Klondike and that there would be no reconciliation with Will, her parents gave her their blessing to apply for a divorce and return to Dawson with her eldest son. A year later they escorted the younger boys to Dawson and stayed long enough to get Martha set up as the manager of a sawmill.

Socially, Martha's position was an odd one. As a wife and mother she was accorded the utmost respect. Yet her having a baby with no husband in sight raised a few eyebrows. Had she not been living under her brother's roof, her situation would have been considered far more scandalous. Although the scarcity of women in the Klondike fostered a tendency to overlook unconventional behaviour, many people would not have condoned Martha's opposition to her husband's wishes and stubborn insistence on going her own way. Knowing this, she probably kept the full story of her separation from Will to herself for many years.

The ultimate proof that Martha's past would not interfere with her acceptance into the upper crust of Dawson society came when she married George Black—a lawyer and one of the town's most eligible bachelors—in 1904. George went on to become Territorial Commissioner in 1912, giving Martha the prestigious position of chatelaine of Government House for the next four years. After World War I, Martha supported George through four terms as federal member of parliament for the Yukon. When illness forced him into temporary retirement from politics before the 1935 election, she ran successfully in his place, taking her seat in the House of Commons two weeks before her seventieth birthday. She continued to make the Yukon her home until her death in 1957 at the age of ninety-one.

With her first marriage in shambles behind her, remarrying was the last thing on Martha's mind when she first went to the Klondike in 1898, but for a number of women, the potential for matrimony was the prime motivating force that propelled them northwards. When Portus Weare's cook, Bridget, announced her intention to go to the gold fields, he scoffed at her and pointed out that she could not mine. "That's true," she replied, "but there's them that can."

A few months later, "a woman of stylish appearance and haughty demeanor swished her silken skirts past the admiring office boy in Mr. Weare's office . . . and extended a primrose-gloved hand" to her astonished former employer.[21] The transformed Bridget told Portus that before she had gone fifty miles down the Yukon River she had received 125 proposals of marriage. She finally accepted the offer of an Irish man with a mine that was earning fifty thousand dollars a month.

While Bridget held out for proven wealth, others were willing to gamble by marrying any man who was Klondike-bound, and hoping he struck it rich. In the August 22, 1897, San Francisco *Examiner*, a journalist revealed that he had run an advertisement seeking "a young lady or widow, not over 30, unincumbered and matrimonially inclined" to accompany an anonymous prospector to the Klondike, and received thirty-four applications within a week.

Many of the women who responded to the advertisement were quite frank about their objectives. "Yes, I am willing to get married and go to

Donning a skirt, the miner on the left demonstrates the Klondike bachelor's predicament: no women to do household chores.

Alaska," one stated in her reply. "I have read everything in the papers about the gold up there, and I am free to confess I want some of it." Another explained that she was eighteen and none of her family were living. "I think I could be a helpmate to you," she wrote, "and the union would be of advantage to me, for I find it a hard struggle in this world, without relatives, though my friends are kind; it is not like having some one all your own."

The economic realities that influenced most of the applicants were most clearly articulated by a twenty-eight-year-old widow.

> I look at the matter this way. Knowing what I can do myself, I think that if you are the right sort of man we could go up to Alaska, and by getting right down to hard work could in a year or two accumulate enough to live in comfort the rest of our days. Even if we do not go prospecting up there the chances are infinitely greater for a young couple to succeed in a new country like that than here. We are both young enough to see a good deal of happiness, and yet old enough to have gotten over romancing. Yes; if you come up to my expectations—and, by the way, I don't look for perfection in any man; we all have our faults; I am willing to chance it—you, marriage, Alaska and all.

Although it was a fake, the *Examiner* advertisement was similar to others that appeared in personal columns and classified sections of newspapers from coast to coast. Often the men were looking for women with capital, as well as a willingness to marry. Some women also placed ads of their own.

⌘

Matrimonial agencies provided an alternative to advertising in the newspapers. One Detroit agency promised that, for only ten cents, it would send Klondike miners a long list of names of honest young women who wished to marry. They also offered to find "rich husbands for poor girls,"[22] if they would only part with a dime for a register of gentlemen's names.

Some entrepreneurs saw the importation of marriageable young women to the gold fields as an easy way to make money. One elderly woman who calculated that there were at least two thousand prospectors in the Klondike who wanted to get married immediately and would be willing to pay a good price for the proper kind of helpmate, approached Portus Weare for an endorsement of her endeavour. Weare's North American Trading and Transportation Company would make money off the women's transportation and board, she explained, while her own profits would come from commissions paid by the miners. Despite having heard his former cook's description of the Yukon's desperate bachelors, Portus wanted nothing to do with the undertaking and quickly ushered the woman out the door.

An even more questionable scheme was that of Mr. C. Carrington, an ex-minister from New York State who proposed to auction off wives to Klondike men. In the fall of 1897, Carrington announced his plan to induce two to three hundred unmarried women to sign an agreement binding them to go to the Yukon with him the following spring. He would pay their travelling expenses.

"The girls will then be put on the auction block," explained the *Seattle Daily Times* on November 26, 1897, "and sold to the highest bidder for nuggets. He expects some of the girls will be worth almost their weight in gold. They will have nothing to say as to whom their husbands will be. His disposition, color of hair and eyes, nationality, age, etc., will not be taken into consideration. . . . The gold goes to Carrington and the girl owns the Klondiker."

Carrington told the *Daily Times* he had already enrolled eleven women. He defended his venture, saying it was "a perfectly legitimate business," but it is doubtful the Canadian authorities would have agreed. In any event, there is no evidence that Carrington's Dawson wife auction ever came to pass.

Self-serving as Carrington's proposal was, his assertion that he was responding to the needs of "thousands of young women in the East who are unable to find husbands in their own communities, and would avail themselves gladly of the opportunity," did have some validity. The American Civil War had killed more than 600,000 men, dramatically skewing the sex ratio throughout the country. In 1869, females outnumbered males by a quarter of a million on the eastern seaboard, and thirty years later, there was still an imbalance between the sexes in this region.

Not only was this situation a cause for concern for women who might never find husbands—in an era when marriage and motherhood were held as the highest goals for women—it also had broader social and economic implications. Complaints were frequently voiced about the impact of women entering the labour force and depressing wages for all workers. Meanwhile, social reformers worried that single women who could not count on their families for support were condemned to slaving for meagre earnings under terrible working conditions. One proposed solution to the problem was to relocate the women to the west, where men were more numerous. This idea gained new life with the sudden concentration of men in the Klondike. The line between employment and matrimony was often blurred, but either way the objective was economic security.

Charlotte Smith, an American sociologist, wanted to transplant four thousand or more working women from sweatshops and factories of the eastern United States to the Klondike. She had no interest in personal gain, but was, according to one journalist, "laboring solely in what she thinks the best interests of humanity. Transportation from a life of drudgery, with a bare pittance in the way of wages, to homes in Alaska would, in Miss Smith's opinion, be a blessing which thousands of women would be glad to embrace."[23]

Even some promoters who were not acting entirely altruistically showed some concern for the feelings of the women they proposed to send north. One noted that many "poor but thoroughly respectable girls" would be willing to go to the Klondike "if they were assured they would be properly cared for."

> In the towns and villages of New England the number of women is far in excess of the men and employment so hard to get that thousands would be willing to go to Alaska under proper conditions. I propose to secure places in advance for companies of, say, 100 girls, and have their employers advance money for their transportation from the States and recompense me for my trouble besides. No girls will be accepted except such as can bring the highest recommendations as to character and respectability. Arriving at the gold district each one will be assigned to her place, but all will be located within a short distance of each other, so they may have association and be able to counsel each other. Under their influence the camp would take on a homelike appearance, and the miners would not feel that sense of isolation which sends so many to their graves. They would be served with well-cooked food, and the general health of the camp would be vastly improved.[24]

Although many men learned to be competent cooks in the Klondike, there was some truth to the notion that men fared better when there were women around. Labourers at Clarence Berry's mine could look forward to

Edna's regular visits with a batch of fresh doughnuts. Similarly, the products of Emma Anderson's kitchen were widely acclaimed. Within days of the arrival of the Swedish woman and her three children on Eldorado Creek, miners from nearby claims were following the aroma of her spicy cinnamon rolls and crusty brown bread to her door and begging her to bake for them. So desperate were they for a change from flapjacks and sourdough bread that they agreed to supply the flour and salt, in addition to paying a dollar a loaf.

Besides baking, homemakers often grew precious vegetables in carefully tended gardens. A common method of roof construction was to lay poles across the top of the walls, cover them with canvas and then pile dirt on top. Emma and others planted seeds on their roofs, and the heat from the house allowed their families to enjoy fresh lettuce, radishes, and onions early in the spring when the ground was still too cold for planting. Women also added variety to the diet by picking wild berries and using them in pies, jams, jellies, and sauces.

Apparently the schemes to import large numbers of impoverished spinsters and widows never proceeded beyond the planning stages, for no great influx of single women was ever recorded. It is more difficult to determine whether any mail-order brides found their way to the Klondike gold fields, but most likely the majority of the husband-seeking women who took advantage of the situation did so on their own initiative. They certainly had lots of encouragement from the press, which constantly reminded readers how difficult life was for Klondike bachelors and how eager these men were to marry.

On February 7, 1898, a San Francisco *Examiner* story on "opportunities for American girls" made much of the fact that culinary skills were the most sought-after quality in a Klondike bride, but also implied that a natural female talent for cooking made any woman a good candidate. Just imagine, the writer urged,

> six thousand rich men, compelled to do their own cooking, [and] longing for the refinements of home life and something good to eat. It isn't so bad a place for a woman to live. . . . Short provisions, you know; and dry goods and delicacies pretty high; but a woman in the cabin makes living economical. A woman that knows how to cook doesn't waste things like a man.

Plain cooking is all that is expected on the Klondike, so a woman doesn't have to be very expert to please first-rate. Up there we eat mostly bacon, canned meats, beans, canned fruits, dried fruits, bread, evaporated potatoes, rice and tapioca. Almost any woman can cook these things well, and a girl that can't cook them well can at least do better than a man.

"The crop of Klondike millionaires promises to be a big one," the writer concluded, "and the girls are not showing the interest that might be expected." Perhaps they weren't. Or maybe they had assessed the situation and seen a golden opportunity to cash in on their domestic skills without necessarily tying themselves to a husband. Heedless of Ethel Berry's warnings that the Klondike was no place for a single woman intent on making a living or a fortune, there were many who had exactly that in mind. For female stampeders with entrepreneurial instincts, matrimony was often a secondary consideration.

4

MINISTERING TO
—the wants of—
HELPLESS MASCULINITY

rances Dorley, the Seattle dressmaker and milliner who talked her parents into letting her join the stampede in 1898, knew from her three-week visit to Skagway the previous year that there would be a great demand for women and their domestic skills in the Klondike. Although she could have made a living in Dawson with her needle and thread, she instead packed pots, pans and extra food. In Skagway she found a party of men bound for the gold fields who were willing to take her with them if she did all the cooking en route. She agreed to use her provisions during the journey, on the understanding that they would replace them in Dawson.

For a young, single woman to travel unchaperoned in the company of male strangers was very daring. Yet the only unwanted attention Frances reported was from a group of native men who asked if they could buy her from her companions. The members of her party were dumbfounded and speechless, until one gallantly declared that she was his "squaw" and not for sale. Frances gratefully accepted this rescue from what they all perceived as a threatening situation, but when she got to Dawson she was unfazed by the prospect of making her way alone among some thirty thousand men.

Frances spent the first three months after her arrival in Dawson reassembling her stock of food and equipment, and searching for a cabin she could turn into a roadhouse. In October she found a suitable building near the junction of Bonanza and Eldorado creeks. "It was hard work," she recalled fifty years later.

A constant stream of men passed up and down the two creeks, both of which were always lined with miners determinedly shovelling the pay dirt into their sluice boxes. I baked tons of bread and pies and made millions of doughnuts which I sold to the men who stopped for a hot meal or a fresh supply of cooked grub.

Butter was shipped up from the States in wooden buckets which contained five pounds each, at about five dollars a pound. I saved all the empty butter tubs I could find and filled them with baked beans. To the hungry men, starved for good, well cooked food, they were worth many a dig in their gold pokes.[1]

That first winter, Frances was too busy to be lonely, but by spring she was ready for more female company and more refined living. She returned to Dawson where she teamed up with Mrs. Moore, a middle-aged widow she had met on the trail to the Klondike. The two became close friends and successful business partners. Hard work and high standards—they catered only to "the more respectable element of Dawson commerce"—made their Professional Men's Boarding House a lucrative operation.

At twenty-six, Frances was regarded by many as an old maid when she left Seattle in 1898. It was her spirit of adventure, however, not a desire to find a husband, that led her to the Klondike. Then romance unexpectedly came her way when a broken tooth took her to see Dr. Alexander John Gillis, a Dawson dentist, in December 1899. Although she and A.J., as he was universally known, took an instant liking to one another, Frances was in no hurry to give up her independence. Only after a three-year courtship did she consent to become Mrs. Gillis.

After fifteen years of marriage, Frances had undoubtedly abandoned all thoughts of having children, but at the age of forty-five she gave birth to a baby girl. In 1919, concerns about their daughter's health prompted the Gillises to leave their beloved Dawson and move south to Victoria.

From the moment the Klondike discovery was announced in the newspapers, women like Frances Dorley began making plans to go north for the purposes of "ministering . . . to the wants of helpless masculinity,"[2] but they were not the first to have this idea. There had been women providing domestic services for profit in Alaska and the Yukon almost as long as there had been prospectors in the region searching for gold.

One of the Yukon's early female entrepreneurs was a stocky blonde by the name of Mrs. Willis. Before the Klondike strike, Mrs. Willis ran a laun-

Hungry men with no cooking skills gladly paid for restaurant meals.

dry and a bakery in Circle City, which, in 1896, was the main mining centre in the Yukon River valley. On her first trip in, she travelled with a party of four prospectors and pulled her own 250-pound sled the entire seven hundred miles from Lake Lindeman to Lake Laberge. On another occasion, she and two sled dogs hauled in a 750-pound load, which included a sewing machine she had just purchased in San Francisco. When word of the Bonanza Creek strike reached Circle, this hardy forty-five-year-old packed up her washboard, baking tins, and sewing machine, and joined the exodus to Dawson.

Mrs. Willis's sewing machine was one of about forty in the Yukon and Alaska in the pre-Klondike era. One of the others was owned by Anna DeGraf, a widow who went north in 1892, in search of her twenty-three-year-old prospector son. Prior to setting off on her quest, she had been supporting herself with a dressmaking business in Seattle. "I took my sewing machine along," she explained, "for I felt that I was going to an unknown land, where women and their work would be scarce, and it might be necessary for me to earn my living by sewing."[3]

The first time Anna crossed the Chilkoot Pass, at the age of fifty-five, she used a crutch because she was troubled by a broken leg that had not healed properly. Nevertheless, she kept up with the others in her party, walking twenty to twenty-five miles a day.

Two years in Circle City brought her no closer to solving the mystery of her son's disappearance, so she moved to San Francisco where her daughter lived. Anna ran a boarding house there until the Klondike stampede gave her an excuse to go north again. As before, her main purpose was to look for her son, but she also admitted that the north had cast a spell on her and she was feeling restless.

The outfit Anna put together in 1898 weighed three thousand pounds and included a sewing machine, numerous bolts of cloth, and a good stock of buttons, stays, and lace. Unfortunately, a late start prevented her from getting to Dawson before freeze-up and she was forced to return to California for the winter.

Anna finally reached the Klondike in the spring of 1899 and was immediately struck by disaster. The day after she found a cabin to rent and moved in, it burnt to the ground. She escaped unhurt, but all her dressmaking supplies and most of her personal belongings were destroyed. When the sun came up on the morning of April 27, it found the little, grey-haired woman sitting on a chair in the middle of the street, numbed by cold and shock. She was not alone in her despair. Dawson had suffered heavy losses from fire before, but this conflagration was its worst. Strong winds and problems pumping water from the frozen river had confounded the fire department and the hundreds of volunteers who had worked frantically through the night trying to save the town. By the time the battle was over, half of Dawson's business section lay in ashes.

The day after the fire, Anna met an acquaintance from Seattle who offered her a job as a cutter and fitter in the fur department of the Alaska Commercial Company. She accepted without hesitation. Anna was never one to shun hard work, and when word of her skill as a dressmaker got out, she began taking on extra commissions in her free time.

I would work all day at the store and go home and have a bite of supper and sew late into the night for my customers, many of whom were the dance hall girls, and early in the morning I would go and fit the dresses on the dance hall girls, after they had come home from their all-night work at the dance hall. This work was very hard on me, especially during the winter on account of the short days and extreme cold. . . .

In summer, I didn't mind the night work very much, for I could see to sew without a lamp, until midnight. There I would sit by the window and sew, and sew, and friends going by would call to me, "Don't you ever go to bed?"[4]

Despite her demanding schedule, Anna's long-lost son was never far from her thoughts. In summer, she got up early every Sunday, her only day of rest, and walked out to the creeks to see if he might be among the miners there.

Anna's early months in Dawson were lonely, but she quickly made many friends and was often invited out to dinner after church on Sunday. She became acquainted with another widow who kept a small store, and through her found a close circle of friends. The widow's fiancé and three other men had formed a group to study theosophy and they invited the two women to join their meetings. Anna approved of the men right away—they were well educated, interesting, and refined—and so, throughout the winter, the six of them met every Sunday evening. The gatherings alternated between the women's homes and followed the same pattern each week: readings from the works of Madame Blavatsky and other theosophists, followed by discussion, then tea and cakes. Anna found the evenings delightful.

At Christmas, Anna and the widow planned a surprise party for their male friends. They let one of the men in on their plans so they could use his house. On the afternoon of December 24 the women left work early, and went out to their co-conspirator's cabin.

We had gotten together some little gifts, and toys such as one would buy for small boys—a drum, a watch, a little horn, and so on; and I took along a pair of clean curtains and put them up in place of the ones that had done service for many months. We put strings across the room near the ceiling and hung greens and toys on them; set up the Christmas tree, trimmed and lighted it, had a fire going and supper on the way, when we heard the other men coming. We hid behind the door and waited. . . . On opening the door, they exclaimed "Oh, what a transformation! My land! this is wonderful!" . . . Then the widow tittered and they discovered us. We danced around and laughed from sheer delight. The miner lay on the floor, kicking his heels together, and tooting on the little horn, as his way of showing joy. We put big aprons on the men and they finished getting the supper, while we set the table.[5]

After dinner they sang hymns and every other song they could think of, read from Shakespeare, and recited poetry. When someone suggested dancing, the lack of musical instruments was no hindrance; they simply provided the music with their own voices. Their noisy celebration attracted attention from their neighbours, and soon there was a crowd outside the cabin, singing along with them. The festivities continued until one o'clock in the morning, and before the women left, the men made them promise to come back for another party on New Year's Eve.

During her second winter Anna received a marriage proposal which she firmly declined. "I assured him I was too busy making a living to take unto myself a husband, and I made it so clear to him that I could not think of having such a luxury as a husband, that . . . the subject was never mentioned to me by him again."[6] She gave a similar answer to a later proposal from another man.

Dressmakers were in great demand throughout the gold rush. Madame Rousseau's store was one of the first in Dawson.

Anna never completely gave up hope of finding her son and stayed in Dawson until 1917, when the birth of a great-granddaughter enticed her back to San Francisco. She died there in 1930 at the age of ninety-one.

Skilled dressmakers like Anna were in great demand from the very beginning of the gold rush. Mrs. Chester Adams went to the Klondike in 1897 expecting to make a few hundred dollars and cleared ninety dollars within three days of arriving. She charged eight dollars for a plain wool skirt, ten dollars for a fitted blouse known as a waist, and up to twelve dollars for a dress. None of her prices included the cost of materials. Women who took in mending typically earned $1.50 an hour.

At the end of the nineteenth century, seamstresses throughout North America and Europe began facing competition from the emerging ready-made garment industry. The Klondike was no different. Most clothing importers were men, because of the capital investment required, but a few women also profited from the tremendous demand for the latest fashions. In 1897, an attractive young Australian named Nellie Humphrey invested about two thousand dollars in gowns and lingerie and spent a month in Dawson selling her stock at what even she thought were ridiculously high prices.

The *Seattle Post-Intelligencer* of September 2, 1898, portrayed her business venture as something of a rescue mission: "It was the quick wit, business sagacity and, last but not least, the pluck of Mrs. Humphrey that enabled the fair sex of Dawson to revel again after months of deprivation in the frills and fancies of dress so dear to the feminine heart." A year after her first successful trip, Nellie travelled to Dawson with another consignment of ladies' wear.

<hr>

While some entrepreneurs made small fortunes by satisfying the fashion whims of those Dawson women who had money to spare or jobs that required stylish apparel, others placed their bets on the provision of basic services. The Klondike was swarming with men had always depended on mothers, wives, and other female relatives to take care of their domestic needs, and many of them had plenty of money to buy what they wanted. On the eve of her departure from San Francisco, Bessie Thomas explained why she had decided to journey to the gold fields and open a restaurant.

Miners have got to eat and I think there is more money to be made in feeding them than in slaving my life away here. I have got to earn my own living, and I don't see why there shouldn't be just as good a chance for me in a mining camp as there is for a man. . . . Here I just do my work for the pittance accorded me, and don't know I am doing anybody any especial good or myself either.

I do know that one of the most important things in a mining community is for the men to have good, wholesome meals, properly cooked and served. In the diggings, I am told, the diet is almost exclusively one of fish and canned goods. A diet of this sort becomes very monotonous, and if a few good, whole-souled women would go up north and look after the culinary end of camp life, there would be a great sight more happiness as well as a great deal less disease.[7]

Women like Bessie were found everywhere along the routes from Skagway and Dyea to Dawson, all up and down the creeks, and in Dawson and the smaller settlements. The scale of their businesses varied and successful enterprises were often expanded and upgraded. The term roadhouse was used to describe anything from a simple grub-tent with a few rough-hewn tables to an inn with a well-appointed dining room and sleeping rooms with feather beds. Roadhouses were generally located along the trails or on the creeks, while restaurants and hotels were more often found in town. Regardless of what they were called, liquor was served in virtually all such establishments.

Although women did not have a monopoly on the hospitality business, the feminine touch was often credited with making the difference between mediocrity and excellence. Mrs. J. Carroll, who started selling meals from a tent in 1899 and within two years owned part interest in three roadhouses, was one of the Klondike's best-known and most-respected roadhouse keepers. She personally supervised operations at one of her three establishments, where her efforts won rave reviews in the 1902 "Golden Clean-up Edition" of the *Dawson Daily News*.

The dining room service of the Dome roadhouse is excellent, for she herself attends to all cooking, and sees that nothing but the best quality of goods is used. The sleeping apartments are neat, clean and cozy and the beds are warm and comfortable.

A store in connection with the roadhouse handles goods of all kinds and supplies the miners with goods at Dawson prices, with a low rate of freight added. The bar dispenses the best brands of liquors and cigars.

Mrs. M. P. Rothweiler, a Seattle milliner who had improved her position in life through shrewd real estate dealings, also gained renown in the roadhouse business. Mrs. Rothweiler arrived in Dawson in June 1898 after spending a bleak winter on the shores of the Yukon River, trapped by ice halfway between St. Michael and Dawson. By the time they got to the Klondike most other members of her party had lost their taste for adventure and immediately booked passage on outgoing boats, but Mrs. Rothweiler liked what she saw in the booming gold rush town and began assessing business opportunities.

In the spring of 1899 she found what she was looking for on Bonanza Creek: "a sod shanty that bore the sign 'Mary's Place,' where a sallow-faced little drudge of a woman doled out 'coffee and sinkers at two-bits a throw.'"[8] Mrs. Rothweiler bought Mary out, demolished the shack, and replaced it with a fine log structure which she christened the Magnet Hotel after nearby Magnet Hill.

At Mary's Place on Bonanza Creek, miners tired of sourdough bread could buy doughnuts and coffee for twenty-five cents.

Mrs. Rothweiler's Magnet Hotel was renowned for good cheer, bountiful meals, and comfortable accommodation.

Over the summer she added a couple of large, two-storey log buildings, covered and lined with asbestos to reduce the fire hazard, and lit by electricity. The new buildings contained the bar, dining room, kitchen, sitting room, and barber shop attended by a resident "tonsorial artist." There was also a library stocked with several hundred volumes which Mrs. Rothweiler made available to hotel guests and local miners. Overnight accommodations included a separate bunkhouse with spring mattresses on the beds, "a most elegantly furnished bedroom" on the first floor of one of the main buildings, and a number of second-floor bedrooms "furnished in the most modern style."[9]

When Mrs. Rothweiler first purchased Mary's Place, neither she nor anyone else knew the potential of the area. As surrounding claims began to yield rich stores of gold, however, the thriving community of Magnet City took shape around her roadhouse. In 1902, the "Golden Clean-up Edition" of the *Dawson Daily News* described her influence on the development of Magnet City.

Gradually about the hotel there grew up a settlement; stores followed, other hotels, until today Magnet is the best and busiest of Bonanza settlements between Dawson and Grand Forks; and the whole is due to the genius and foresight of a woman, and that woman one to whose business ability many mine operators of that vicinity owe, not only encouraging words, but actual help in credit extended to them during the arduous period of developing their mines. What fortune Mrs. Rothweiler has gathered is due to her own untiring exertions and personal efforts, and if Magnet Hotel is popular, that popularity is based on the good substantial reason that within that hostelry three things are certain to the traveller. First, good cheer; second, well-cooked, well-served and bountiful meals; third, comfortable, cleanly sleeping quarters.

Grand Forks, the second-largest community in the Klondike after Dawson, also owed its origins to a roadhouse owned by a woman. Belinda Mulrooney, a petite, round-faced Irish American, arrived in Dawson on June 10, 1897, before most of the world even knew about the Klondike gold discovery. She had heard rumours of the rich diggings while working on one of the steamers that plied the waters of the Pacific north coast. Without delay she outfitted herself and convinced a group of Klondike-bound miners to let her join their party. Their reluctance to be burdened with a woman changed to admiration when she demonstrated her hunting and fishing skills, keeping them well supplied with fresh meat on the Yukon River portion of the journey.

The first thing Belinda did when she got to Dawson was throw the last of her money—a twenty-five-cent piece—into the river, "just for luck" as she put it. That may have been her last coin, but Belinda was far from impoverished. At twenty-six, she was already an experienced entrepreneur. Since leaving home five years before, this Pennsylvania coal-miner's daughter had run a sandwich stand at the Chicago World's Fair and an ice-cream parlour in San Francisco.

After losing her entire investment when the ice-cream parlour burnt to the ground, she found work as a stewardess for the Pacific Coast Steamship Company. This job brought her into contact with native women who were happy to trade furs for hats and dresses that Belinda brought up from the south. She then turned around and sold the furs to passengers for a tidy profit. Before leaving for the Klondike, Belinda spent all her savings, which amounted to five thousand dollars, on hot water bottles and bolts of silk and cotton. Within days of her arrival, she had sold her whole stock and was thirty thousand dollars richer.

Belinda then opened a restaurant in Dawson, but was forced to close it in the fall because she was unable to get enough provisions. Not one to get discouraged, she turned her attention to other schemes. She was certain that a flood of gold seekers would hit the Klondike the next summer, but instead of making preparations to meet their needs in Dawson, as others were doing, Belinda chose a site fourteen miles out of town. Late in 1897, she bought a lot at the junction of Bonanza and Eldorado creeks and began organizing the construction of an elegant two-storey hotel and a store.

The Dawson businessmen shook their heads at her folly, but when spring—and the first major wave of stampeders—arrived, she could hardly keep up with the demand for food, drinks, and rooms. The sale of land around Belinda's Grand Forks Hotel was soon brisk, with new buildings going up daily. Slightly more than a year after opening, Belinda sold her hotel for twenty-four thousand dollars. By this time the town of Grand Forks contained more than a thousand residents and about four hundred buildings.

A woman with Belinda's energy and flair for business could not be content with a single enterprise. Indeed, as soon as the Grand Forks Hotel was established, she began looking for opportunities in Dawson. In July 1898 she opened the Fairview Hotel in a prominent location on Front Street, close to the post office, government offices, banks, and major stores. The three-storey, thirty-bedroom building was the largest structure in town, and Belinda spared no expense in furnishing it. The lobby was lit with cut-glass chandeliers; the dining-room tables were laid with linen tablecloths, bone china, and silver cutlery.

Belinda no longer worked behind the bar as she had done at the Grand Forks. She hired a manager to look after the day-to-day operations, but had her own office and kept an active hand in running the hotel. Several times she travelled to Skagway to personally secure the best food, liquor, and furnishings for the Fairview, and in September 1899 she went to Seattle to bring back plate glass windows, a steam-heating apparatus, and fine lumber for finishing the interior.

Belinda began her Klondike career as a simple restaurateur, but quickly rose to the top of the local entrepreneurial elite. She played an active role in promoting the introduction of telephone service, and was instrumental in concentrating the telephone business into one company by purchasing the opposition line. She was also involved in the Hygiea Water Company, which was formed in response to a severe shortage of safe drinking water. As the *Dawson Daily News* expressed it, Belinda possessed "a business foresight that would do credit to any business man," and had "outstripped those of the sterner sex who have been connected with large business enterprises on the outside."[10]

One thing that set Mrs. Carroll, Mrs. Rothweiler, and Belinda Mulrooney apart from other women was that they had capital to invest when they arrived in the Klondike. The majority of female stampeders lacked this advantage, but since most men could not afford to stay in hotels or eat in restaurants night after night, there were abundant opportunities for housekeepers.

Some housekeepers worked for straight wages. Others agreed to accept a portion of their employers' earnings after clean-up in the spring. The latter arrangement was somewhat of a gamble as more than one unscrupulous miner tried to weasel his way out of paying the woman who had washed,

Miss Anderson's London Cigar Store was one of many Dawson businesses owned and operated by women.

mended, and cooked for him all winter long. Housekeepers were also vulnerable to pressure from men who thought sexual services should be included in their job descriptions. Alice McDonald found this out the hard way when she went looking for work in the Klondike.

Alice was a young Swedish woman who had immigrated to the United States in her late teens and settled in Ohio with her sister. Her decision to join the gold rush was a sudden one, precipitated by seeing a picture of a cozy log cabin in Dawson. As soon as she saw it, Alice told her sister she was going in search of a happy home like the one in the photograph. Two weeks later she was on her way.

Before her hasty departure for the gold fields, Alice earned a scant four dollars a week doing housework. Like one in five working-class families in the United States at the time, she and her sister supplemented their income by taking in boarders. Despite her limited command of English, she felt confident that her domestic skills would support her in the Klondike, but it was not quite as easy as she had imagined.

The day after she arrived, Alice applied for a position as a waitress in a Dawson restaurant. She was hired on the spot, and then fired half an hour later because she was unfamiliar with the "Alaskan" names of the dishes being ordered and could not work fast enough to serve the long line of customers. The next day she found a job in a slower-paced restaurant where she washed dishes, scrubbed floors, and was only occasionally called upon to wait on tables.

Preferring to find a position cooking for a group of miners on the creeks, Alice asked everyone she met whether they knew of an opening. Over and over she heard that miners would rather hire male cooks because they could split wood and carry water, in addition to preparing meals. No one took her seriously when she told them she could do the heavy chores as well as any man. Several men pointed out, however, that she would have no trouble finding a position as a housekeeper if she was willing to sleep with her boss. She answered that she had not come all the way from Cleveland to be insulted.

After a month or two of fruitless searching, Alice turned to the "situations wanted" section of the *Klondike Nugget*. Alice's advertisement, which read "A respectable girl wishes a position to cook for a party of miners on some of the creeks," had plenty of company. Women looking for cooking jobs far outnumbered all others, male or female, advertising their services.

Fortunately, there were also more vacant positions listed for women than for men. Cooks were paid in the range of sixty to a hundred dollars a month. This was high compared to wages in the rest of North America, but with the cost of living in Dawson running at about $180 a month, a single woman could only support herself with this sort of job if room and board were included.

While the advertisement did not get the hoped-for response, it did lead to an offer to cook for a woman who owned a roadhouse. The job was fine, but Alice soon realized that unless business picked up, her employer would not be able to pay her very much, so she continued making inquiries about other work. This led to yet another proposition that insulted her virtue.

> A man came to [the] roadhouse . . . and he told me that he had something most important he wanted to talk to me about in private. So I took him into the next room and he said that he was a married man with a wonderful wife and two daughters in the convent. He said he knew what kind of girl I was, and he would not want to bring any illness to his wife, as she was too fine a woman. He asked me to be his housekeeper and mistress for a year. He said he would make me independent for life, as he had a very rich claim he was working. He said I could go back to Sweden and no one would ever know. He told me . . . he would be back in a few days for the answer. I told him I could give him the answer right away. . . .
>
> "Suppose your wife were dead," I said, "and you were dead and your two beautiful daughters in the convent were now ready to leave and go into the world and make their own living. They went to a foreign country where they couldn't speak the language, but in time acquired a little knowledge of the language. Suppose that a man of your caliber would step up to one of your two girls and make her this proposition that you have just made me."
>
> The tears ran down his cheeks and he apologized profusely. I told him his tears didn't mean a thing to me, that he tried to put me in the lowest gutter, and that was my answer, so to please leave.[11]

Although many people insisted that Klondike men always treated women with courtesy and respect, the kind of offers and suggestive remarks Alice encountered were probably all too familiar to other lone women. Assault charges were laid in a few cases, but most women kept quiet about the milder, everyday harassment they experienced, for there was still a strong bias in society against women who ventured out in the world without the protection of a husband, father, or brother. Complaints were often greeted with suspicion that the victim had brought the unwanted attention on herself. Wives and widows were generally treated with more respect than unaccompanied single women, prompting some spinsters and divorcées to disguise their marital status by calling themselves "Mrs."

Alice herself temporarily employed this tactic to counter the censure of people she met during her journey. The first day on the train she discovered that her travelling companions' eagerness to discuss her Klondike plans changed abruptly when they learned that she knew no one in the Yukon. This fact obviously made them doubt her morals and they invariably became distinctly chilly towards her. After changing trains in Chicago, Alice started saying that she was on her way to join her husband in Dawson. This fabrication had the desired effect and she may have regretted dropping it when she reached the Klondike.

After some months at the roadhouse, Alice found a position cooking for a group of miners. She found this situation satisfactory and kept it until she married Dan McDonald, a Nova Scotian she had met shortly after her arrival in Dawson. Matrimony did not put an end to her days of wage-earning labour, however, for Dan was one of the many men who had failed to realize their Klondike dreams. Optimistic Alice encouraged him to continue prospecting, while she took in washing to pay the bills.

After a few years of getting nowhere in the Klondike, the McDonalds moved to Alaska to try their luck in the newly discovered Tanana gold fields, but fortune continued to evade them. In 1910, Alice, who had been doing everything from picking blueberries to running a hotel, took their two young children and went to live with her sister in California. Eight years later, Dan was drowned at sea while on his way to rejoin his family.

Even if they were willing to do their own housekeeping, most men hated doing laundry, and little wonder, for washing clothes was pure drudgery. Hauling water, stoking the stove to heat the water or to melt snow in winter, and scrubbing, rinsing and wringing out each item by hand could take up the best part of a day.

Although the hours spent bending over the washtub left them with raw hands and aching muscles, industrious washerwomen could make thousands of dollars a year. There was a long tradition in the mining camps of prospectors' wives, like Alice McDonald and Kate Carmack, taking in laundry, but their contribution to the family coffers was often overlooked. Consequently, when Mrs. John N. Horne got the chance to tell the world about how she and her husband had made their fortune in the Klondike, she made sure her role in their success was not ignored.

The Hornes first went looking for gold in 1895 and not until 1899 did they strike it rich. The only thing that carried them through the lean years and allowed Mr. Horne to keep prospecting was his wife's work as a laundress. Mrs. Horne made no attempt to hide her humble beginnings. "Just say that I was long a Yukon washerwoman," she admonished a reporter when she and her husband arrived in Seattle with fifty thousand dollars in gold. "We have plenty of money now, but I am proud of the fact that I washed and sewed for the Yukon miners."[12] So proud in fact, that she planned to have a piece of gold jewellery made for herself, with a washboard for the design.

According to one journalist who visited the Klondike, only the most fastidious miners changed their underwear more than twice a month, because at fifty cents per item they could not afford more frequent laundering. Whether or not this was true, the gold rush also brought another type of man to the north, the type who wore clean, starched, white shirts when he went to the office or out for an evening's entertainment. Mrs. J.P. Wills, a stout, jolly laundress who had been in the north for six years before the Klondike discovery, saw the change coming and was the first to supply these "boiled" shirts to Dawson dandies.

Mrs. Wills was married to a blacksmith who was unable to work because of crippling rheumatism. In about 1894, when she was nearly fifty, she left him at home in Tacoma and went to Circle City where she struggled along as a washerwoman. When news of the Klondike strike broke she was among the first to head to the new gold fields.

In Dawson, Mrs. Wills opened one of the town's first laundries. It was a prosperous enterprise despite high costs: thirty-five dollars a month rent; $225 for her winter wood supply; $2.50 for a box of starch; $1.50 for a washboard that would have cost twenty-five cents in the south. She had more work than she could handle alone, and hired a native woman as an assistant, paying her four dollars a day plus room and board.

There is no record of what Mrs. Wills charged for boiled shirts or other

Industrious washerwomen could earn thousands of dollars a year, but the work was pure drudgery.

items, but in 1898 an employee of the U.S. Department of Labour who had gone north on a fact-finding mission reported that laundries charged four to six dollars per dozen items, although prices fluctuated depending on the demand for the service. Another account mentions charges of seventy-five cents for laundering a dress shirt and three dollars per dozen for linen collars. These prices often equalled the original cost of the garments.

Since any woman with a washboard and soap could go into the clothes-washing business, some looked for ways to keep ahead of the competition. One Dawson laundress specialized in washing ladies' fine garments, while another carved out a lucrative niche for herself with an exclusive contract to do all the washing for the North-West Mounted Police barracks.

Mrs. G.I. Lowe had one of the more imaginative approaches to attracting customers. In addition to mending articles of clothing at no extra cost for customers, she told fortunes for a dollar a piece on the side. In the fortune-telling department, however, she was no competition for Mrs. Slaydon, who announced her arrival in town with the following advertisement in the August 5, 1899 issue of the *Dawson Daily News*:

> Extraordinary! Mrs. Dr. Slaydon, The World's Greatest Palmist and Medium, recognized by all as the wonder of the age. Don't fail to see this wonderful woman. Consult her on any and ALL affairs of life.

Steam laundries showed up early in Dawson's history, providing employment for some women, but also competing with the smaller, home-based businesses. Men generally had more money to invest in these equipment-intensive operations. A few, however, were owned by women such as Ellen Gibson, who bought the Montana Steam Laundry in December 1899 and ran it successfully for three years.

Ellen went to the Klondike in 1898, one year behind her husband Joe. Travelling north with the couple's two teenage sons, she faced her first set-back when they and the rest of their fellow passengers learned that their tickets were only good as far as St. Michael, not Dawson as they had been led to believe. Under duress the captain promised a free return trip to California to anyone who wanted it, but was adamant that fares for the remainder of the journey up the Yukon River would have to be paid in cash. Penniless though she was, Ellen refused to give up and go home. She and the boys stayed in St. Michael and worked at whatever odd jobs they could find until they made enough money to get to Dawson.

Before her departure from San Francisco, Joe had written and suggested Ellen bring a sewing machine and a clothes wringer. This proved to be good advice, for she soon realized she could not count on Joe's efforts alone to win the fortune they sought. Soon after her arrival she started taking in laundry. When the Montana Steam Laundry came up for sale she did not have the asking price of five hundred dollars but, in her usual determined manner, she made arrangements to pay it off in monthly instalments. Unable to afford an assistant, Ellen did most of the work in the laundry single-handed, sometimes recruiting her sons to make deliveries or wield the heavy flatirons.

In contrast to Ellen's driving ambition, Joe put little effort into working his claims. He was less of a gambler than his wife and preferred the security of wage labour, with its regular but relatively low pay. As tensions between the couple grew, Joe spent more and more time drinking in the saloons.

Finally, late in the summer of 1902, Ellen packed her bags and set off with another couple for Fairbanks. Although the Montana Steam Laundry was doing well, she could see that Dawson was beginning to decline and she believed she could find a brighter future in the north's new boom town. Her sons, now eighteen and twenty years old, stayed with their father. Ellen never returned to the Yukon and the Gibsons divorced six years after her departure.

While laundries solved the problem of dirty clothes, personal hygiene also presented a challenge for Klondikers, especially in winter. A number of entrepreneurs operated bath houses in Dawson and the surrounding communities, typically charging one dollar for a plain bath and a rubdown, and two dollars for a Turkish bath. Regardless of the expense, many men and women welcomed bath houses as an alternative to heating water on the stove and then crouching in a tin tub, trying to wash away the sweat and grime without flooding the floor.

Mrs. A. Wilson, proprietor of the Stockholm Baths, was a graduate of the Stockholm Massage Institute in Sweden. She offered both plain and Turkish baths, as well spruce steam baths, "the great fever and scurvy destroyer and skin beautifier."[13] Attendants of both sexes were on hand to administer "scientific and facial massage," shampooing, hair dressing and manicuring, from noon to midnight every day except Saturdays, when the baths stayed open right through until Sunday noon.

Marie A. Riedeselle also featured the luxury of massage at her bath house. Marie, a French Canadian who had been raised in New York State, was a woman of many talents. By the age of thirty she had trained as a nurse, gained fame as a professional masseuse and facial specialist, and won a prize for designing a bicycling outfit for women. In 1893, she left New York City and bought a farm in Connecticut, announcing that she was going to live there alone, with only her dog, horse, and chickens as companions. True to her word, she built fences, ploughed the fields, and marketed the products of her labour by herself. Four years later the Klondike called and she was off on a new adventure.

Independent as ever, Marie resolved to make the journey alone because she preferred not to be "encumbered with the rivalries and discussions that naturally arise in a party." Her unassailable confidence in her ability to succeed was backed up by a great deal of planning. For three months, the small, slim, grey-eyed woman attracted attention in Seattle, as she went about preparing for the trip and life in the north.

"She has studied every phase of life from Dyea to Dawson," a *Seattle Daily Times* reporter wrote on February 1, 1898,

> [and] knows accurately the geography of the country, knows the customs and habits of the people there, the kind of garments best adapted to the climate and the work, how to handle dogs, manage a loaded sled, propel a boat; in fact, how to do everything a human being needs to do in that country. She says she came to Seattle to learn these things and has mastered the situation. . . .
>
> During her sojourn in Seattle she has made her Klondike suit, superintended the selection of her outfit, tent, sled, etc., and has devoted one hour each day to medical gymnastic exercises, and her muscles are in perfect condition for her great undertaking. She knows the difficulties and has prepared for them.

Marie reached Dawson in the spring of 1898 and opened a business on Front Street, where she offered massage treatments, and both Russian and plain baths. Besides the obvious benefit of getting clean, she claimed that a visit to her establishment could cure rheumatism, prevent or cure scurvy, and restore lost vitality. In 1899 she moved her business temporarily to Grand Forks, but soon returned to Dawson and found a new space for her business in the Spokane Hotel.

Barbers, including at least one woman, came early to the Klondike, but similar services for women were rare at first. By the summer of 1899, two hair-dressing parlours had been established. Many of the customers were women who worked in dance halls and theatres.

On November 24, 1899, a writer for the *Dawson Daily News* lamented the passing of the "good old days of '96, '97 and '98 [when] the dance hall queen cared not so much for personal adornment, but rather prided herself on her staying powers for drink and revelry." Changing standards had led to the opening of a number of beauty parlours, he complained, where

> the dance queens and soubrettes skip every afternoon to have their tresses fashioned in the latest Greek and Turban knots, the braided pug,

chignon puffs, scallops and loops both bewildering and fetching. . . . There the jaded complexion is rejuvenated by liberal applications of washes, lotions, powders and cosmetics until the fairies hardly recognize themselves in the transformation.

But the dance hall queens and soubrettes were not simply indulging their own vanity. They knew what their audiences liked, and they understood their job: ministering to the other wants of the male population.

5

COME AND DO
—a shuffle—
WITH ME, SAM

I n August 1900, twenty-four-year-old Kathleen Eloisa Rockwell, a veteran of dance halls and theatres in New York City, Washington State, and British Columbia, landed at Dawson with a travelling theatre company. Over the next few years she adopted the nickname Klondike Kate and gained modest fame. In addition to acting in plays, she danced and performed specialty acts such as her appearance as "The Fashion Plate Artiste" at the Savoy Theatre during the week of October 8, 1900. For the most part, Kate was just another pretty face, but the night she introduced her flame dance to Dawson, she ensured her place in Klondike history.

Heads turned the moment Kate walked out on stage in her brief, form-fitting costume covered with red sequins and glittering rhinestones. Pink tights sheathed her legs, and a black satin cape hung from her shoulders. She stopped in the centre of the platform and faced the men who packed the theatre. As she stood there, motionless, staring out into the darkened hall, voices hushed, and the clinking of bottles and squeaking of chairs ceased. The room grew charged with anticipation as the seconds ticked by. Kate held her stance, riveting the audience with her gaze.

Suddenly, with one fluid movement, she let the cape slip from her shoulders and plucked up a cane attached to more than two hundred yards of red chiffon. Arms outstretched, she started to turn, and the gauzy material slowly rose in the air. Offstage, a single violin cut the silence, its long, keening notes sending shivers up every spine.

She floated dreamily about the stage in a rising tide of crimson, until, all at once, the rest of the orchestra broke loose. Lifted by a whirlwind of music, she began to leap and twirl, weaving the fabric this way and that.

Faster and faster she spun and the stage became a sea of fire as the blazing cloth surged around the red-haired, red-garbed dancer. Sweat glistened on her face. The watchers in front could almost feel the heat. And then, as if consumed by the fire of her passionate performance, she dropped to the floor, motionless once more, while the chiffon drifted down around her.

The audience response to Kate's spectacular dance was wildly enthusiastic. In keeping with Klondike tradition, the cheering men deluged the stage around her feet with gold coins, nuggets, and bags of gold dust. But there was no lingering in the limelight for Kate. In vaudeville theatre, one solo act followed quickly after another, and her turn on stage was done.

Klondike Kate, Fashion Plate Artiste.

Once the final curtain fell at midnight, the canvas floor covers were rolled up and the chairs and benches that had seated the audience were piled to one side to clear the dance floor. As a variety girl, Kate's job was to spend the rest of the night mixing with the patrons, encouraging them to spend their money at the bar. Variety girls lacked the social status of so-called legitimate actresses and singers who confined their professional activities to the stage. On the other hand, they considered themselves a cut above percentage girls, whose only source of income was the commission they received from dancing and drinking with the men.

Stage performers required at least a modicum of talent and good looks, but the most important qualification for being a percentage girl was stamina. Their only day of rest was Sunday, when dance halls, theatres, and saloons were required by law to close. Every other day the percentage girls were on the job from five or six in the evening until the doors closed twelve hours later. For this they received a weekly salary of forty to fifty dollars, plus a commission on all the dances and drinks they sold. By comparison, men working as waiters, bartenders, card dealers, and musicians were paid $90 to $120 a week, while actresses and actors earned in the range of $150 a week.

Dance music—waltzes, polkas, reels, and schottisches—was provided by bands such as Professor A.P. Freimuth and his eleven-piece orchestra. As they struck up the opening notes any percentage girl who had not been spoken for would urge the nearest man to "hit this one a whirl" or "come and do a shuffle with me, Sam."[1] The men paid the cashier a dollar for each dance and were given ivory or cardboard chips which they handed over to their partners before the music began. At the end of the night the women cashed in their chips, receiving twenty-five cents a piece.

Although each number lasted only a minute or two, percentage girls required considerable endurance to keep going through all 125 to 150 dances

Percentage girls wore typical Victorian attire on the dance floor.

called in a night. Between tunes the caller directed the participants to promenade to the bar, where the men were expected to buy refreshments for themselves and their dance partners. Every drink a man purchased earned the woman accompanying him a 25 percent commission. Beer, whisky, brandy, and gin cost between fifty cents and a dollar, while a quart of champagne went for about thirty dollars or two ounces of gold. The women generally quenched their thirst with lemonade or ginger ale, but sometimes drank champagne, or at least made a show of drinking it to encourage their companions to buy the more expensive libation.

Observers varied widely in their assessments of percentage and variety girls. Martha (Purdy) Black, the fashionably attired stampeder who struggled over the Chilkoot Pass in a heavy skirt and tight corsets, thought they were "often beautiful, invariably had good figures, and many were clever and resented the stigma generally attached to their profession."[2] On the other hand, American physician Dr. Luella Day was not so kind. "The women in these dance-halls were not what you would call raving beauties," she opined, "but there was frank exposure of such charms as they imagined they had, for they wore dresses abbreviated at both ends, thus displaying their necks and arms and their legs up to their knees."[3]

Revealing costumes, such as Dr. Day described, were common on the stage, but were never seen on the dance floor. Percentage girls wore typical Victorian attire: long-sleeved, high-collared blouses and long, flared skirts. The most daring ones revealed a bit of ankle, but hems were never shorter than mid-calf length. Variety girls always changed from their stage outfits for the latter part of the night when they mingled with the men. Their fashionable Parisian gowns, which they could afford because of their higher salaries, set them apart from the ordinary dollar-a-dance girls. There was, however, little difference between their jobs once they were no longer behind the footlights.

Larger halls, such as the Palace Grand and the Orpheum, had second-storey boxes or balconies that overlooked the main floor. These offered patrons a view of the action below, or privacy if they wished to draw the curtains. Men celebrating fortunes won at the gaming tables or excavated from rich claims, and weary miners trying to forget their lonely, miserable existence on the creeks rented these boxes by the night and invited percentage or variety girls to keep them company. The role of the women was to talk to

A Klondike-era dance hall girl.

and amuse their escorts, provide a listening ear or a shoulder to cry on, laugh at their jokes, and above all, keep the liquor flowing.

Drinks served in the boxes were sold at premium prices, with champagne going for twenty dollars a pint. The women kept the corks from the bottles ordered by their male companions and traded them in at the end of the night, earning $2.50 to $4.00 on each one.

Some dance hall women earned a name for themselves as box rustlers because of the dubious tactics they used to increase the number of corks they collected. One of their tricks was to pour their drinks into a spittoon when the men were looking the other way and then ask for a refill. If a box rustler had a waiter as an accomplice, she could distract the unwitting reveller while the waiter removed half-full bottles of champagne from the box along with the empties. Part bottles were combined or topped up with water and resold, sometimes even to the same customer. The privacy of the boxes also lent itself to rolling, the not-so-subtle art of getting a man drunk and emptying his pockets.

Klondike Kate never stooped to rolling, but she admitted later in life to box rustling with the help of her lover, Alex Pantages, who was a waiter. Her skill in showing men such a good time that they failed to realize or care how much money they were spending contributed to the $150,000 nest-egg she took with her when she left the north.

Of all the men Kate bestowed smiles upon in the Klondike, only Alex won her heart, but love was not all he wanted from her. He also took much of her fortune. After they went south, Kate willingly invested large sums of money to help Alex on his way to becoming one of the leading theatre magnates on the west coast. Since they presented themselves to the world as husband and wife, she assumed they were working in partnership. Alex saw things differently, and in 1905, with no warning, he married another woman.

A successful breach of promise suit restored some of Kate's lost riches, but her broken heart was not so easily mended. To make things worse, it was becoming increasingly evident that she was never again going to match the glory of her Dawson days. After a few years of trying in vain to rekindle her flagging career, she turned to polishing and promoting the legend of Klondike Kate. She did an excellent job of convincing a generation of journalists, Hollywood screen writers, and television producers that she had been hailed as the Belle of Dawson, the Queen of the Klondike, and the Flower of the North. In reality, however, there were other women with equal or better claims to fame.

One title taken long before Kate ever set foot in Dawson was Princess of the Klondike, which belonged to Marjorie Newman. Nine years old when she went to Dawson in 1898, Margie soon became the toast of the town. Her parents put all three of their young children on the stage, but their only daughter was unquestionably the most popular member of the family. Whether dressed up in tartan to sing "Annie Laurie" and dance the highland fling, or playing innocent Little Eva in *Uncle Tom's Cabin*, she never failed to delight audiences. Margie Newman, declared the *Klondike Nugget* on September 21, 1898,

> is positively the sweetest and as clever a child as it has ever been our pleasure to listen to and watch on the stage. The charm of the little maid grows on one the oftener she is seen. She appears sometimes with her brothers, and they are both clever boys, but there is a natty neatness and grave conscientiousness about the little girl which has endeared her to the hearts of the big men who go so often to see her.

Margie's singing, dancing and acting talents were almost beside the point. She was adored, and reaped rich rewards, simply for reminding the homesick men of their loved ones far away. In 1899, when there were only 163 children under the age of fourteen in Dawson, one of her admirers penned the following tribute, published in the May 6 edition of the *Klondike Nugget:*

We see our own dear children by the magic of your art,
And affection's fire's relighted with a fierce and sudden start,
And you help us bridge both time and space 'twixt we and
    those apart.
    O Little Margie Newman

God bless you little Margie for you make us better men,
God bless you little Margie for you take us home again,
To Nona, Otto, Ruth or Bert or darling little Ben—
    O Little Margie Newman

And we love you for your own sweet self and for the good you do,
To the best that's in our natures we cannot but be true,
When we find our hearts a softening with a love inspired by you.
    By Little Margie Newman.

Two of the Klondike's favourite adult entertainers were Polly and Lottie Oatley, who opened the Oatley Sisters' Concert Hall a week after their arrival in mid-June 1898. The June 28 edition of the *Klondike Nugget* raved about their inaugural show, expressing great surprise that "such talent could find its way to this quarter of the globe."

> With splendid voices and the latest songs and being excellent dancers they made a decided hit. They danced the buck-and-wing together in a manner that pleased the admiring spectators. Then dog Tiny, a mite of a canine comes in for his share of praise for he sings a little himself, much to the wonderment of everybody.

Between appearances on the stage, Polly and Lottie joined the customers on the dance floor and at the bar. The sisters gained a perhaps unjustified reputation as heavy drinkers, who were put to bed drunk every night, yet retained "the bloom of youth, bright eyes, good voice and lively heels."[4] If the Oatley sisters were truly believed to be such dissolute characters it seems unlikely that forty "ladies" would have attended a Sunday evening benefit concert at their hall, as reported in the *Klondike Nugget* of September 21, 1898. The event, organized to raise money for Dawson's hospitals, featured recitations, songs, dances, and impersonations. Both amateurs and professionals performed. The latter included the Oatley sisters, the Newman children, and variety girls Daisy D'Avara and Kitty Howard.

After establishing themselves in their own concert hall, the Oatleys went on to headline programmes at major theatres around Dawson for several years. They took breaks in the south—sometimes leaving for many months—but kept coming back to the town where they were so well received.

Lottie Oatley's sense of humour was very much in evidence on one occasion when she returned from a trip outside. As the steamer *Anglian* drew close, the crowds along the waterfront noticed the popular variety girl leaning on the railing, carefully cradling something wrapped in a blue cloth. She was met at the foot of the gangplank by a friend of the man most people assumed was her lover. With great solicitude, he took the blue bundle from her arms, and they proceeded up the dock. Observers exchanged knowing glances. The departure of any single woman from town was always cause for speculation; this only confirmed their suspicions. One bold character pointed to the bundle and asked if it were hers. "Certainly," she replied, and carried on, ignoring the smirks. But she got the last laugh a few minutes later, when the mewing of a kitten from within the blanket gave the game away.

Popular as they were, the Oatley sisters were no match for Cad Wilson, who outshone all the other Klondike stars during her ten-month sojourn in Dawson. Although neither her singing nor her looks were remarkable, she had expressive brown eyes and a captivating stage presence. It was rumoured that Cad was enticed to Dawson by the highest salary ever offered to a performer in the Pacific northwest. Men loved the way she delivered the suggestive lyrics of her catchy theme song, "Such a Nice Girl, Too," and other provocative numbers in her repertoire. When she sang "Just a Little Lingerie," for example, she illustrated the words by lifting her skirt "much higher than was necessary to show her lingerie, or even the diamond garter which encircled her left nether limb, just above the knee."[5]

Cad and other entertainers flirted with their audiences and showed more leg on stage than was considered proper at a time when piano legs were still being covered in some parlours for the sake of decency, but baring of breasts or stripping were never tolerated on Dawson stages. Even the high kicks and other daring moves that some female dancers included in their routines were relatively tame. Celebrated high-kicker Lottie Salter considered the lavish ruffles and yards of lace that trimmed her skirts "absolutely nec-

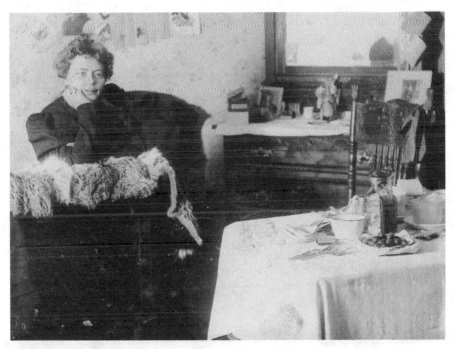

Entertainer Cad Wilson relaxing in her room.

essary to get the billowy cloudy effect, which pleases the audience, and at the same time removes any suggestion of indelicacy. Should a bit of ankle peep through the maze of lace it makes the kick more piquant."[6]

When dancer Freda Maloof went on stage at Dawson's Novelty theatre and did the hootchie-kootchie, a daring scarf dance that had been made famous at the Chicago Exposition by a woman called Little Egypt, the police quickly stepped in and charged her with committing an indecent act in a public place. Despite Freda's imaginative defense that she was executing a Mohammedan religious dance, and her offer to demonstrate in court so the judge could see for himself that there was nothing obscene about her performance, she was fined twenty-five dollars and prohibited from continuing her act.

Cad's performances were never so risqué as to get her in trouble with the police. She was, however, taken to task by the editor of the *Klondike Nugget* on October 29, 1898, after one of her early appearances in Dawson. The occasion was a benefit concert at which respectable women were in attendance, having been assured there would be no offensive acts. All went well until Cad took the stage. Apparently she misjudged the audience, because shortly after she began singing, a number of women stalked out in disgust. "Her audacity called out applause in the rear of the hall," the editor observed, "but the ladies in front hung their heads and their escorts wished they had never brought them."

Cad left Dawson on August 17, 1899. Two days later the *Klondike Nugget,* which seemed to have forgiven her earlier faux pas, lamented the departure of one who had "contributed no small amount of happiness since her arrival here last year." She took with her $26,000 and an elaborate belt fashioned entirely from gold that was the envy of every female performer in town.

The belt, a gift from some of her many fans, was a magnificent piece of craftsmanship. Front and centre it featured a gold pan the size of a dollar coin, flanked on either side by a pick and shovel; inside the pan were a windlass, a rope, and a bucket, tools used to bring up the paydirt from the mine shafts. Five chains of nuggets hung down from the belt, each one bearing a golden trinket: a perfume bottle flecked with gold dust; a monogrammed watch; memorandum tablets; a pencil and pencil case; and a bon-bon box with a quartz nugget on its lid and the words "Klondike, N.W.T." written in gold around its circumference. Nugget belts adorned with charms were worn by many Dawson variety girls, but none compared to Cad's prize.

Plenty of leg was seen on Klondike stages but stripping was never tolerated.

Like Cad, Violet Raymond—"a prepossessing blonde, jovial in nature [and with] a graceful and well-developed figure"[7]—profited greatly from her time on Dawson's stages. Violet's northern career began in Alaska in 1895. Arriving in Juneau at the tender age of eighteen, she took the region by storm, and reigned for two years as the Queen of Burlesque.

Burlesque, more commonly known as vaudeville, was the most popular form of western frontier theatre in the 1890s and dominated Klondike stages throughout the gold rush era. An evening of vaudeville typically featured a play, usually a melodrama, comedy, or farce, followed by solo acts by singers, dancers, comedians, jugglers, gymnasts, acrobats, and magicians. Some burlesque performers were genuinely gifted, but talent was not necessarily a requirement for the job. H.B.S. Marcus, a New York vaudeville entrepreneur who owned Dawson's Combination Theatre for a time, admitted: "We don't go in much for talent. All we want is plenty of lungs and legs to make the show a go."[8]

When news of the Klondike gold strike reached Juneau in the spring of 1897, Violet Raymond was among the first to pack her bags. Joining a vaudeville company of six other women and seven men, she travelled over the Chilkoot trail and down the Yukon River. They arrived in June and were immediately engaged to perform at Dawson's brand-new Opera House, the first permanent theatre in the Klondike. Despite its grand name, the Opera House was nothing more than a two-storey log building. The front was fitted out with a bar and gambling tables, while the back housed a combination theatre-dance hall, which held no more than one hundred people.

The Juneau vaudevillians had been playing the Opera House for only four weeks when Violet abruptly announced her retirement. After a month of wooing her with gold and diamonds, Antone Stander, a quiet, unassuming Austrian who was one of the richest men in the Klondike, had won her hand in marriage.

In November, Violet left Dawson and moved with her new husband to his cabin on Eldorado Creek. It was a difficult transition. "The life was pretty lonely at No. 6," she told a reporter for the San Francisco *Examiner* in July 1898 when she finally returned to civilization. "I was obliged to keep house all day, while Mr. Stander worked the claim." The erstwhile Queen of Burlesque spent her evenings reading, thankful that Antone had coal-oil lamps and could afford unlimited fuel for them, even at fifteen dollars a gallon. Occasionally she rode into Dawson on horseback for a change of scenery and to visit friends.

The Standers left the Klondike in July 1898 with nearly $200,000 in gold dust and nuggets. Of this, $75,000 was Violet's personal property, given to her by Antone. When asked by the *Examiner* reporter what she intended to do with her money, Violet replied sensibly that she planned to bank it and draw interest until she saw a good opportunity for investment.

Antone was not as well equipped to cope with his sudden affluence. Although he invested some of his gold in a Seattle hotel, he also drank much of it away. Violet finally left him when his jealous rages, usually precipitated by drinking, became too much to endure. He died penniless, while she hung on to her fortune, leaving an estate of fifty thousand dollars.

Blonde, blue-eyed Gussie Lamore—a banjo-playing singer and vaudeville actress who hiked over the Chilkoot Pass with Violet Raymond—was also courted by one of the Klondike's wealthy mining men, but in the end she spurned his advances. It was a wise move, for Swiftwater Bill Gates was a heartless charmer who wrecked the lives of several other women who failed to see through him.

Swiftwater Bill made no secret of his infatuation with the winsome entertainer. One day he decided to indulge Gussie's extreme fondness for fresh eggs, a rare and precious commodity in the early days of the gold rush. He bought every egg in town and presented them to her. Unfortunately, his grand gesture failed to impress Gussie, once she realized that every one of the eleven eggs—for which he had paid twenty-five dollars—was rotten. Nevertheless, the incident was instantly embellished and incorporated into the Klondike mythology.

For months Bill wined and dined Gussie, while she led him on, hiding her contempt for him. Before she left Dawson at the end of the summer, he set a sack of gold dust at her feet and asked her to marry him. Whatever her answer, Bill watched her steamer pull away firmly believing she had agreed to tie the knot later that fall when he came south. Within a month, however, her true feelings were plainly stated in the San Francisco *Examiner*. "He's as stupid as an owl . . . and as rich as—anything," she candidly told reporter Alice Rix. A million dollars, Bill's expected earnings from his claim over the winter, was a good deal of money, she admitted, "but independence is a good deal too. If I could take the million off to one end of the world and have the man at the other—[but] Swift-water Bill isn't so stupid as all that."[9]

Gussie's comments in the *Seattle Daily Times* on February 2, 1898, were even more dismissive.

> Pooh! I wouldn't have had him for a million. . . . I thought I'd get his money when he came out and then let him go. He was too easy—the easiest thing you ever saw. Why in there, all you had to do was touch him for $500 and get it. But I wouldn't have married him if he'd owned the Klondike.

When Bill arrived in San Francisco and discovered Gussie had no intention of becoming Mrs. Gates, he turned his charm on her older sister and soon convinced Grace Lamore to join him at the altar. He spared no expense in setting up a home for his new bride and showered her with expensive gifts. Within three weeks of the wedding, however, she was demanding a divorce on the grounds that he was excessively affectionate. "He squeezed and hugged me from morning till night," Grace complained. "Now no woman could endure such treatment as that, could she? It was positively cruel. Because I refused to return his caresses he slapped my face. He needn't think because he is worth all kinds of money he can bore me to death."[10]

Twice rejected, the irrepressible Bill then began pursuing eighteen-year-old Nell, the youngest Lamore sister, who wisely resisted his advances. In the spring of 1898, Gussie took Nellie, who was no stranger to the theatre, and returned to Dawson. Finding that Bill's amorous exploits were the talk of the town, both sisters used the stage to indulge in some good-natured teasing of their former suitor and brother-in-law. In an inspired piece of casting, Nellie was chosen to star in *The Adventures of Stillwater Willie*, a thinly veiled satire about Swiftwater Bill, which played to sell-out crowds at the Combination Theatre. In the sequel, *Stillwater Willie's Wedding Night*, Gussie revelled in her role as the bride. Far from being annoyed, Bill attended both plays and reportedly found them quite amusing.

The worldly Lamore sisters knew how to handle a man like Swiftwater Bill, but two other young women were less fortunate in their dealings with him. One was Bera Beebe, an impressionable fifteen-year-old whom he met in Seattle. On his second attempt he managed to run off with her to Dawson, despite Iola Beebe's best efforts to protect her daughter's virtue. One month after Bera gave birth to their son, Bill convinced his adolescent wife to leave the infant with her mother, who had followed them to the Klondike, and go south with him for the winter. A year later Bill abandoned Bera, who was once again pregnant, and eloped with his fifteen-year-old niece. Iola spent many years trying to make Bill pay support to Bera and his sons, but never succeeded.

❦

Not all dance hall and theatre women were as protective of their autonomy as Gussie. Many gladly relinquished their single status when given the opportunity, even though marriage usually marked the end of their stage careers. Although a husband who was in the entertainment business often allowed a female performer to continue her vocation if she wished, a man who had only spent time in the theatre as a member of the audience rarely approved of his wife appearing on stage.

Like Violet Raymond, Priscilla Hetherington Hanby Payton of Scotland, better known in Dawson as Sid, forsook the footlights when she married local businessman Robert Burnham. Priscilla and her sister, who performed under the stage name Jacqueline, made their Klondike debut at the Monte Carlo Theatre in July 1899. They quickly established themselves as audience favourites. Seven months later, on January 8, 1900, the *Dawson Daily News* announced with a touch of disappointment that, after a quiet wedding at the Presbyterian manse, Mrs. Burnham had given up the stage and would "hereafter devote herself to domestic affairs."

Matrimony was seen by many dance hall and theatre women as a route to acceptance in Dawson society, but those who stayed on in the Klondike found it difficult to erase all traces of the past. Even the most respectable performers carried some taint of impropriety. Beatrice Lorne, a singer almost universally regarded as being above reproach, discovered this sad truth the hard way.

Beatrice was a young widow with a child to support when word of the opportunities in the Klondike reached her in Australia. Deciding to try her luck, she left her daughter with relatives and sailed for the distant gold fields, arriving in Dawson in 1899. With her exquisite soprano voice she had no trouble finding work and was soon being billed as "the Klondike Nightingale." While other vocalists emphasized the erotic in their performances, Beatrice appealed to the men's nostalgia for home and their longing for wives and sweethearts left behind. Night after night, she brought tears to their eyes with her lovely renditions of sentimental favourites like "Swanee River" and "Don't You Remember Sweet Alice, Ben Bolt."

There was never a hint of scandal attached to Beatrice's name. Often she was invited to sing at benefit concerts and other performances where "ladies" would be in attendance. After several years in Dawson she married veterinarian George Smith and sent for her daughter, Connie, to come from Australia.

Once married, Beatrice no longer sang for her living. She had no regrets about quitting the crowded theatres that smelled of cigars, booze, and men who needed to bathe. But Beatrice missed seeing the pleasure her singing brought to the faces of listeners. Consequently, she was delighted to be asked to perform at the Methodist Sunday School Christmas entertainment. Connie and Dr. Smith would be in the audience, along with other Sunday School pupils and their parents.

The event was a success, and the Klondike Nightingale was as well received as ever. The next day, however, large, hand-written signs appeared all around town castigating the concert organizers for inviting "a woman of the dance halls" to sing in front of children. Beatrice's outraged husband tracked down the perpetrator and gave him a thorough horse-whipping. No further comments of this sort were ever voiced by him or anyone else, but the Smiths must have been happy to leave such narrow-mindedness behind when they moved south in 1905.

Martha (Purdy) Black, who separated from her husband on the way to the Klondike and later put a few noses out of joint when she married lawyer George Black, openly defied the social code that relegated former dance hall women to the fringes of Dawson's polite society. In 1912, George was appointed Commissioner of the Yukon Territory, and during their time at Government House in Dawson the Blacks hosted numerous parties. Among the invited guests at one evening reception were C.W.C. Taber—a prominent Dawson lawyer and long-time friend of George's—and his wife. It was the presence of the latter that roused half the town to righteous indignation, for no one could forget that Mrs. Taber had once been Diamond Tooth Gertie Lovejoy, a popular soubrette famed for the glittering jewel fastened between her two front teeth. To one of the Tabers' fellow guests, Gertie was "a demure little woman, quite pretty and very self-effacing,"[11] but others saw only the diamond that still sparkled between her teeth, reminding them of her suspicious past.

Because of the small non-native female population in the Klondike, all women attracted attention, but actresses and dance hall girls endured the greatest public scrutiny. Little they did went unnoticed by Dawson's newspapers, which were especially vigilant in keeping their readers informed about the romantic affairs of the demimonde. Sometimes the tone of the stories was light. On August 19, 1899, for example, the *Klondike Nugget* reported that Jack Glover had thrown all of actress Babette Pyne's possessions out of the cabin they shared, because he had discovered she was only living with him to make one of her former lovers jealous. Often, however, newspaper articles revealed the shadows that darkened many of these women's lives.

A Klondike dancer known as the Belgian Queen, circa 1900. Entertainers' lives seemed glamorous on the surface, but were often darkened by tragedy and despair.

Suicide was a relatively common occurrence in the Klondike, a place of shattered dreams for many men and women. Women intent on killing themselves often swallowed chloroform, morphine, or laudanum. Kitty Stroup, who was only nineteen when she died in 1898, four days before Christmas, chose strychnine.

Since the age of fifteen, Kitty had been working in Yukon and Alaska dance halls and living off and on with a man named Charley Hill. Although not married to Charley, Kitty went by the name of Stella Hill. Like many women in her position, she used a pseudonym either to protect her family back in Boon's Ferry, Oregon, or to keep them from finding her. When Kitty and Charley came to Dawson from Circle City he found work tending bar at the Pioneer Saloon and she was hired as a percentage girl at the Monte Carlo Theatre. Her excellence as a waltzer ensured she was never short of partners.

Whether or not her feelings were justified, Kitty came to suspect her lover of planning to leave her for another woman. One morning after work she left the dance hall and went to the Pioneer Saloon to see if Charley would go out for breakfast with her. He refused to speak with her and sent her home because she had been drinking. Hurt and angered by his rejection, she went instead to the nearest drug store and purchased an eight-ounce bottle of strychnine.

On the way back to her room on the upper floor of the Monte Carlo, Kitty encountered several co-workers. She told one that she and Charley had been together four years and she was not going to have him toss her aside now. To another she mentioned that Charley would never see her alive again. Worried about her air of despondency, her friends tried to stay with her. She managed to evade them, however, and locked herself in her room. Charley was quickly summoned. He broke down the door, just in time to see Kitty down a glass of colourless liquid. Correctly fearing it was poison, he called for a doctor, but within twenty minutes of swallowing the fatal dose she went into convulsions and died. It was her second or third known suicide attempt.

The majority of females who took their own lives in the Klondike were dance hall women, like Kitty, or prostitutes. Failed love affairs, shame, and despair about future prospects were the reasons most often given for their rash acts. A few days before Myrtle Brocee, another nineteen-year-old, placed a pistol to her right temple and blew her brains out, she told a friend that she had attempted suicide on a previous occasion before coming to Dawson. Myrtle also confessed that she would try again "unless something turned up to rid her of the life which she hated and which brought her the importunities of the men."[12]

Myrtle and her older sister, Florence, performed a duo singing and dancing act at the Tivoli Theatre. Three weeks before her death, Myrtle came down with a severe case of pneumonia. She recovered from her illness but, according to some of her friends, was dreading returning to work. Unfortunately, medical bills and lack of earnings had consumed nearly all her meagre savings and she knew no other way to support herself.

At 2:00 A.M. on December 9, 1898, as Florence was returning home from work, she stopped by to see her sister. To her horror, she found Myrtle's lifeless body in bed, propped up by a couple of blood-spattered pillows, the gun still clutched in her hand.

Unable to protect Myrtle from suffering during life, Florence poured all her resources into a final gesture. She ordered the finest coffin available, trimmed with silver and lined with blue and white silk. Then she dressed her sister in a white satin dress and slippers, and laid her to rest in the snow-shrouded Dawson cemetery.

Compared to the gold rush towns of California and Alaska, there was relatively little violent crime in the Klondike, but assaults and murders of women by jealous men were not uncommon occurrences. The majority of victims were percentage and variety girls, as they often became objects of infatuation. Dora George's relationship with J.R. Armstrong was characteristic of the kind of troubled alliance between dance hall women and their lovers that both shocked and titillated the Klondike's more upstanding members of society.

In March 1899, Armstrong was charged with assaulting Dora, a pretty, twenty-three-year-old variety girl. The two had lived together for a while before their relationship soured and Armstrong started talking of killing Dora because he feared losing her. After Dora moved out of the room they shared, Armstrong alternately threatened her and begged her to come back. He demanded she return a pair of diamond earrings he had given her, then visited her bedside when she was sick and tenderly put them back on her ears, asking her forgiveness. His letters revealed the depths of his desperation. "Dear Dora," he wrote on January 25, 1899,

will you let me send a dog for you tomorrow and you come and see me. . . . Please don't get mad at what I said it was much better for me than to kill some one for talking about you on Saturday eavening. When I was down at your place I was crasey and had no sence. . . . will you forgive me and be good friends. . . . if you want to sing on the stage all right. I thought that the gang was turning you against me you can come here and I will put all my money in the bank in you name. Dear sweathart answer this and let me know whether you will come and see me I will lay here and cry all day long for you. I never said any thing to do you any harm . . . the hapies days of my life was spent with you when we lived together down over the restaurant. . . . I will help you and your childrean out. you can send some money at once if you like. I will give you my money and you can bank it in your name . . . I wish you was here so I could talk to you. . . . I remain your J.R. Armstrong Many Kiss to you.[13]

Although Dora took to keeping the doors locked when alone in her cabin, Armstrong broke in one morning and confronted her. Revolver in hand, he ordered her to hand over the diamond earrings. She complied, but he continued ranting and waving the gun about. Dora managed to flee to a neighbouring cabin, barely escaping the fate of a number of other dance hall women who died at the hands of the men who claimed to love them best.

Maud Roselle, a popular actress at the Monte Carlo, was shot and killed by her lover, Harry Davis, in August 1899. On the morning of the tragic shooting, Harry followed Maud to her room above the theatre when she finished work. Blanche Lamont, who lived across the hall, heard Maud telling Harry she wished to end their relationship and trying to mollify him by saying they could meet that afternoon. "You will see me now," Harry shouted back, "and you will never leave me." Moments later a terrified Maud ran into Blanche's room with Harry close behind her. He caught her and threw her to the ground, and, without hesitation, put a bullet through her head. Then he turned his gun on himself. The two died instantly, a gruesome duplication of another murder-suicide that had taken place in the same room a few months earlier.

In October 1900, variety girl Pearl Mitchell was murdered by James Slorah, a bartender whom she had met in Dawson and lived with for a few months. He shot her three times, then tried and failed to kill himself. After a long and sensational trial, Slorah was condemned to hang, but his sentence was later commuted to life imprisonment.

Nobody ever tried to stop actress Mae Meadows's husband from shooting at her, but theirs was a unique situation. Charley Meadows was one of the Klondike's most flamboyant showmen. Not only did he build Dawson's largest theatre, the Palace Grand, but he regularly appeared on its stage to display the skills he had perfected in his days with Buffalo Bill's Wild West Show. In one of his specialty acts Charley demonstrated his marksmanship by shooting glass balls that Mae held between her fingers or placed on top of her high-piled hair. This routine was discontinued after he shot off the tip of her thumb one night. Although Charley insisted the accident was the fault of a defective bullet, Mae refused to take any more chances.

Few dance hall women took the kind of risks Mae did, but they did endure long hours and low wages. In 1901 they formed a professional asso-

For the ladies of the Women's Christian Temperance Union, dance halls, prostitution, and drinking were inseparable. This photograph, taken in the red-light district, was probably staged.

ciation. After threatening to withdraw their services, they won their first victory—a moderate increase in their minimum salary and the guarantee of a one-hour break for each meal. By this time, however, the very existence of dance halls with women working on commission was under attack.

Women who made their living in dance halls or the theatre were regarded with a great deal of suspicion in the Victorian era. Their greatest transgression was that they mixed freely with male strangers. Those women who dressed provocatively, drank heavily, or lived in common-law relationships provided further proof of their wickedness. Most contemporary observers tended to put the majority of actresses, singers, and percentage girls in the same moral category as prostitutes. But dance halls and theatres were not brothels, and any female employee of these establishments who engaged in sexual commerce did so on her own time.

In the early days of the gold rush, pragmatism forced the authorities to turn a blind eye to activities that would have been prohibited elsewhere in

Canada. In August 1900, however, Clifford Sifton, the federal minister of the interior, wrote William Ogilvie, commissioner of the Yukon Territory, to say that he was receiving numerous complaints about Dawson's dance halls and gambling houses.

Among those petitioning Sifton on this matter was the Social Purity Department of the Women's Christian Temperance Union. The ladies of the WCTU were distressed about the official tolerance of dance hall women and prostitutes. "This matter is of deep interest to us all," they explained, "as many boys from all parts of Canada are in the mining regions, and make Dawson their permanent or temporary headquarters. For the sake of our Motherhood, for the sake of our wifehood, for the sake of our boyhood, we pray you act speedily in this matter."[14]

Ogilvie's response to Sifton's letter was an attempt to shed some light on the realities of northern life. Originally, all members of the territorial council had been "strongly of the opinion that these vices should be stamped out," he noted, but time had changed their minds.

> Dance halls are an evil . . . but at the same time they are like many other evils, considered absolutely necessary under certain conditions. To abolish them would be to throw a lot of women into a more vicious life, as many of these women would not resort to ordinary prostitution but would be leeches on the general mining public. Box rustling, as it is called here, that is dance hall girls and theatre girls selling liquor in the boxes, has been often discussed, with a view to its suppression, but no decisive step was taken, as it could not be very well seen what could be done to suppress it entirely. As long as human nature is what it is, this evil will exist in some form or another, and no legislation can be enacted which will abolish it.[15]

Meanwhile, the number of women of ill repute in the Klondike region was declining for reasons that had nothing to do with Sifton or the WCTU. Rich, new gold deposits had been discovered in Alaska and many people were leaving the Klondike to seek their fortunes elsewhere. An official count by the North-West Mounted Police in July 1900 identified only two dance halls operating in Dawson, with forty-two dance hall girls employed in these establishments.

Pressure to uphold the moral standards of the rest of Canadian society continued to be exerted on the Yukon Territorial Council. As a result, the government introduced a new Liquor License Ordinance in 1902 that, among other things, prohibited public dancing in licensed premises, and stated that "no licensee shall pay or permit to be given to any female any percentage for any liquors sold or delivered to any person on his premises, and no female will be allowed in any licensed premises for the purpose of soliciting or inducing others to drink or buy liquor." Inspector Routledge applauded the new ordinance in the annual police report for 1902.

> This dance hall problem has been a thorn in our side since the earliest days of Dawson; we could not prohibit them under the law, and yet we were well aware that a greater part of the crime committed in the country was caused, either directly or indirectly, by the dance halls and their quota of women; the women employed in these places were of the very lowest order, but strange to say in many cases they were surprisingly good looking, and this fact would enable them to get the men drunk and then rob them. After robbing the men, if the matter was reported, the women would always have sufficient evidence forthcoming from the human parasites, and hangers on, of the place to swear that the man who had been robbed had been drunk and spent the money.[16]

Whatever the reason for the lack of criminal proceedings against unscrupulous dance hall women, it is interesting to note that from 1898 to 1903 there were far more convictions for drunk and disorderly behaviour—the defendants nearly always being men—and for non-payment of wages, than for any other crimes.

As Dawson moved into the twentieth century, the separation between theatres and dance halls became quite distinct, and employment in the latter was increasingly equated with prostitution. The 1903 annual police report labelled dance halls a "grave nuisance," and asserted that "most of the women who frequent these places have, at one time or another, practised another calling openly." Like the dance hall girls, those who practised this other calling saw a tremendous shift in how they were regarded by the police and the public over the years.

Prostitutes were among the first non-native women to reach Dawson in 1896. As soon as news of the Bonanza Creek discovery filtered out to the rest of the North, they joined their clients from gold camps all over Alaska

Prostitutes surveying the street from their cabins.

and the Yukon in the dash for the Klondike. Most prostitutes were American, but like other gold-seekers they were drawn from every corner of the world, including Europe, South Africa, Australia, and Japan.

Klondike prostitutes were "of many grades and classifications," according to one physician who treated some of the "Daughters of Lileth" in his practice, as well as seeing them on the streets.

> Though all of one profession . . . [they were] as far separated in personal allure and personal fastidiousness or character, as heaven is from hell. The gamut ran from the elegance, the social intelligence and the real and regal courtesan-like charm of Dawson's two or three "queens," . . . down to the tawdry, cheap, vulgar and disgusting, sheer dirtiness and sluttish habits of crudely painted creatures.[17]

The majority of Klondike prostitutes were in their twenties or early thirties. A few, such as a fifteen-year-old Japanese girl brought to Dawson by a fellow countryman, had not even reached the age of consent. The lucky ones quit while they were still young and healthy. Those who did not, frequently died of sexually transmitted diseases, violence at the hands of pimps or customers, tuberculosis, or other ailments aggravated by malnutrition and poor living conditions. The life expectancy of turn-of-the-century prostitutes in the north, as elsewhere, was short.

At first prostitutes lived wherever they pleased in Dawson, openly strollling the streets in search of customers. Most settled in the central business district and many of the cabins on Second Avenue bore signs and banners advertising the occupants' names. Before long, however, their freedom began to be curtailed.

Shortly after his arrival in Dawson in September 1898, North-West Mounted Police commander Sam Steele instituted a policy of monthly arrests and fifty-dollar fines for all known prostitutes. Ostensibly to make Dawson a more respectable town, these fines were, in effect, a business tax which provided much-needed funds for Dawson's financially troubled hospitals. Apparently there were no strong objections to the work of the Sisters of St. Ann and their Protestant counterparts at the Good Samaritan Hospital being supported by the town's scarlet women.

Regular medical inspections of prostitutes were also introduced in 1898. In the great Victorian debate about how to deal with prostitution, the Dawson Board of Health took the side of those who maintained it was a necessary social evil—an essential outlet for men's sexual drives—and that medical control would adequately protect the community against any adverse side effects. Following the procedures established under the British Contagious Diseases Act, the territorial health officer and the North-West Mounted Police surgeon examined all prostitutes twice a month. By detaining infected women in custody and giving them treatment, the Board of Health managed to keep venereal diseases under control. Few people questioned the fact that this system penalized the women without holding their customers in any way accountable for their role in the spread of infection.

Although the police generally permitted prostitutes to go about their business, they dealt more severely with pimps, or macques as they were commonly known. A conviction for vagrancy or having no peaceful occupation—legal euphemisms for living off the avails of prostitution—was punishable by fines starting at fifty dollars, combined with jail sentences of at least thirty days. A greater deterrent was the threat of being sentenced to work on the government wood pile. Sawing and splitting the thousands of cords of wood required to heat Dawson's government buildings was hard labour indeed. The worst offenders were given a "blue ticket" which meant they were put on the first boat out and told never to return.

In 1903, the police made a concerted effort to rid Dawson of all macques. More than thirty left the territory—some after being convicted and serving their terms, others because they feared being caught —and at the end of the year, the police expressed confidence that none remained.

As Dawson became more settled, citizens began demanding that the authorities clean up the town's main streets. In the spring of 1899, Steele responded to these urgings by ordering all prostitutes to move to an area bounded by Fourth and Fifth avenues and First and Third streets. The actual number of women involved was not recorded, but was probably less than one hundred, since only eighty-five women were charged with being inmates or keepers of houses of ill-fame in 1898, when Steele's short-lived policy of monthly arrests was introduced. In 1900, the North-West Mounted Police counted only forty-nine prostitutes, nearly all of them living on Fourth Avenue or between Fourth and Fifth avenues.

One of the main justifications for confining prostitution to a single red-light district was the supposed connection between the demi-monde and fires. The May 1899 conflagration that reduced half of Dawson's business district to charred ruins started in the apartments of variety girl Helen Holden, on the second floor of the Bodega saloon. At the inquiry into the cause of the fire, Helen denied leaving any lamp burning in her room and said the stove had last been stoked five hours before the blaze began. She also testified that she did not smoke and, since she had naturally curly hair, did not use a curling iron. Other witnesses swore that the stove pipe had been recently cleaned and had passed a safety inspection. In summing up the evidence, the coroner stated that the cause of the fire was unknown. Nevertheless, the six-man jury recommended that all "women-of-the-town" be excluded from all public buildings other than licensed hotels, a verdict that was widely endorsed.

Banishing all actresses, singers, and percentage girls to the back streets was not considered practical, but the fire provided a good excuse for forcing the prostitutes to relocate. Those who disagreed with this compromise felt vindicated in January 1900 when Dawson's next major blaze was reported to have started in Florence Brocee's apartment above the Monte Carlo Theatre, just down the hall from the room where Kitty Stroup and Maud Roselle had met their tragic ends. In fact, the fire had actually originated in the attic above Florence's room when the creosote-lined stovepipe burst into flames.

It was three o'clock in the afternoon when Florence raised the alarm after noticing sparks falling down from the opening where the stovepipe entered the ceiling. She and most of the others residing in the rooms above the theatre had worked all night and were still in bed. They ran out into the snowy street clad only in nightdresses and other light clothing, and watched helplessly as the flames raced down First Avenue. By the time the fire department brought the blaze under control two hours later, buildings and property worth more than half a million dollars had been destroyed.

The fire claimed no lives, but Conchita and Leo, a vaudeville couple staying at the Monte Carlo, were frantic with worry until they were able to confirm that their young son was not trapped in the burning building. Conchita and Leo, Florence Brocee, Diamond Tooth Gertie, and Jacqueline—all occupants of the Monte Carlo—each lost between one and two thousand dollars' worth of money, jewellery, and clothing. Gussie Lamore and Beatrice Lorne, who were both living above the Opera House, a few doors down from the Monte Carlo, suffered smaller losses because they had more time to rescue their belongings.

In the aftermath of the January fire, the usual accusations were hurled at the dance hall women. Nevertheless, the fire commission recognized where the real problem lay and drafted new regulations requiring a six-inch air space around chimneys at points where they passed through floors and roofs in theatres and other public buildings.

Yet even if a few clear-thinking individuals understood that women were more at risk from, than responsible for, the fire hazard in Dawson's wood-and-tar-paper buildings, no one was about to suggest prostitutes could go back to living wherever they wanted. On the contrary, the construction of a new school a few blocks from the tenderloin district had parents agitating for further restrictions on the prostitutes' activities.

Strict new rules were decreed: the women could not appear at their cabin windows or on the street while "immodestly attired," nor could they do anything to attract the attention of passersby. Limits were also set on the hours when "singing and music and noise" were permitted. These measures still did not satisfy the protesters, so in 1901, the Territorial Council ruled that prostitutes could only reside outside the confines of the city.

Most of those who did not give up and leave the Yukon altogether at this point moved over to Klondike City, a small settlement across the Klondike River from Dawson. The only way to reach Klondike City, or Lousetown as it was less kindly known, was across a long, open bridge. This public approach was a decided deterrent to customers who wished to maintain a puritan image. As business slowed, more prostitutes purchased one-way tickets on outgoing steamers. By October 1901, only about thirty "soiled doves" still lingered on the outskirts of Dawson.

But not all accepted their exile. Some tried to evade the law by posing as respectable entrepreneurs, most commonly cigar-store owners and laundresses. In a crack-down on prostitution in April 1902, twenty-five cigar-store women pleaded guilty to the charge of being inmates of houses of ill-fame within the city limits, and were fined fifty dollars each.

Although some prostitutes renounced their profession to live "private lives," they were spurned by Klondike society even more than were retired dance hall girls. Montreal Marie, a former prostitute who lived with a man by the name of Stammers, knew well what the rest of Dawson thought of her. Although Stammers was a civil servant, which should have placed him in the upper ranks of the local hierarchy, the couple and their two young daughters were consistently ostracized.

One fall Stammers took a trip back to his native Australia, his first visit in fifteen years. Local gossip said Marie had paid his way. The next spring, much to everyone's surprise, he returned with a bride who knew nothing of his other family until she reached Dawson. Despite his duplicity, Stammers was welcomed back into the fold. Women who would have never given Montreal Marie the time of day hastened to invite Mrs. Stammers to tea. Partly they acted out of a combination of curiosity and sympathy for the bewildered young woman, but mostly they were doing what they would have done for any newcomer who fit their definition of a lady. Meanwhile, Marie and her children moved quietly back to Lousetown and she resumed her former occupation.

6

HUNTING FOR SOULS
—in the—
GOLD FIELDS

No one who watched the *Alice* steam in to Dawson on July 11, 1898, could have missed the pair of women who stood together by the railings shrouded in stiff, black habits, the heavy, gold crosses that hung round their necks catching the sun. Their pale, inscrutable faces peered out from the white frames of their wimples, but they carefully avoided meeting the curious eyes of the men and women crowded along the waterfront. When the boat was secured, Sisters Mary John Damascene and Mary of the Cross made their way down the gangplank to the priest who was waiting to greet them. Sister Mary Joseph Calasanctius, who had fallen ill during the journey and was too weak to walk, was brought ashore later.

The three Sisters of St. Ann were no newcomers to the north. All could call themselves sourdoughs since they had seen freeze-up and spring thaw, though Sister Mary of the Cross had only witnessed this cycle of the seasons once. Sister Mary Joseph had a decade of experience behind her, having served at Holy Cross mission on the lower Yukon River since 1888. Sister Mary John had gone to Holy Cross in 1892, immediately after completion of her novitiate. Although far from her native Quebec, she was to find one familiar face in the Klondike. Emilie Fortin, who married Jack Tremblay and faced the repulsive spitting pole in his old bachelor quarters on her honeymoon, had known Sister Mary John as Agnes Ouimette when both were girls.

The nuns were greeted warmly by Father William Judge. The Oblate missionary, a seven-year veteran of the gold-mining communities in Alaska and the Yukon, had made his way to Dawson in March 1897, and immediately begun construction of a church and the Klondike's first hospital. It did not take him long to realize that the population of the region was growing at an unprecedented rate and he could not run the hospital alone. Having worked with the Sisters of St. Ann at various missions, it was only natural he seek the assistance of this group of women whose competence and ability to withstand the rigours of northern life he knew and trusted. It took over a year, however, for them to reach Dawson.

When they received Father Judge's call for help in September 1897, four nuns immediately left Holy Cross and started upriver. Unfortunately, it was too late in the season to make the journey. Low water and shifting sand bars confounded the crew of their steamship. For several days they were stuck on the Yukon Flats, where in places the water was only two feet deep. Finally they were forced to turn around.

The next spring, three of the sisters managed to find places on the first steamer bound for Dawson. Again there were delays when their boat grounded on sand bars, but this time their prayers were answered and they succeeded in reaching Dawson. At the end of August their numbers were reinforced by the arrival of Sisters Mary Zephyrin, Pauline, and Prudentienne from Akulurak. Situated on a vast tundra plain on the windswept coast of the Bering Sea, Akulurak had seemed a bleak and lonely place when they first went there, but the nuns had left with sad hearts. They felt they were abandoning the native people with whom they had worked, and that the Akulurak mission was being sacrificed for Dawson. There was never any thought, however, of disobeying orders.

Although the sisters were used to modest accommodations, they were taken aback when they saw their Dawson residence: a former cold-storage room with no windows. Their living situation improved slightly when they moved into a two-storey cabin, although they had to share it with the hospital's female patients who were housed on the second floor. Doctors and friends visited the patients until late at night, making sleep difficult. A few months later the nuns relocated again, this time to a room over the kitchen that barely held their six beds and left almost no space for eating, washing, or sitting to write letters or read. It was over a year before they got a separate dining area. Living under such crowded conditions added a great deal of stress to the sisters' lives, but they understood that space was at a premium.

The original St. Mary's Hospital was a two-storey log structure, fifty

One of the Sisters of St. Ann attends to a patient in a crowded ward.

feet long and twenty feet wide, with little in the way of equipment or supplies, and no running water. Sacks of sawdust took the place of mattresses on the beds, and the only patients who had sheets were those who brought their own and had them privately laundered.

By the time the first nuns arrived, work was under way to expand the hospital with a seventy-by-twenty-foot, three-storey addition, and a smaller main-floor wing. The increased space, which more than doubled the capacity, was desperately needed to deal with the victims of a typhoid epidemic that was raging through the Klondike region. Each new floor was filled to capacity as soon as it was finished. A rainstorm in early September caused delays and increased costs because all the carpenters working on the second level were diverted from their work to mop up the water and prevent it from leaking through and soaking the patients installed below. At the time there were eighty-nine patients in the hospital. Seven of these were women, grateful that the presence of the nuns allowed them to be accommodated. By October 1898, construction was complete and the hospital was bursting with 140 people, mostly typhoid sufferers.

The opening of the Good Samaritan Hospital by the Presbyterians in mid-August 1898 took some of the pressure off St. Mary's, but demand for beds remained high. The Klondike, in the early days, was an extremely

Sisters Mary Prudence, Zenon, Edith, Benedict, Pauline, Prudentienne, Jules of the Sacred Heart, and Coeur de Jésus (left to right from top), 1900.

unhealthy place. At the peak of the stampede Dawson was the largest city west of Winnipeg and north of Seattle, yet it was entirely lacking in proper sanitary arrangements. The swampy lowlands on which the town had been built, the rotting garbage thrown into the rivers that supplied the residents' drinking water, and the stinking sewage running freely in the gutters created perfect conditions for the spread of the deadly typhoid bacteria.

Health problems were compounded by severe shortages of fresh food during the first two winters of the gold rush. Malnutrition made people susceptible to illness, and dietary deficiencies frequently resulted in scurvy, scrofula, and anaemia. Sister Mary Zephyrin had herself suffered from scurvy in 1894, causing her to lose all her teeth at the age of thirty-nine. Other common winter complaints included frostbite, gangrene, rheumatism, and pneumonia.

For more than a year before the arrival of the sisters, Father Judge ran the hospital almost single-handedly, while still finding time to minister to the spiritual needs of his flock. His assistants were a few men with as little medical training as himself, and a couple of American doctors who left in the spring of 1898 because they were not licensed to practise in Canada. Shortly after their departure, Dr. W.T. Barrett arrived in Dawson from Manitoba and accepted Father Judge's plea that he take over as the hospital's head physician.

The staffing situation at St. Mary's improved over the summer of 1898 as more well-educated gold seekers poured into the region, discovered there were no more claims to stake and began looking for other employment. The hospital's nursing staff included a veterinary surgeon, at least one fully qualified male nurse, and several foreign doctors who were unable to meet the Canadian licensing requirements.

The nuns themselves had no formal training in nursing, but in Dr. Barrett's opinion this was of little concern. He found them to be extremely competent in caring for patients, noting that they brought with them "a vast storehouse of knowledge, and a legacy rich in experience in dealing with humanity in the raw, a solid foundation on which to build a more advanced technical education for hospital nursing." He had special praise for Sister Mary John Damascene who was given full charge of the operating theatre. She was, he thought, "an outstanding example of aptitude and thoroughness in mastering the technique of surgical nursing. . . . Her work in St. Mary's will remain a monument to her zeal and attention to detail in preparation of the patient and the operating theatre."[1]

Soon after arriving in Dawson the nuns discovered that Father Judge's health was failing. A frail man at the best of times, he had worked himself to the point of exhaustion and neglected his own well-being. In this weakened state he was unable to withstand an attack of pneumonia that struck him during the winter. On January 16, 1899, at the age of forty-nine, he passed away. The whole community, Catholics and non-Catholics alike, mourned the beloved priest's death. For Sister Superior Mary Zephyrin his demise meant more than the loss of an old friend and respected colleague. It represented an enormous new challenge, for she was now responsible for managing the hospital and dealing with its crushing burden of debt.

Due to high operating costs and Father Judge's refusal to turn away any sick person as long as there was space available, St. Mary's had run a deficit from the day it opened its doors. Neither he nor the nuns received a salary, but cooks, laundresses, water carriers, lay nurses, and consulting doctors all had to be paid at the Klondike's usual exorbitant rates. Building materials and supplies were also expensive.

Patients paid for their care in one of two ways. Those with foresight and spare cash purchased a type of medical insurance known as a hospital ticket for fifty dollars a year. Ticket holders were entitled to full board and medical care for an unlimited amount of time. Other patients paid five dollars a day. Unfortunately, the Klondike was full of people who had spent their last penny to get there and then not found the riches they had expected. When the Sisters of St. Ann took over the hospital, it was forty-five thousand dollars in the red. Despite several emergency appropriations from the government and a decision by the Yukon Council to start paying the hospital $3.50 per day for each bed occupied by an indigent patient, the situation improved only marginally.

The only way to keep the hospital running was to raise funds privately. After discussions among themselves, the nuns decided that they would have to go out and appeal directly to the miners for donations. Early in May 1899, Sisters Mary of the Cross and Mary John Damascene left for a tour of the creeks, with a man by the name of C.H. Higgins as their guide.

For their first day's journey to Hunker Creek they rode on a pair of borrowed horses. After that they walked through the snow and mud, with their habits pinned up to clear the top of their rubber boots. The second day they covered thirty miles, arriving at midnight at a cabin on Dominion Creek where they had been promised a place to stay. As the three weary travellers prepared for bed, Higgins overheard the nuns conversing in French. He could not understand their words, but he sensed something was wrong. In response to his inquiries, Sister Mary John showed him her badly blistered feet, and her boots, which had worn through. Higgins immediately put his own boots back on and retraced their steps to a dance hall and store, seven miles back down the trail.

He knew the chances of finding footwear small enough to fit the nun were few. Much to his surprise, however, one of the female employees of the establishment—a woman of ill repute in his eyes—heard his request and offered a pair of her own boots. When he pulled out his sack of gold dust to pay, she asked if he was the man who had passed earlier with the two nuns and whether the boots were for them. Upon hearing his answer, she pushed away his poke and told him just to ask the sisters to pray for her.

The new boots got plenty of wear over the following weeks, as the sisters and their loyal guide worked their way up and down Dominion, Bonanza, and Eldorado creeks. Everywhere they stopped they were met with generosity, and by the end of their twenty-eight-day excursion they had covered about 475 miles and collected ten thousand dollars.

Concerned citizens also helped finance St. Mary's with their own initiatives, such as benefit performances and raffles. In the fall of 1899, when the hospital's finances looked particularly grim, a group of Dawson women came to the rescue with plans for a grand Christmas charity bazaar that was a resounding success.

The gala, week-long affair was held at the Palace Grand Theatre. Each day's activities were chronicled in *The Paystreak*, a daily newspaper published for the duration of the bazaar. Editor Faith Fenton, a respected journalist who had come to the Klondike as a correspondent for the Toronto *Globe*, described the bazaar's opening night in the December 25 *Paystreak*.

> Anything prettier than the scene of Saturday evening can hardly be imagined. . . .
>
> Looking down from the boxes or up from the floor, from the stage or entrance, whatever the point of view, the picture was one of glowing color, light and warmth, vitalized by laughter, music and the hum of speech. . . .
>
> From eight o'clock onward guests arrived in a continuous stream. They crowded galleries and boxes, then overflowed down to the main floor. They laughed and chatted, drank cafe noir and fished in the water lily pond; they tried the wheel of fortune, visited the gipsy proprietress, purchased bon-bons, listened to the music, and when it grew irresistible, threw severity and formality to the winds, and danced— making the pretty picture more charming yet.
>
> Twelve o'clock brought Sunday morning all too soon.

The bazaar provided a welcome break in the midst of the darkest, coldest month of the year. People happily paid the price of admission to the brightly lit hall, and then made the rounds of the stalls, spending money freely on an impressive selection of handmade and donated items, lottery tickets, and food.

Although far too busy with hospital duties to help organize the event, the nuns still found time to do their part. Sister Mary Pauline made candies for Mrs. Mahoney's Confection Booth. A new arrival, Sister Mary Jules, roasted turkeys for the Christmas dinner. For the Fancy Work Stall, Sister Mary Joseph trimmed a handkerchief with Brussels lace, and several other sisters made wax-dipped paper flowers.

One of the highlights of the fair was the Turkish Booth, which occupied much of the theatre's upper floor and was "most effectively furnished with low divans, nooks and corners, and the dim, tinted lights affected by the Orientals."[2] There, café noir and cigars were served by "fair women, bewitching as any Eastern houris." Despite the hint of naughtiness in *The Paystreak's* depiction of the Turkish Booth, there was nothing risqué about the bazaar. The ladies' organizing committee was headed by some of the most respectable women in the district, including the wives of Captain Cortlandt Starnes of the North-West Mounted Police and Judge Dugas.

At the end of the week Mrs. Dugas and Mrs. Starnes presented twelve thousand dollars to a delighted Sister Mary Zephyrin. Although this did not solve all the financial troubles at St. Mary's, it relieved much of the pressure.

The hospital's debt was not Sister Superior Mary Zephyrin's only trial during the year after Father Judge's death. She also found herself dealing with a wayward nun. Sister Mary of the Cross, who had charmed the miners out on the creeks, was also a favourite with patients and hospital staff. She laboured tirelessly on the floor, cheering those around her with her lively and joyous manner. She even found time to give religious instruction to one of the interns who expressed an interest in the Catholic faith. While Sister Mary Zephyrin heard nothing but praise for the young nun's work, she also noticed that she was increasingly absent from scheduled prayers and seemed remote when she spent time with the other sisters.

Finally, when Sister Mary of the Cross and the intern could no longer hide their feelings for one another, she requested permission to leave the order. Not even Mother Mary Angel Guardian, who came up from Victoria to talk with the rebellious nun, could change her mind. Sister Mary of the Cross left the Yukon in the summer of 1899. When her vows expired and she was once again simply Mary Peterson, she and the intern married and returned to Dawson. They soon moved away again, however, after realizing that the town's Catholic community would never accept them.

In November 1899, the Sisters of St. Ann opened the Yukon's first school, next to the hospital and the church. Only one nun could be spared from the hospital, so Sister Mary Joseph Calasanctius taught all the classes, assisted by Mamie Connor, a former student of St. Ann's Academy in Victoria. Their teaching supplies consisted of four or five readers, a few arithmetic books, and a blackboard, which they were unable to use until someone in town found a box of chalk.

Twenty pupils appeared for class on the first day, and over the next few months, enrollment grew to forty six. In order to qualify for government funding, religious education was restricted to after school hours; this satisfied a number of Protestant parents who sent their children to the school. The growing number of families in Dawson soon compelled the sisters to assign two full-time teachers, and in 1904, St. Mary's School was moved to a new two-storey building in the centre of town.

In 1906, St. Mary's Hospital also relocated. The new facility was a large, modern structure, with electricity, steam heat, running water, and an X-ray machine. Ironically, the Klondike's population had, by this time, dwindled considerably. The Good Samaritan Hospital closed its doors in 1918, but the nuns stayed on and continued to make their hospital one of the best in the north.

By 1948, when St. Mary's celebrated its golden jubilee, it had a maternity wing, a children's ward, and a tuberculosis annex. Eighty-year-old Sister Mary Prudentienne, who had come to Dawson from Akulurak fifty years previously, was still an active member of the staff. A disastrous fire in 1950 marked the end of an era. The nuns operated for the next thirteen years out of temporary quarters, but finally acknowledged that St. Mary's Hospital would never be rebuilt. The last sisters packed their bags and said good-bye to Dawson in 1963.

Like the Roman Catholic church, the Church of England had a long history in Canada's northern regions. The two denominations were highly competitive when it came to claiming converts, and in 1861 the Anglicans won the race to send the first man of God to preach in the Yukon Territory. Throughout the following decades, the Church Missionary Society periodically dispatched others to continue spreading the word. Nearly all were male. Then in 1893, a diminutive, young Irish woman arrived in Forty Mile to answer the bishop's call for assistance.

Although Susan Mellett was only twenty-two years old, she had travelled alone across the Atlantic, across the continent, up the Pacific coast to St. Michael, and then on to Forty Mile. When she finally reached the end of her long journey, she discovered Bishop William Bompas was none too pleased that she was his only new recruit for the year. Ideally, Bompas was looking for men to carry out the work of the church in the vast wilderness under his jurisdiction. Furthermore, he preferred his missionaries to be married, or at least engaged. Fortunately, Susan possessed two other qualities that the bishop considered essential: sterling piety and a hardy constitution.

Susan also brought with her some practical skills. In Ireland, she had taught in the Ragged Schools, charitable institutions that provided basic education, industrial training, and religious instruction for poor children. Based on this experience, and the fact that she was female, she was given the job of teaching the native children who lived at the mission. It went without saying that she would also help Charlotte Bompas, the bishop's wife, with household duties.

Once she had proven herself, Susan was transferred to Rampart House to teach. While serving there she met Reverend R.J. Bowen, a young English clergyman who had come north in 1894. They married in 1897, and shortly afterwards received orders to move to Dawson.

The Bowens' first task in Dawson was to build a church. Despite the scarcity of glass window-panes, they managed to obtain a few, but when it came to putting them in place there was no putty to be found anywhere in town. Someone suggested using bread dough, so Susan mixed up a batch. The dough was quite effective through the winter, but had to be replaced with a more conventional substance after the first spring thaw.

The new St. Paul's church was proudly inaugurated in the fall of 1897. In addition to being used for Sunday services, it also served as a schoolhouse, and as lodgings for the Bowens until a proper rectory could be built. Their bed was a shelf over the chancel which they reached by a ladder. "We were always thankful we were not sleepwalkers," Susan recalled, "as there was no railing, nothing but space." Down below, a partition was put in to separate the area they used as a living room, kitchen, and vestry from the place of worship. Although they had so little room that they had to keep their personal belongings under their makeshift bed, there was always room for lonely men to stop in for a chat and a cup of tea.

Like most ministers' wives, Susan Bowen worked hard and received no pay. Her duties included teaching day students through the week, organizing Sunday-school classes, and visiting sick parishioners. Special events, like Dawson's first children's Christmas party, took weeks of planning. In preparation for this event Susan went to all the shopkeepers, Protestant and Catholic alike, asking for gifts and candy to distribute to the children. Although hardly anyone had any children's playthings in stock, one generous store owner donated an entire shipment of toys, before they even arrived.

In May 1899, Reverend Bowen contracted typhoid malarial fever. His recovery was slow and it eventually became apparent that he needed a longer period of convalescence. The Bowens spent the next year in England, returning to the Yukon in August 1900 when they were called to establish a new parish in Whitehorse. They left the north permanently in 1903, when Reverend Bowen again fell ill.

Another Anglican missionary wife was Sarah Stringer, better known as Sadie. She and her husband Isaac had grown up on neighbouring farms in Ontario. When Isaac graduated from theological college he asked her to marry him and go with him to the Arctic. Sadie accepted his proposal. Rather than marrying right away, however, she prepared herself for her new role by studying nursing at Grace Hospital in Toronto for two years, and then taking missionary training from the church. In March 1896, Isaac came south on furlough and they tied the knot. Two months later they left for Herschel Island in the high Arctic, both "burning with a missionary zeal laced by a sense of adventure."[3] Sadie was twenty-four; Isaac twenty-six.

In 1905, the Stringers and their two children moved to Dawson, following Isaac's consecration as the new Anglican Bishop of the Yukon diocese. As wife of the first bishop to make Dawson his headquarters, Sadie was assured a place in the upper ranks of Dawson society, but she was not one to put on airs. Sadie was "the sort of woman who immediately hands you a piece of pie as soon as you cross her threshold."[4] The fact that many of those who crossed the threshold of the manse were native people coming to speak to her husband, and that she often sat with them in her kitchen, feeding them pie and plates of beans and pouring endless cups of tea, was not to everyone's liking.

On one occasion she managed to offend almost the entire membership of the Women's Auxiliary by seating the wife of Julius Kendi, a visiting native minister, in the place of honour at her right during afternoon tea. Oblivious to protocol, Sadie simply thought Mrs. Kendi would be more comfortable sitting close to the only person she knew at the gathering.

In addition to her social obligations, Sadie actively supported her husband's work and kept the home fires burning during his many trips to visit the territory's far-flung missions. Dawson remained their home until 1931, when Isaac became Archbishop of Rupertsland and they moved to Winnipeg.

Unlike the Catholics and the Anglicans, the Salvation Army never bothered with the few inhabitants of Alaska and the Yukon prior to the gold rush. But news of the tens of thousands congregating in and around Dawson, all lusting after wealth and vulnerable to the evils of mining-camp life, convinced them to turn their attention northwards.

The idea of a Salvation Army Klondike expedition originated with Evangeline Booth, the Canadian Field Commissioner and daughter of the organization's founder. A first-hand look at the "teeming multitudes mad for gold,"[5] whom she encountered during a visit to British Columbia in the early days of the stampede, convinced her of the necessity of a Dawson mission. Thirty-one-year-old Eva was a dynamic and charismatic individual who knew how to get things done. She wrote at once to the Army's chief of staff explaining her vision:

> I have pictured the city whose wickedness and flagrant wrong is already so extreme that a returned miner told me himself, with a hopeless accent, when I pleaded with him to live there for God and goodness, "An angel couldn't keep good in Dawson City." I felt that I could never know rest again till I had done something to stay the sin and alleviate the suffering which the great mass of undoctored and unnursed humanity must mean.[6]

Her plan was soon approved and eight Soldiers of Christ chosen to "go hunting for souls" in the gold fields.[7] Included in the party were two women, Emma Matilda Aiken and Rebecca Ellery. Emma, or Lillie as she was usually known, was recruited for her training as a nurse. Forty-year-old Rebecca, one of the senior members of the group, was selected for her maturity and her years of missionary experience. She had converted in her mid-twenties and had earned the rank of ensign after serving as an officer for ten years.

Rebecca Ellery (left), Lillie Aiken, and the men of the Salvation Army Klondike contingent before leaving Toronto in April 1898.

The daughter of a large Ontario farming family, Rebecca had never married. She took great pleasure, however, in mothering the younger members of the expedition.

Because of the anticipated hardships, the members of the Klondike contingent were better paid than other Salvation Army missionaries. Rebecca received a weekly salary of nine dollars, just one dollar less than the group's leader. Lillie and most of the men in the group were paid eight dollars a week. Although they were each required to return $4.50 for board, the Army provided them with food and other necessities, such as postage for personal letters.

The Army also supplied each member of the expedition with a complete wardrobe, but being more accustomed to sending missionaries off to tropical locations in Africa, India, and China, the official clothiers had little idea what would be required in the Yukon. Like many female stampeders, Rebecca and Lillie realized soon after their arrival in Dawson that aside from wearing warmer coats in winter, women dressed no differently in the Klondike than at home. "The outfits we came in are the most foolish I have ever seen," Rebecca admitted in one of her rare moments of discontent. "I've not a thing fit to put on except what I brought on my own."[8]

The expedition's send-off was a grand event, full of typical Victorian theatricality. Unlike most Salvation Army meetings, this one was held in Toronto's prestigious Massey Hall. The evening featured the usual songs, prayers, and sermons, but the highlight was the introduction of the expedition members themselves. A murmur of excitement rolled through the hall, and people craned their necks and peered over the balconies as a large dog trotted down the aisle pulling a sled heavily laden with essentials for wilderness living. Then the expedition members appeared and were greeted by thunderous applause. The men unloaded the sled and erected the tents. Once "camp" had been set up on the stage, the Hallelujah Lasses—sweltering in their heavy wool "Klondike suits" and fur hats—tossed flapjacks in the air as they demonstrated how they would prepare meals on the trail.

On April 15, 1898, the day after the Massey Hall meeting, the group boarded a westbound train. Rebecca felt her first twinges of trepidation. "When leaving the station," she wrote in her diary, "I seemed to realize what it meant to say goodbye to all near and dear to me, but my faith is high. I believe God will help. He is on our side. If I don't forget to pray as I ought, it will be well with me."[9]

The trip across the continent was broken periodically to stage farewell gatherings. The Klondikers were accompanied during the overland portion of their journey by Eva Booth and one of her several adopted children, a blond, blue-eyed, four-year-old known as Little Willie. Every time the cherubic orphan took the stage to sing "Let a Little Sunshine In," hearts melted and donations poured in. The expedition members also sang at the meetings, their special number being a song composed in honour of their adventure. Audience members were encouraged to join in the chorus:

We're going to the Klondike,
We're going to the Klondike,
We're going after sinners in that land.

We're happy lads and lasses,
We're not afraid of passes.
We're going to the Klondike at God's command.[10]

One month after leaving Ontario they sailed from Victoria, arriving in Skagway on May 27. The next day they began their trek over the Chilkoot trail. Arrangements were made for the women to travel as far as Canyon City in a horse-drawn carriage, a vehicle not well designed for the rough trail. As they jolted along over rocks and holes, Rebecca and Lillie kept getting thrown into the laps of the eight men with whom they shared the carriage. Rather than being annoyed or distressed by the impropriety of the situation, Rebecca wanted to laugh. She suppressed this urge, however, since the men were strangers and sharing a joke with them could have been construed as loose behaviour. At last she asked the driver to stop so she could get out and walk, and she and one of the men proceeded on foot.

As soon as the Salvation Army party reached Lake Bennett they assembled the two sectional wooden boats they had carried over the pass and loaded their supplies. The women were assigned to separate boats since they were not expected to take turns rowing. They were in no danger, however, of having the devil make work for their idle hands; there was often mending to be done as they floated down the river, and their time on shore was filled with cooking meals and baking bread.

Rebecca was in her element. Her diary entry for Sunday, June 14, hums with contentment.

> Truly we are a family now. I have just as much interest in them as if they were my brothers, in cooking, mending, fixing for them in every way I can to make them comfortable. Mrs. Aiken said to me one day, "I believe you would give them your head." I replied, "I don't think anything is too good for them." There is none of the lads I could fall in love with so I feel free to do anything for them. . . . We got up about eight this morning, had breakfast, prayer, and Mrs. Aiken washed up. Someone was playing the organ before I was up. It is just lovely over here, away from everybody but our own party. . . . I feel so happy and am just where God wants me.[11]

Three weeks later, having reached Dawson, Rebecca's enthusiasm for her role was as solid as ever.

I believe my work has been to look after the lads for I don't know what they would have done if they had not had someone to see to their needs who could rough it better than some of them. I look after their clothes and cook for them just as if I was paid to do it. I love it and never feel better than when I am helping them.[12]

Lillie, on the other hand, did not agree with Rebecca's assessment that "wives or sisters could not be better treated by our lads than we two women are."[13] Lacking her older companion's ability to joke with the men and look cheerfully upon their demands, she cried herself to sleep on more than one occasion. "I don't seem to be a satisfaction," she sobbed to Rebecca one night. "If I had the money I would go home."[14] At that point, however, there was nothing to do but go forward.

Inspired by the prospect of thousands of sinners awaiting them, the Salvationists hastened to Dawson. Rather than floating with the current, they rowed most of the way and made record time. Although the men's hands were blistered and bleeding when they reached their destination, they held an open-air meeting that evening and collected sixty-five dollars in gold dust and nuggets.

The Salvation Army expedition en route to Dawson.

After this first successful gathering they held meetings nightly and three times on Sundays. One evening a man approached Rebecca and asked if he could shake her hand. He had not shaken hands with a good woman in twelve years, he explained. Such moments were heartening, but the Salvationists were generally discouraged by the lack of interest in their mission. Not until October did they get their first convert. "It is hard to get people into our meetings," Rebecca wrote a year after their arrival. "We have had such a few souls. A number of those who kneel at the Penitent-form we never see again."[15] When Rebecca and Lillie initiated women's prayer meetings on Friday afternoons they also found there was limited interest. The first meeting drew only one woman, but the following week there were seven, and then nine.

While the men built barracks and a meeting hall, the women attended to invalids in their cabins and tents and visited prisoners in the jail. Rebecca also went out collecting funds to support their work, even daring to enter Dawson's dens of iniquity. Any fears she had about entering these establishments were quickly dispelled. "I collected from the saloons and hotels about $50," she reported after her first foray, "and not one word said to me was out of the way."[16]

Late in the summer, Rebecca and two of the men walked up to Grand Forks to solicit donations from the miners. Like the Sisters of St. Ann, she found the men courteous and generous. In one saloon two young men treated her to lemonade. Another miner insisted she stay and have dinner with him in his cabin. She noted that it was the best meal she had eaten since coming to the north.

Saving souls was not the Salvation Army's only concern. They offered free meals and beds to destitute men, and kept a supply of clothing on hand for anyone who needed it. They also operated a labour bureau, and ran a wood-yard where the unemployed could earn a little money sawing and splitting logs. All services were available to any needy person, regardless of race or creed. On December 25, 1898, they began a tradition of serving a free Christmas dinner to all who wished to partake. Rebecca, Lillie, and three male volunteers spent days in the kitchen preparing enough food for the three hundred men who ultimately showed up.

All members of the Salvation Army expedition had signed on for a minimum twelve months, but none felt inclined to leave after their first year. In 1900, however, Lillie departed under a cloud of shame. Although married to a man in Ontario, she fell in love with a Klondiker, resigned, and went south to obtain a divorce so she could marry him.

Rebecca remained at the Dawson mission until she received orders to return south in July 1900. She left with regrets. "I felt we were saying good-bye to people we would never meet again till the Judgement Day,"[17] she wrote in her diary as she sat on deck watching the wide, slow Yukon River flowing back towards Dawson. Then she pulled herself together and turned her attention to shedding Christ's light on her fellow passengers.

7

THE NEW WOMAN
—in—
THE NORTH

One of the most important contributions of women like Rebecca Ellery and the Sisters of St. Ann to Klondike society was the care they gave many of the unfortunate stampeders who fell ill. The secular counterparts of these angels of mercy were the women who went to the gold fields as trained nurses and doctors. Like the church women, they were few in number, but the services they rendered were invaluable.

In 1897, nursing was still a relatively new field for women. Florence Nightingale's work on the front lines of the Crimean War in the 1850s and in England over the following decades had done much to establish nursing as a decent vocation for women. Many doctors, however, resented the increasing professionalism of nurses and regarded them as a threat. It was into this environment that Ishbel Aberdeen, wife of John Campbell Aberdeen, Governor General of Canada, launched her notion of a national organization of visiting nurses, to be known as the Victorian Order of Nurses (VON) in honour of Queen Victoria's diamond jubilee.

Lady Aberdeen's proposal was widely opposed at first. The medical establishment objected on the grounds that the nurses would undercut doctors by charging lower fees, and would endanger the public by practising medicine when they were not qualified to do so. Doctors and others also expressed concerns about the morality of sending young, unchaperoned women to remote locations. Eventually, however, enough of the critics were won over. In November 1897, the first recruits were accepted into the VON and assigned to postings across the country.

Knowing the north was in dire need of professional medical care, and that Canadians had an insatiable appetite for anything to do with the gold rush, Ishbel decided to send four nurses to the Yukon. Part of their job would be to draw attention to the fledgling organization. In January 1898, Ishbel spoke at a meeting of doctors and nurses in Toronto and called for volunteers to join the Victorian Order of Nurses' Klondike contingent. Candidates had to be unmarried, at least twenty-eight years old, and have graduated from a recognized nursing school. Ishbel also warned that they would be expected to dress very plainly, and not curl or crimp their hair.

Among those who heard Lady Aberdeen's call for recruits was thirty-nine-year-old Rachel Hanna, who had trained at Toronto General Hospital. The idea caught her fancy, as she was adventurous and enjoyed the outdoors. Rachel sent in her application at once and soon found herself preparing to journey northwards. The other three women selected to represent the Victorian Order of Nurses in the Yukon were Georgia Powell of New Brunswick, Margaret Payson of Nova Scotia, and Amy Scott, a recent immigrant from England. All were experienced nurses, highly recommended by physicians they had worked alongside.

In March 1898, the four met in Ottawa, where they signed their contracts and were outfitted by members of the National Council of Women. The VON contract specified that nurses would receive three hundred dollars a year, plus expenses for board, maintenance, uniform, and travel. Any woman who married before her two-year term was completed was expected to resign and her husband was to pay back the money that had been spent transporting her from headquarters to her posting. Lady Aberdeen took a personal interest in the Klondike nurses' preparations and arranged a lavish farewell dinner at Rideau House, the governor general's official residence.

The nurses made the first part of their journey in the comfort of a private railway car that carried them from Ottawa to Vancouver. Travelling with them were two other Klondike-bound women: Faith Fenton of the Toronto *Globe;* and Mrs. Starnes, who was going to join her husband, Inspector Cortlandt Starnes, in Dawson. In Vancouver, the women met the Yukon Field Force, a two-hundred-man unit that was going north to establish a Canadian military presence in the new territory.

Lady Aberdeen had thought it prudent for the VON contingent to travel with the Yukon Field Force so the soldiers could protect them. In return, the nurses would help keep the troops healthy. Concerns for the women's safety were probably exaggerated, but the nurses certainly upheld their part of the bargain, treating a number of soldiers for a variety of ills during the journey. Their ministrations were also eagerly sought by ailing civilians they met along the way.

On May 14, the two hundred men and six women boarded the *Islander* which would carry them to Wrangell, near the tip of the Alaska panhandle. Five days later they were steaming up the Stikine River on their way to Glenora and the start of their arduous overland trek.

At Glenora, the women were divided into two groups that travelled separately. Georgia Powell, Amy Scott, and Mrs. Starnes were assigned to the advance party, while Rachel Hanna, Margaret Payson, and Faith Fenton followed behind with another detachment. Each trio of women shared a horse. Georgia had little use for their mount, "a stupid, lazy, old pony, whose one ambition was to bang up against every available tree."[1] She gave her turns to the other two women, preferring to walk, even on the day when they covered seventeen miles of muddy trail in the pouring rain. Georgia described their daily schedule as

> up at 2 in the morning, breakfast at 3, tent down and everything packed at 4 and everything on the trail before five. Our lunch . . . consisted of two hard biscuits and a cup of water from the nearest spring. . . . we had dinner just when the [last of the men] came in, sometimes 8 or 9, sometimes as late as 11 p.m.[2]

When they reached Fort Selkirk, Amy stayed behind with the main body of the Yukon Field Force, while Georgia and Mrs. Starnes continued on to Dawson, arriving on August 8, 1898. Like the Sisters of St. Ann who had arrived a month earlier, Georgia found her skills desperately needed to care for the many victims of the typhoid epidemic that was raging through the region. She was immediately installed as matron of the Presbyterian-run Good Samaritan Hospital, which was still under construction.

The hospital consisted of two log buildings, each twenty-five feet wide by fifty feet long. During its first week of operation, eighteen men were admitted. The number doubled in the second week, and by December, seventy-five patients crowded the wards. Georgia made no secret of the conditions in her first report to Ishbel Aberdeen in Ottawa.

> I thought I had seen something of typhoid fever, but nothing like this. Of severe hemorrhage cases, we had six at one time. Typhoid with pneu-

By 1900 the Good Samaritan Hospital had fewer patients and more supplies, but the nurses still worked hard.

monia, with malaria, congestion of the liver, rheumatism, neuralgia, sore throat, discharge from the ears, and sore eyes. Such sick men! nor was the sickness all, but the filth and the vermin; and we had so little to do with. . . . The few mattresses we had were taken from the convalescing men and given to the very sick men. Often a patient lay for days with only a blanket between him and the boards, thankful if we could give him a sack of shavings. And yet I must say not one of these patients had a bed sore, or even a chafe, so closely were they watched and attended.[3]

Georgia's own bed was a sack stuffed with wood shavings and, for some inexplicable reason, with boards, but as the hospital's only trained nurse she had little time for sleep. After a month of exhausting work and poor food, she too fell ill with typhoid. Fortunately, the other three nurses arrived a few days later.

Amy was assigned to nursing duties at the North-West Mounted Police barracks, while Margaret was sent to staff the hospital at Grand Forks. This left Rachel to care for Georgia and take over temporarily as the Good Samaritan Hospital's head nurse. Originally the Dawson nurses slept in a small tent. Before winter set in they moved into a log cabin, which speeded Georgia's recovery, but there was little improvement in their working conditions during the first year. Disinfectants, dressings, sheets, and gowns were all in limited supply, and they had only candles to light the wards during the long winter nights. The patients' beds were so close together that they had to turn sideways to pass between them.

The arrival of winter saw a reduction in the number of typhoid cases but an increase in scurvy victims. "Nursing scurvy patients at best is disgusting work," Georgia noted in her report, "under these circumstances, doubly so. The scrubbing and cleaning of these miserable creatures—and how some would fight against the bath!"[4]

The spring of 1899 brought relief to the nurses as new shipments of fresh food and advancements in Dawson's sanitary arrangements led to an improvement in the public health situation. Typhoid broke out again that summer, but fewer people were affected. In November 1899, there were only twenty-seven patients at the Good Samaritan Hospital: seven suffering from typhoid, two from scurvy, and the rest from other ailments.

Although the four nurses received nothing but praise, their time was devoted almost entirely to hospital work rather than the district nursing which was the Victorian Order of Nurses' primary mandate. This prompted a decision to withdraw the VON from the Klondike in May 1900. By this time only Georgia remained on the Order's payroll.

Margaret had resigned after six weeks at the Grand Forks hospital, a deplorable facility with even fewer conveniences than the Good Samaritan. At night Margaret had slept in a corner of the ward, the only woman in a room full of men with only a curtain for privacy. Since there was no bed, she rolled out her sleeping bag on the cold, bare floor. Georgia reported sympathetically on Margaret's resignation, noting that the hardships and privations she had endured "were many, and almost degrading enough to make one doubt the 'blessedness of drudgery.'"[5] Margaret accepted a job at the Dawson post office, and later married a wealthy miner.

Amy was invalided home to England during the summer of 1899, while Rachel resigned from the VON at the end of the year. Rachel was not unhappy with the organization, but she knew if she stayed with the Order she would be transferred elsewhere. She loved life in the north and her work at the Good Samaritan Hospital, so she chose to remain at the hospital as an employee of the Presbyterian Mission Board. In 1904, when the Good Samaritan became a civic institution, Rachel moved to Atlin, where she worked as matron of another Presbyterian hospital for the next fourteen years.

Georgia also resigned and stayed in Dawson. She was reluctant to part company with the man she would eventually marry, Sergeant Bates of the North-West Mounted Police. Nevertheless, the wedding was postponed in 1900 when she went off to care for soldiers fighting in the Boer War. In South Africa she was happily surprised to be reunited with Amy, as both were serving with the 10th Canadian Field Hospital.

With St. Mary's and the Good Samaritan Hospital both swamped with patients in the early years of the gold rush, a number of men and women with medical experience took the opportunity to open their own infirmaries. Throughout 1898, six private hospitals did a flourishing business in Dawson, although by the end of 1899, only one remained. At least one of these pri-

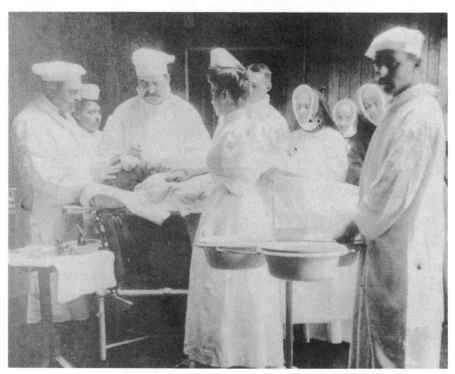

Sisters Mary Damascene, Prudentienne, and Zenon (left to right) look on while a lay nurse assists in an operation at St. Mary's Hospital.

vate hospitals was operated by a woman: Mrs. R.A. Edgerton, a professional nurse from England who had gained field experience while working for the Red Cross. Mrs. Edgerton later became matron of the Good Samaritan Hospital.

A few women who worked as nurses in the Klondike were actually fully qualified doctors. Canadian law stipulated that foreigners could practise medicine only if they were graduates of four-year programmes and could pass a certifying examination. A number of American doctors failed to meet these requirements, which caused a great outcry from those who saw this as unfair discrimination. Many members of the public also complained that the policy made no sense, given the shortage of physicians in the north. Some of the unlicensed doctors left the Yukon, while others advertised their services as nurses. A few, like Dr. Luella Day, were charged with unlawfully practising medicine.

Dr. Day's activities came to light when one of her patients died during childbirth. Luella had met the woman, Belle Conder, on the trail to Dawson. She was called to Belle's bedside to attend to a difficult labour because no licensed doctor was available. Luella did what she could, but was unable to save Belle's life. Although the charges against her were eventually dropped and she was permitted to work in Dawson as a nurse, the experience left Luella bitter and resentful.

Another American woman, Dr. C.M. Haynes, tried to convince the authorities that her wealth of experience compensated for her inability to meet the licensing requirements. Although she had graduated from a three-year programme, she had been a doctor for twenty-five years. The board of examiners refused to make any exceptions to the rules.

One of the few American doctors to pass the certification exam and be allowed to practise medicine in the Yukon was Dr. Mary Mosher, a Boston homeopath. She travelled to the Klondike in 1898 with an unmarried sister and remained there for at least a year.

In March 1899, Mary rented the Family Theatre for an evening and invited nearly one hundred friends to help celebrate her recent admission into the ranks of Dawson's practising physicians. Although many of the town's leading citizens were in attendance, the guest who attracted the most attention was the doctor's two-month-old, adopted daughter. The baby's natural mother, twenty-three-year-old May Edgren, had died of typhoid fever shortly after giving birth. Unable to give the newborn the care she needed, Jessie Edgren agreed to give his daughter up for adoption and chose Mary out of the fifteen women who volunteered for the job.

It was only in the last two decades of the nineteenth century that the majority of North American medical colleges ceased to exclude female students. Even then women often constituted only 10 percent of medical school classes.[6] Teaching, on the other hand, was well established as a respectable way for women to enter the work force and ranked as the favoured profession for middle-class women. Not until 1899, however, were any teachers able to find work in the Klondike.

When Mrs. L.C. Howland left Seattle in 1897, she hoped to open a school "to teach the forty children unfortunate enough to live in Dawson City something besides the way to cook beans . . . or to pan gravel."[7] Mrs. Howland was on her way to join her husband who managed a Yukon River steamboat, but having graduated only four years earlier from Harvard University she had aspirations beyond housekeeping.

In preparation for her venture, Mrs. Howland equipped herself with an extensive library of textbooks for her prospective young students. She also packed a selection of higher-level works on science and history, essays by Charles Lamb, and literary works by Nathaniel Hawthorne and Walter Scott. These were intended for the men whom she expected would wish to brush up their education during the winter months. When Mrs. Howland's teaching plans foundered she turned instead to writing for the San Francisco *Examiner* under the pen name Molly Glenn.

The Klondike's first successful private school was probably one run by an American teacher, Miss Lind, who went north to visit her sister—the wife of a wealthy Eldorado miner—in the summer of 1899. Although Miss Lind arrived fully intending to return to her teaching job in the United States, life in the Klondike so intrigued her that she resigned from her position at home and stayed to teach in a tent schoolhouse on Eldorado Creek. Among her pupils were Ethel and Dewey, the oldest of the three Anderson children who had come from Seattle with their seasick mother, Emma, to join their father the previous year.

In 1899, when the Sisters of St. Ann opened St. Mary's School, there were 163 children living in Dawson, with a few hundred more in the surrounding region. Although the nuns welcomed pupils of all denominations and restricted religious instruction to after-school hours, only a small

Schoolteacher Miss Lind and students, circa 1899. The blonde girl in the black dress (centre) is Ethel Anderson; her brother Dewey is on the far right.

number of Protestant children attended St. Mary's. Total enrollment during the first year ranged from twenty to forty-six.

Agitation by non-Catholics finally convinced the territorial government to open public schools in Dawson and several communities on the creeks in August 1900. For many years, the majority of Klondike teachers were single women, attracted by the novelty of living in the north, the relatively high pay, or both. When Toronto kindergarten teacher Laura Thompson received a phone call during the summer of 1907, asking if she was interested in a job in Dawson, the mention of wages convinced her immediately. In Toronto she was earning $480 a year; in the Yukon her annual salary would be $2100.

There was a high turnover among Klondike teachers, the most common reason for leaving being a change in marital status. The idea of respectable, single women pursuing careers was just beginning to gain general public support at the turn of the century, and few people were ready to accept that married women might work outside the home by choice rather than necessity. School boards throughout North America imposed their values on their female employees, forcing them to leave their jobs when they married, and the authorities in the Yukon were no less conservative.

One of the first women hired to teach in the Klondike's public school system was Maude Edwards, daughter of a Dominion Land Surveyor who was working in Dawson. In September 1902, the Yukon school inspector reported that Maude showed "good teaching ability and a good manner before the class," and he judged her work to be "very satisfactory." She intended to marry soon, however, and the inspector adamantly opposed her wish to keep her job. "It would not be desirable to retain her services after her marriage," he argued "as we could only expect a part of her attention to be given to the school."[8] Unable to convince the school board otherwise, Miss Edwards became Mrs. Hutcherson and retired.

Another early teacher was Winifred McLellan. Born in 1877, teaching had been her dream since childhood. She had already been teaching for several years in her home town of Noel Shore, Nova Scotia, when her brother, a Dawson grocer, wrote and suggested she come north. Winifred arrived in 1900, and taught in Dawson and the surrounding area until 1907, when she left to get married. She later spoke of her time in the Klondike as the happiest years of her life.

While in Dawson, Winifred lived with her brother over his store. Her accommodation at Bonanza Creek was a small cabin next to the school. Although she was only five-foot-two and weighed ninety-eight pounds, she was not afraid to live alone in the mining district. She did, however, call on some of her older male students to keep her door and windows shovelled clear of snow, and to chop kindling for the stoves in her cabin and the school.

A number of educated women who were unable to get jobs in the public schools or unwilling to live with the dictates of the school board gave private lessons in specialty subjects. Miss R.A. Mackie tutored students in French, while Katherina Kreig, a "prima donna soprano" who had graduated from the Leipzig Conservatory of Music, gave lessons in voice culture and study of harmony.

One of the greatest breakthroughs for working women in the late Victorian era was their entry into the offices of government and business. The labour shortage caused by the Civil War had given American women their first opportunity to prove themselves in clerical positions, an advance that had an impact north of the border as well. The introduction of the typewriter in the 1880s, and the corresponding need for nimble-fingered operators, assured women's place in the white-collar workforce. In 1900, females held 77 percent of all typists' and stenographers' jobs in the United States, compared to 5 percent three decades earlier.[9]

While female clerical staff were becoming a common sight in most North American cities by the end of the century, they were slower to appear in Dawson. In December 1897, newspaper correspondent E. Hazard Wells remarked on the absence of women in the town's offices.

> There are a number of bald-headed gentlemen in Dawson engaged in business, but not a single pretty typewriter girl to sit industriously by, reflecting the bewitching beauty of her countenance in one of those polished and hairless domes of knowledge. Yet there are several writing machines in the town . . . and boys who are attempting to operate them earn from $8 to $10 per day. An excellent opening exists for a few lady stenographers. At present they could command $15 to $20 per day.[10]

Despite his disparaging tone, Wells obviously considered experienced female clerical workers to be more valuable than untrained men, and was

Dawson staff of the Canadian Bank of Commerce in 1907. Female clerical workers held positions in many government offices and private businesses.

correct in his assessment of the job opportunities for women with the appropriate skills. Within a year both the gold commissioner's office and the post office had hired female employees. By 1903, the most common occupation listed for women in the Dawson city directory was stenographer, and women outnumbered the men who earned their living this way. In addition to those working in government offices and private enterprises were several women who ran their own businesses doing freelance typing and stenography.

For women without higher education or clerical training, retail work was considered one of the more genteel employment options. Among those who went to the Klondike and found jobs as saleswomen or cashiers was Mary Fellows. Working in the North American Trading and Transportation Company's Dawson store certainly did no harm to Mary's social position: she went from cashier to wife of Ely Weare, the acting president of the firm and a prominent Chicago businessman. Their wedding was, according to the *Klondike Nugget* of February 18, 1899, a "social event of importance to Dawson's most exclusive circles."

Another career which opened up to women in the late Victorian era was journalism. Although the Klondike gold rush was an overwhelmingly male event, women were sent by several eminent newspapers, as well as a number of smaller publications, to cover the story. The end of the nineteenth century was a time of rising prestige for reporters. What had once been a low-class occupation became a glamorous pursuit for the well educated. The men and women who wrote for the top newspapers were adventurous and resourceful. Instead of watching from the sidelines, they helped make the news by participating in events. Toronto *Globe* correspondent Faith Fenton epitomized this new breed of journalist.

Thirty-eight-year-old Alice Freeman, who wrote under the name Faith Fenton, was no rookie when she travelled to the Klondike with the Victorian Order of Nurses and the Yukon Field Force in 1898. In announcing her arrival in Dawson, the September 28 edition of the *Klondike Nugget* called her "a brilliant Canadian writer of magazine and newspaper fame." Before joining the staff of *The Globe*, she had been editor-in-chief of *The Canadian Home Journal*, and her byline had appeared in both the New York *Sun* and the Toronto *Empire*.

Faith's first report on her Klondike journey was filed from Wrangell on May 16, 1898, with others following every few weeks thereafter. Her lengthy dispatches were rich with detail about fellow travellers, sights, scenery, weather, trail conditions, and amusing, dramatic, or tragic incidents. One character she sketched for her readers was a packer by the name of Murphy, a rough, weather-burnt giant of a man. One night as they sat by the campfire she probed him regarding his thoughts on women.

"White women are not much good," says Murphy, "savin' your presence. They won't work. A klootchman (Indian woman) is best. She don't ask no questions, and she does what she's ordered. A klootchman's worth five dollars a day to any man out in these parts. . . . Can you cook?" he queried. "Can you wash blankets? An' I suppose you couldn't round up cayuses? No? Well, you see, you really wouldn't be no use to a packer."[11]

VON nurses (from left to right) Margaret Payson, Rachel Hanna, Georgia Powell, and Amy Scott with journalist Faith Fenton (far right).

What the soldiers thought of having a "New Woman" like Faith along can be surmised from a diary entry written by Private Edward Lester half-way through the trek.

The women have not come in [to camp] yet which is a blessing, as in the other camp they were an infernal nuisance their tents being so close to ours that they could overhear all that went on, & they were continually making complaints, Tommy's language not being always the choicest. If they were so modest they should have had their tents pitched away from our lines. . . . I think Faith Fenton is at the bottom of it all.[12]

When Faith donned her walking skirt in Wrangell, the commander of the Yukon Field Force, Lieutenant-Colonel Thomas Evans, may have also regretted the decision to allow women to accompany his troops. Although the skirt came down well past her knees, she did not hide her lower legs with bloomers and gaiters as the nurses did. The bachelor colonel was too embarrassed to approach Faith about the delicate subject of her exposed ankles himself, so he delegated the task to Mrs. Starnes. The problem was solved by sewing a band of material to the hem of Faith's skirt.

Aside from these minor conflicts, Faith got along well with her military travelling companions. At the end of the journey she declared that the men were "good fellows every one," and thanked both officers and privates for the courtesy they had extended to herself and the other women.

By the time Faith reached Dawson on September 15 it was too late to return south, so she found herself a cabin close to the Good Samaritan Hospital and happily settled in for the winter. Her work was sometimes hampered by frozen ink, but it was the unreliable postal system that gave her the most problems. Her worst experience occurred when she prematurely filed copy about a hanging that never took place.

Four Tagish men had been sentenced to death for murdering a white miner the previous summer. The execution was set for the morning of November 1, which presented Faith with a dilemma. The next official mail was not due to be sent out for another two weeks, but an experienced traveller who was about to leave for Skagway was willing to carry letters for a fee. Unfortunately, he was determined to make an early start—one hour before the hanging was scheduled to occur. After much deliberation, Faith decided to get her scoop by sending a story that read as though it had been written after the fact.

Forty-five minutes after the mail carrier left Dawson, Colonel Sam Steele announced a twenty-four-hour reprieve for the condemned men. This did not worry Faith unduly, but the next day, when Steele postponed the execution for another four months, she realized she had made a serious error in judgement. Without delay she hired a runner to retrieve her story, then waited anxiously for a day and a half until he returned, envelope safely in hand.

By the time the rivers were free of ice in the spring, Faith had decided to stay in Dawson. She continued to send stories to *The Globe*, although most were short news items rather than the long, detailed pieces she had written as the newspaper's Klondike correspondent.

Like most other professionals and white-collar workers, Faith was welcomed into Dawson's inner circle, where she met Dr. John Nelson Elliott Brown, secretary of the Yukon Council, and medical health officer for the territory. Romance soon blossomed between the two, and on January 1, 1900, the couple exchanged wedding vows at St. Paul's Anglican church. Faith spent the week before her wedding editing *The Paystreak*, a daily newspaper published during the week of the St. Mary's Hospital fundraising bazaar.

Marriage did not bring Faith's journalism career to an immediate end. She wrote occasionally for both local and outside newspapers. In September 1901, she had the honour of sending the first press dispatch from Dawson on the new telegraph line. The Browns remained in Dawson until 1905, when Elliott accepted a position as superintendent of Toronto's General Hospital.

One of the most renowned foreign correspondents to cover the Klondike gold rush was Flora Shaw, who had spent years in various parts of the British empire writing for the London *Times*. According to one Canadian newspaper, Flora was "perhaps the most distinguished lady journalist in the world."[13] In 1898, the senior editor of *The Times* asked her if she would be interested in going to Canada to investigate conditions in the Klondike, just as she had done when she visited the gold fields of Australia in 1893. After five years as the newspaper's colonial editor, she was ready to get back in the field. The trip to Canada was exactly the type of adventure she thrived upon, and she jumped at the opportunity.

Flora left England at the end of June and arrived in Dawson less than a month later, on July 23. Her extensive reports to the newspaper made almost no mention of her personal experiences along the way. In a speech given to the Royal Colonial Institute in London after her return, however, she described the steamer that carried her down the Yukon River to Dawson. It was one of the least pleasant modes of transportation she encountered during her journey. Not only was the food practically inedible,

> no accommodation for sleeping was provided, machine-steam puffed in our faces, machine-oil dropped on our shoulders, black bilge-water ran around our feet, and the smell of freight, of which salt fish formed part, mingled with the smell of as much unwashed humanity as could be put in the available space.[14]

Yet she also noted that as a woman she received special considerations, including a berth in the captain's cabin when he was on duty at night. While being female may have helped smooth the way for Flora, her position as a representative of a prominent newspaper likely contributed to the treatment she received from those she met along the way.

Because of a desire to also visit and write about other parts of Canada before returning to England, Flora stayed only three weeks in the Klondike region. As soon as she got to Dawson she found a place on the hillside above the town to pitch her tent, and hired a man to prepare meals and do household chores, leaving her free to conduct interviews, make observations, and prepare her reports. She spent four days—two of them in heavy rain that turned the trail to mud—on a walking tour of the creeks. Travelling alone, she talked with mine owners and labourers, watched them work the sluice boxes, and tried her hand at panning and shovelling. Her research in Dawson was equally thorough. She even visited several gambling and dance halls one night between midnight and two in the morning. "It was not a pretty sight," she reported, "but it enabled me to form a more complete estimate of the miner's life."[15]

In contrast to the often lyrical tone of Faith Fenton's dispatches to *The Globe*, and the human-interest stories favoured by American papers like the San Francisco *Examiner,* Flora's letters to *The Times* bordered on the scholarly. Flora was a highly intelligent woman and she knew what interested her erudite readership. Her three long features on the Klondike were packed with facts and figures about geology, topography, climate, mining methodology, and economics.

Flora also looked closely at government administration in the Klondike, and her assessment was sharply critical. After hearing endless stories about corrupt, incompetent, and careless officials, she concluded that "the relations which exist between the representatives of the Government and the public leave almost everything to be desired."[16]

Although Flora later clarified her position saying that she had the utmost respect for Canada's civil service and that only a few individuals were guilty of the offenses she had mentioned—publication of her comments in England quickly made news on the other side of the Atlantic. When newspapers from the outside finally reached Dawson, many readers responded with outrage. Faith Fenton offered a vigorous defence of the Klondike administration in one of her reports to *The Globe*, pointing to the limited duration of Flora Shaw's stay as the reason for her failing to fully appreciate the situation.

The trip to Canada was Flora's last overseas newspaper assignment. Years of driving herself to excellence had left her fatigued, so in 1900, at the age of forty-eight, she retired from *The Times*. In 1902, she married Sir Frederick Lugard and began a new career, as wife of the British High Commissioner to Nigeria.

One of the first newspapers to send correspondents to the Klondike was the San Francisco *Examiner*. Within a week of the *Excelsior*'s arrival in San Francisco in July 1897, the newspaper had recruited a team of four men and one woman to travel to the gold fields and provide first-hand accounts of conditions. The men included a mining expert and a poet who was to tell of the "picturesque side" of Klondike life. Helen Dare's assignment was to offer a feminine perspective, although she also wrote numerous pieces of a more general nature.

Helen's view of the gold rush was less than enthusiastic. "It sickens the heart to look close at this gold seeking," she wrote from St. Michael on her way to Dawson. "Gold is pretty and good to have, but one grows to hate its yellow sheen when one sees how it draws men on and pranks with them like a mocking devil."[17] As she travelled up the Yukon River towards the Klondike she grew pessimistic listening to the disheartening tales of men who had already given up and were leaving before winter set in. The men on the outward steamers looked "grimy, rumpled and unkempt," she thought, "and every Klondyke-bound woman's soul shrivelled at the sight."[18]

Not wanting to be trapped in Dawson by freeze-up, Helen stayed in Dawson only long enough to confirm the scarcity of provisions in the town and make dark predictions about the probability of suffering, and perhaps even starvation, in the coming winter. When she finally got back to San Francisco in October she wrote rapturously of the joys of returning home.

> What a joy and a delight and a blessed boon civilization is, with its swift and easy modes of travel, its soft beds, delicate foods and sweet flowers, its warmth and beauty and comfort and cleanliness, and, above all, its fresh white napkins and tablecloths![19]

Although not part of the official San Francisco *Examiner* expedition, Mary Holmes was also enlisted by the newspaper as a correspondent. Her journey over the Chilkoot Pass trail with her husband provided a striking contrast to Helen's relatively easy trip. Mary's most harrowing experience was a close escape from drowning when she and five of the men in her party attempted to get their heavily laden and cumbersome boat across the swiftly flowing Taiya River, just above the town of Dyea. She turned this episode into an *Examiner* story entitled "A Woman's Ride in Mad Waters" which appeared on August 29, 1897.

> This thing began by wading in gum boots over a mile, through icy water up to my waist, clinging to a rope lest I lose my footing in the swift stream. . . . Soon the stream got too deep for wading and we resolved to float the scow across to the other side.

Mary and two of the men climbed into the scow. The others held onto the tow line and tried to ease them across the river, but as the boat moved out from shore, the current wrenched the rope from their hands. Suddenly Mary and her companions were speeding downstream towards a treacherous log jam that had already been responsible for numerous wrecks and at least two deaths.

> I will not deny that . . . I was frightened just a "wee bit." Of course, I did not let my companions know my innermost feelings, because it was plainly to be seen that they, too, were anything but comfortable over the situation. . . . We hit broadside on. . . . Half over we went and then the rebound of the log sent us back again with such force that we shipped fully a barrel of water. Then the prow was carried under by the current, but almost at the same instant a huge wave struck the stern, wheeling

us half way around and lodging us safely against the remnants of the old bridge. We were safe enough, but the sensations of the previous fifteen seconds had left us physical wrecks. . . .

The most embarrassing part of my adventure is that people will insist that I am a heroine, because I neither fainted nor cried out when apparently about to lose my life. . . . all who pass my tent stop to get a look at "the brave, cool woman," as they call me.

Despite the example set by female journalists like Mary Holmes, Flora Shaw, and Faith Fenton, the Klondike's own newspapers hired only a few women. One of these was Belle Dormer who became the first editor of the *Klondike Nugget's* society column in November 1900. She continued to keep the town informed about social happenings until 1903 when the *Nugget* ceased publication. At least two Dawson women worked on the technical end of newspaper production as typesetters and printers: Della Kelly was employed by the *Yukon Sun* between 1902 and 1906, and Anna Caskey worked at the News Publishing Company, where her husband was the foreman.

The Klondike gold rush had a way of attracting educated eccentrics, as well as fortune seekers, and not all of these were men. Alice Rollins Crane, the California ethnologist who claimed to have been the first white woman to run the Whitehorse Rapids, spent at least one year in Dawson pursuing a vague scientific assignment. Alice was a member of the Southern California Academy of Sciences and went "armed with a Government Commission from the Smithsonian Bureau of Ethnology [and] credentials from several newspapers and journals."[20] On July 30, 1898, she was introduced by the *Klondike Nugget* as a "valued new arrival" to Dawson: "Mrs. Crane has lived with Apaches and Sioux besides being acquainted with many other tribes, and is a delightful conversationalist on such matters."

Ostensibly Alice's mission was to gather information about "the little known northern tribes of Indians," but her research en route to Dawson was limited by her determination to get there as quickly as possible. During a pause in the journey when she was forced to camp and wait for the ice to clear off the lakes, she had a skirt, blouse, and jacket custom-made from moose-hide by native seamstresses. "The Labarge Indians are very expert with their needles and in dressing hides," she reported in "Our Klondike

Success," an account of her adventures published in *Wide World Magazine* in June 1901. "They caught the idea quite readily when I ordered my suit, although it was the first of that kind they had ever made for a white woman." Alice called the moose-hide suit her "Pocahontos outfit," and proudly wore it all the way to the Klondike.

Alice also purchased a caribou-hide canoe from local natives for the river portion of the journey. Alice and her guide, Fox, travelled from Whitehorse to Dawson in this "kiak," she paddling and he steering. "Of course this was a dangerous mode of navigation," she admitted, "but it seemed the only way by which I could save time." And time was, apparently, of the essence. Looking back on her expedition Alice remarked that "no one can be more surprised than myself at my endurance and courage through it all; but I love adventure; I love my work, too, and I have such a short time in which to accomplish so much, that I cannot afford to lose a moment or an opportunity."

Despite Alice's professed love of her work, it is unclear how much ethnological research she actually did while in the Klondike. Shortly after arriving in Dawson she had a cabin built for herself in West Dawson, a satellite community across the Yukon River, to serve as her winter quarters. Then it seems she was sidetracked by other concerns.

> I was delayed somewhat in my mad career by taking care of poor men who had succumbed to scurvy and typhoid fever. I took two at a time in my little 15ft. by 16ft. cabin, and had five serious cases, but did not lose a patient. Of course I expected nothing for my trouble, and got it! I had the satisfaction, however, of occasionally returning the slur from the majority of the men, that "this is no place for a woman," by replying that "they sometimes needed one to take care of the sick men!"

By the time Alice left the north she had obtained interest in a number of valuable mines. She had also collected enough material about miners and Dawsonites for a book of gold rush stories—*Smiles and Tears from the Klondyke*—but any scientific papers she might have published remained obscure.

The latter part of the nineteenth century saw many women with advanced educations and professional careers becoming involved in the women's club movement in the United States, and to a lesser extent in Canada. These clubs were mostly unaffiliated and had various objectives: sponsoring literary and cultural activities; campaigning for the right to vote and other legal rights; working actively for social reform; and fostering career opportunities for women.

A number of new clubs, such as the Woman's Alaska Gold Club and the Woman's Klondike Expedition Syndicate, were formed during the gold rush to assist women who wished to join the stampede. One of the founders of the Woman's Alaska Gold Club was Florence King, a patent lawyer from Chicago who found it difficult to get information about the Klondike because she was female. About 150 club members planned to set off for the Yukon in March 1898. In the end the expedition was cancelled, but meeting with other club members may have helped launch some individuals towards their goal through the exchange of information and mutual encouragement.

Another party of American women did set off for the Klondike, but were thwarted by misfortune along the way. The women had come together under the leadership of Hannah Gould, a fifty-year-old widow. Most members of the group were businesswomen, including one Bostonian who planned to open a library and charge a fee for joining her "circle of intellect." To this end she took with her twenty-five thousand books, ranging from poetry to dime novels. Two trained nurses from the Brooklyn Hospital also signed on, but Hannah refused all applications from stenographers because she did not believe their training prepared them for the rigours they would face.

On December 16, 1897, Hannah's thirty women and forty-one other passengers, mostly male, boarded the *City of Columbia* and steamed out of New York City harbour. They were to travel around Cape Horn and up the Pacific coast to St. Michael, where they would transfer to a river boat and complete their thirteen-thousand-mile voyage to Dawson. It was an ambitious undertaking which failed spectacularly.

Shipwrecked in the Straits of Magellan near the southern tip of South America, the passengers were forced to spend three days and nights on a rocky island while the crew attempted to mend the damage to their vessel. During this time they lived in constant fear of attack from the island's inhabitants, whom they were convinced were cannibals.

The travellers left their dubious refuge with the boat still leaking in seven places, but managed to stay afloat until they reached Valparaiso, halfway up the coast of Chile. There they discovered that the *Columbia*'s owners had gone bankrupt, leaving the captain unable to secure funds for provisions or repairs. The passengers managed to raise enough money between them to continue sailing north. Upon arriving in Seattle they were told that if they still wanted to go to the Klondike they would have to make their own arrangements, despite having paid for passage all the way to Dawson. The majority, having by then had enough adventure to last a lifetime, abandoned their quest and headed back home.

8

WITH SHOVEL
—and—
GOLD PAN

In the spring of 1898, Ethel Berry, the Bride of the Klondike, brought her younger sister, Edna, north to spend a few months on Eldorado Creek. The moment they arrived at the famous claim that had made Ethel and Clarence Berry rich and helped start the Klondike stampede, Edna asked if she could try panning for gold. She had seen the jam jars filled with nuggets collected by her sister the previous year and had read the newspaper stories that described Ethel picking up ten thousand dollars in gold "as easily as a hen picks up grains of corn in a barnyard."[1] No matter how often Ethel and Clarence told her such accounts were exaggerated, she couldn't wait to see for herself.

One of the men showed Edna how to fill the pan with gravel and water and then shake it with a swirling motion so the heavy metal settled to the bottom. Her brother-in-law, in an expansive mood, told her she could dig any place she wanted and keep all the gold she panned.

I took my pan over near the bank, poked around a bit with the shovel, looking for a prospect, and then started digging. All of a sudden the fine gold, looking much like gravel, came rushing down as sugar would pour from a sack if you punched a hole in it. I had sense enough to know that was not the way it was done, and I called: "Someone come here and look, or did you just salt this for me?"

You should have seen the expressions on their faces when they saw the results. One said: "I'll be jiggered." Another said: "Ye Gods! the luck of a tenderfoot!" Then Clarence spoke up. "Go ahead, take your pan. That's what I said you could do."[2]

Thousands were lured north by visions of gold dust pouring into their open hands and nuggets lying on the ground just waiting to be gathered, but no one ever made a fortune that way. Even Edna, after her first thrilling introduction to prospecting, turned to cooking for the mining camp labourers. Nevertheless, the desire to own more of the gleaming metal was in her blood. To this end she insisted on receiving her fifty-dollar monthly salary in gold dust, and often took her shovel and pan down to the creek on her free afternoons.

Sooner or later, most women who went to the Klondike were given an opportunity to pick nuggets out of a sluice box or wash out a few pans full of gravel. Regardless of whatever other occupations they may have engaged in to make a living, many also staked claims.

Anyone, male or female, over the age of eighteen could purchase a free miner's certificate for ten dollars. This certificate was valid for one year and granted the holder the right to prospect and mine for gold and other minerals anywhere in the Yukon. Claims were staked—in person only—by hammering four-foot posts into the ground and writing the date, the details of the claim, and the locator's name on one side. Locators had ten days to record their claims after staking, except for claims located more than ten miles from the nearest government Mining Recorder's office; in those cases, one extra day was granted for every additional ten miles of distance.

Once a claim was recorded and a fifteen-dollar fee paid, the locator received a placer mining grant, conferring the exclusive right to work the property for one year. Placer mining grants had to be renewed annually. Any claim for which the grant was not renewed, or which remained unworked for more than three consecutive days during the mining season (except where reasonable cause could be shown), was declared vacant and could be staked anew.

Claims were numbered as being above or below the discovery, or first, claim on a creek. Although the allowable dimensions of claims were carefully described in government regulations, inaccurate measuring and topographical peculiarities led to many boundary disputes. Races to stake and record claims were also common. Mrs. E.P. Minor and Mrs. J.T. Kelly, both miners' wives, were involved in one such incident.

The property in question was No. 13 above upper discovery on Dominion Creek, which was open to relocation because the man who had

Clarence Berry shovels paydirt into the gold pans of his wife, Ethel (left), and sister-in-law Edna Bush, 1898.

staked it had left the Yukon. The original title lapsed at midnight on August 31, 1898. As the appointed hour neared, three people converged on the site. At exactly midnight, Mrs. Kelly and Mrs. Minor pounded their stakes into the ground, one at either end of the 250-foot-long claim. Then they mounted their waiting horses and galloped down the trail towards Hunker Creek. As they left they saw Donald McDonald arrive and begin hammering in his own stakes next to theirs.

The two women reached the mouth of Hunker Creek in record time. As arranged, a boat was waiting there to carry them down the Klondike River to Dawson. They sped down the short stretch of river wondering if McDonald was behind them, or whether he had taken the alternate trail along Bonanza Creek, which was slightly shorter but overland all the way. He had, it turned out, chosen the latter route, but the women still managed to reach town first. They arrived breathless and jubilant at the office of Gold Commissioner Thomas Fawcett and filed an application to record their claim.

Mrs. Minor and Mrs. Kelly had staked first and applied to record first; No. 13 above should have been theirs, but Donald McDonald had another card to play. The man who had originally staked the claim owed Donald's brother, Alex, two thousand dollars, and in consideration of this debt had given him permission to relocate the claim when it became vacant. According to the letter of the law this fact was irrelevant, yet the gold commissioner ruled in McDonald's favour. It was a perfect example of the type of administrative wrongdoing that London *Times* correspondent Flora Shaw would expose a few weeks later in her controversial Klondike report.

Seeing they would get no satisfaction from Fawcett, the two women negotiated directly with the McDonalds and were eventually granted the claim. In the meantime, the Minor Case, as it came to be known, and other alleged incidents of misconduct by civil servants, led the federal government to set up a commission of inquiry in October 1898. Only a few junior officials were found guilty of corrupt or unethical behaviour, but the inquiry clearly showed that Fawcett was incapable of handling the extremely challenging job of gold commissioner. He was subsequently dismissed.

Bachelors and men whose wives had not accompanied them to the Klondike often resented the fact that married couples like the Kellys and the Minors could stake twice as many claims as single individuals. These critics tended to see the wives' claims as bonuses awarded to husbands, rather than property belonging to the women or shared in an equal partnership.

Generally the role of wives in these partnerships was to keep house, cook, and provide companionship, but some women also participated in the manual labour. Mrs. John N. Horne—the laundress who commissioned a gold washboard brooch in honour of the profession that had once supported her and her prospector husband—did every type of mining camp work when she first went to the north. She liked to boast that with her muscular washerwoman's arms she could operate a rocker, a cradle-like device for washing gold out of large quantities of gravel, as well as any man.

Women also occasionally helped during spring clean-up when all the rock and dirt that had been extracted from the mine shafts over the winter

During spring clean-up women sometimes worked alongside their men.

had to be shovelled into wooden flumes so running water could separate out the precious nuggets and grains of gold.

Like mining, prospecting was considered man's work and few women chose this direct approach to getting rich. Mrs. Woods and Nellie Cashman were two of the rare female prospectors of the Klondike era. In 1898, Mrs. Woods owned fifty-eight claims on creeks along the Yukon River valley, although possibly not any in the Dawson area. She had spent time in mining camps in Montana and elsewhere before going north, where she was determined to win a fortune that she could leave to her two daughters in California when she died.

According to one man who met Mrs. Woods near Forty Mile, the tall, muscular woman was as rough and tough in both speech and actions as any seasoned miner. Once, during one of the winter's coldest snaps, she left her travelling partner in a fit of anger, taking no blankets or provisions. She and her dog team covered thirty miles before they found food and shelter. Although in her mid-forties, "her step was springy as a young girl and every movement was swift and graceful."[3] Her face, however, was coarsened by years of exposure to the elements.

Both Mrs. Woods and Nellie Cashman abandoned women's clothing when they went prospecting. Mrs. Woods wore knee-length pants with long stockings and a blouse that came down below her hips, while Nellie favoured long, heavy trousers and sturdy boots, but maintained a sense of decorum by donning a long overcoat when she encountered strangers.

Born around 1851 in Queenstown, Ireland, Nellie immigrated to the United States with her sister, Frances, in 1868. A few years later, at the age of twenty-three, she joined a party of two hundred miners from Nevada on a stampede to the

Nellie Cashman in the early days of her gold mining career.

Cassiar district in northern British Columbia. She was unmarried and the only woman in the group, yet no one dared call her a camp follower. Throughout her life, those who knew Nellie agreed that she was ever chaste and pure. "She was unique," recalled one man who knew her in Arizona. "Though she seemed to prefer to associate with men, there was never a spot on her moral character."[4]

Nellie spent several years in the Cassiar district, her time divided between prospecting and running a boarding house for fellow miners. She failed to discover any great amounts of gold, but she did find a way of life that she loved. When the Cassiar gold rush played out, Nellie moved on to the mining regions of California and then to Tombstone, Arizona, where she set up a restaurant. In 1880, Frances was widowed, and she and her children came to stay with Nellie in Arizona. Three years later Frances died, leaving Nellie responsible for the support and education of five nieces and nephews, ranging in age from four to twelve.

It was a duty Nellie took very seriously, but it did not stop her from occasionally indulging in her passion for prospecting. In 1884, she made temporary arrangements for the care of the children and travelled down to Mexico for several weeks to investigate rumours of new gold discoveries there. In 1889, she went looking for gold and diamonds in South Africa. The rest of the time she concentrated on her restaurant business.

When Nellie headed north to the Klondike gold fields in February 1898, she was accompanied by one of her nephews and another young man. They planned to prospect and mine but, like most of the stampeders who arrived after 1897, they found all the good claims were already staked. Undaunted, Nellie opened a grocery store to support herself while she looked around at the mining opportunities.

The luck that Nellie had possessed elsewhere seemed not to have followed her to the Yukon. In July 1898, she bought an undeveloped claim from another woman, Frances Gendreau (or Johndrew). When Nellie sent a hired man out to begin mining, he was ordered off the property by a Mr. M.E. Russel, who insisted that he had staked half the claim before Mrs. Gendreau had put her posts in place. Nellie and Russel took their dispute to the gold commissioner, who found in Russel's favour because he was able to produce more witnesses to back his version of events. Nellie was left with half her claim, but although she worked it for two years, it yielded no gold. During the same time period the half that had been given to Russel produced twenty thousand dollars.

In January 1899, Nellie staked a promising bench claim on the hillside above Bonanza Creek and again became embroiled in controversy. Neighbouring claim owners charged her with encroaching on their properties. Nellie countered that her stakes had been moved. Subsequent surveys denied her even a fraction of her claim.

Protests to the government about these two cases dragged on for several years. Meanwhile, Nellie Cashman became highly respected in the community and well known for her generosity and good deeds. One of her first acts after arriving in Dawson had been to go up the creeks on a fund-raising trip for St. Mary's Hospital. A devout Catholic, she donated liberally to the church and hospital, but did not limit herself to religious charity. On April 22, 1900, the *Klondike Nugget* saluted her, saying

> There is not a mining camp in the country where she is not known and loved, as her many deeds of charity have endeared her to the hearts of

all who ever knew her. . . . Nellie has grubstaked many a prospector and knows more about mining in all branches than many a man who poses as an expert.

Nellie's respected position in Klondike society may have ultimately influenced the gold commissioner's decision on her case more than the verifiable facts. In November 1901 she was awarded ten adjoining claims on Soap Creek, a tributary of Gold Bottom, as compensation for her lost claims.

Nellie made little money from her Klondike claims, but her store and a restaurant she opened later did well. Nevertheless, her heart was always in mining. At least one year she closed her businesses in town for the summer and went out to one of her claims to supervise operations. In 1904, she left Dawson for Fairbanks, the centre of the new Tanana gold-mining district. She spent the next twenty years in Alaska, living much as she had done ever since her Cassiar days. In the summer of 1924, seventy-three years old and sick with double pneumonia, Nellie was brought south to Victoria and left in the care of the Sisters of St. Ann. The nuns did all they could for her, but she died the following winter.

Much of Nellie's pleasure in prospecting came from venturing into the wilderness and living among people who accepted her on her own terms. Other women tended to be more interested in mining as a business, one which they hoped would make them rich. They might stake the occasional claim themselves, but most of their efforts were concentrated on buying and selling claims. They hired men to extract the gold, or developed the properties and sold them at a profit. One of the most successful female mining speculators in the Klondike was Belinda Mulrooney, founder of the town of Grand Forks and owner of the Fairview, Dawson's best hotel.

Within months after arriving in Dawson and throwing her last twenty-five-cent piece into the river for luck, Belinda filed her first Klondike claim. She was a fast learner, and in the year she spent working behind the bar at her Grand Forks Hotel, she listened carefully to her customers' conversations and gleaned a great deal of information about mining. Early in 1898 she entered an extremely lucrative partnership by purchasing a one-sixth share in the Eldorado-Bonanza Quartz and Placer Mining Company.

Belinda's investments reflected her shrewd business sense, and the way she managed her properties showed a thorough understanding of placer mining procedures. By 1899, she owned or had part interest in at least ten valuable claims. Sometimes she took lays on other people's claims and hired men to work them. A lay was a short-term arrangement whereby the property owner allowed another person to mine a portion in exchange for a share of the gold extracted. One five-hundred-square-foot lay that Belinda took for a month yielded one thousand dollars' worth of gold a day.

Whenever possible, Belinda personally directed the work on her properties. As she explained to a reporter for the *Dawson Daily News* who expressed surprised at finding her supervising a twelve-man crew, "I like mining, and have only hired a foreman because it looks better to have it said that a man is running the mine; but the truth is that I look after the management myself."[5] She was a demanding boss who got the best from her employees by paying large bonuses for high productivity.

Belinda may have been a bit too independent for some men's tastes, but many others considered her one of the Yukon's most eligible spinsters for she was attractive and amiable, as well as wealthy. Nevertheless, she had no romantic attachments during her first few years in the Klondike. When she finally married, at the age of twenty-nine, it was to a man who was the antithesis of the rough miners who surrounded her.

Charles Eugene Carbonneau was a French count who had come north as a champagne salesman and become a successful mine owner and promoter. With his stocky build and the beginnings of a double chin, Count Carbonneau was not a handsome man. He was, however, charming, a good conversationalist, and an impeccable dresser with a polished manner. He may also have been a fraud.

Like everyone else in the Klondike, Belinda had heard the rumours that Charles was a French Canadian, born and raised in Montreal, without a drop of aristocratic blood in his veins. Yet doubts about Charles's pedigree did not prevent Belinda from being flattered by his attentions, nor accepting his proposal of marriage. Their wedding took place on October 1, 1900, at St. Mary's Catholic church, and was followed by an elaborate reception at Belinda's Fairview Hotel. During the feast, prepared by the town's best chefs, champagne flowed freely and guests were serenaded by a small orchestra. After dinner, the music continued and they danced until the early hours of morning.

For the next few years, the count and countess spent their winters living elegantly in Paris, with visits to Monte Carlo and other gathering places of the moneyed classes. Each spring, they returned to the Klondike to attend to their mining interests, which included the Gold Run Mining Company. The Carbonneaus, along with several partners, had purchased Gold Run when it was losing money. Belinda took over the management and eighteen months later the company reported a $1.4 million profit.

By 1903, however, the couple were experiencing marital and business difficulties. Charles ceased returning to Canada, leaving Belinda to cope on her own with the hostile environment that was developing within the Gold Run Mining Company. In September 1904, Gold Run's manager, A.E. Wills, published notices in the *Yukon World* announcing that "any contracts or other acts by Mrs. C.E. Carbonneau or others on behalf of the company will not bind the company and will be repudiated." Rather than face the allegations of mismanagement Wills was making, Belinda left the country. In December 1906, she filed for divorce at the U.S. District Court in Alaska. The absent Charles was found guilty of wilfully deserting her two and a half years earlier, and the bonds of matrimony were legally dissolved.

Belinda then spent several years refilling her coffers through successful investments and business ventures in Fairbanks. She eventually moved to Yakima, Washington, where she made a home for herself, her parents, and several siblings. She never returned to the Klondike and never remarried.

Like Belinda, Mimosa Gates was actively engaged in mining, both as a property owner and as a manager. Mimosa—a tall, slender Californian, whose brown eyes gave one reporter "the impression of a restlessness and determination to win her way in this world independent of the helping hand of the sterner sex"[6]—went to the Klondike in the spring of 1898 to visit her brother, Humboldt. A few months after her arrival, a previously unknown coal seam was uncovered on Rock Creek, a branch of the Klondike River. Mimosa was one of the first to reach the site of the discovery and stake a claim, which she later sold for twenty thousand dollars.

During the winters of 1898 and 1899, Mimosa managed one of Humboldt's Eldorado Creek claims in his absence. While in charge she was "never at a loss to give counsel and direct development work when the foreman was at his wits end to overcome some obstacle."[7] Mimosa also bought and sold a number of valuable claims of her own.

In January 1900, Mimosa hired two men to take her on a twelve-hundred-mile journey by dogsled across the Yukon and Alaska. Her purpose

Many women tried their hand at gold panning, but none made a fortune this way. Others had far more success managing mining properties.

was to inspect some mining properties and town lots that had been pur-chased the previous summer on her behalf in the new northern boom town of Nome. The young woman "was a picture for the brush of an artist" as she prepared to depart. Her "mushing costume," consisting of a fur-lined parka, short skirt, bloomers, leggings, and moccasins, was declared "both pictur-esque and sensible" by an admiring reporter on hand to see her off.

> Rebellious ringlets of her black tresses were in confusion about her fore-head, as with the excitement of bidding goodbye to friends and brother, she rose in her seat of soft-clinging robes and waved her hand in fare-well to Dawson, the hidden dangers of a remarkable trip before her evidently unheeded, and intent on making a dash for the glamour and glimmer of another Eldorado.[8]

Another woman who prospered from investing in mining properties was Lotta Burns. Before going to the north in 1895, Lotta lived in Montreal. To support herself and her aging mother, she slaved six days a week in a dingy factory, sweating in summer and freezing in winter. Then one day she decided she had to seek a better future. She made her way across the country and up to Alaska, where she found work in the dance halls of Circle City, and may have engaged in prostitution on the side. Years of living on only a few dollars a week had taught Lotta to be frugal. As the gold poured in, she carefully stowed it away.

Lotta's single-minded pursuit of money did not endear her to the men of Circle City. Unlike the dance hall girls and prostitutes with "hearts of gold" who were always willing to help an ill-starred prospector, Lotta invested her savings in mining properties. To make matters worse, she bought many of her claims from men who had gambled away their earnings and were willing to sell out at bargain prices. Whether or not she actually took delight in ruining men, as some claimed, Lotta was not above tricking an enamoured steamboat captain out of five hundred dollars. She was also accused of fraud by a Circle City prostitute in 1896, and found guilty, although there may have been mitigating circumstances since she was only given a suspended sentence.

When word of the Klondike discovery reached Circle, Lotta joined the exodus to the new mining district. On reaching Dawson she purchased a number of town lots and invested in a variety of business ventures. In the spring of 1897 she made a triumphant return to Montreal, carrying enough gold to place her mother in a comfortable home for the rest of her life.

In August 1897, Lotta headed back to the Klondike. Within minutes of disembarking in Dawson she was putting more money into her pocket. She had brought a bicycle with her from Montreal, the first to be seen in the Yukon. Instantly men began bidding to buy it, regardless of the fact that Dawson's streets were nothing but mud. Lotta had intended to ride the bicycle herself, but when the price reached seven hundred dollars she decided she could part with it.

Lotta stayed in the Klondike through the following year, continuing to profit from her real estate and mining investments. She was no longer called Lottie, as she had been in her dance hall days. When she went south to spend the winter of 1898 in Seattle, the September 28 *Post-Intelligencer* respectfully referred to her as a "young mining woman" and noted admiringly that she was "one of the few unmarried women who have gone [to the north] alone and entirely by their own efforts become rich." Her thoughts on the superiority of Canadian mining laws were quoted in detail. Not a word was mentioned about her shady past.

Many Klondike stampeders, male and female, went north naively believing anyone could stake claims that would yield great riches through their own labours or those of hired workers. Women like Mrs. P. Sutherland of Ballard, Wisconsin, never doubted that they would be miners, at least part of the time. "Of course, I shall mine," she assured a Chicago journalist, "when I can look up from my housework. Why shouldn't I? I'm sure it will be perfectly lovely. Did I ever mine? Well, no; but what difference could that make?"[9]

Georgie Osborne, interviewed on her way to the Klondike with her aunt, Mrs. M.L.D. Keiser, was only slightly more realistic: "Shall we mine ourselves? Well, that is as it may be, but we expect to do so as we have the tools with us. I do not see why we should not. I am looking for gold, and the only way to get it is to work."[10]

Brave words, but neither of these Illinois society ladies ended up doing much digging for gold. Once they reached Dawson they purchased their free miner's certificates and invested in a few mining properties, but made little use of their picks and shovels. As Mrs. Keiser readily acknowledged, she was mainly there for the novelty of the experience. Despite Georgie's vision of herself as a miner, she and her aunt were actually tourists, the first of many.

9

"DOING"

—the—

KLONDIKE

I n the opinion of one Colorado miner who met Mary Hitchcock and Edith Van Buren on their way to Dawson: "Any lady wot leaves a fine home an' fine friends and luxuries to take up with hardships wot's hard enough for strong men to bear ought to be locked up in an insane asylum."[1] The miners of the Klondike probably had similar thoughts about Mary and Edith when they saw these two society ladies making a pleasure trip out of an experience that for many others had been a life-and-death struggle, or a gamble that cost them their entire life savings.

Sometime in the early 1800s, the word "tourism" was coined to describe an approach to travelling that was just beginning to gain popularity. By the end of the century, the affluent elite of Great Britain, Europe, and North America had refined the art of leisurely travel in foreign countries and developed an insatiable appetite for adventure in exotic lands. Scaling icy peaks in the Rocky Mountains, cruising up the Nile, riding elephants in the Punjab—nothing was too daring or outlandish, as long as one did not have to forfeit too many of the comforts of home. Tourists like Mary and Edith may have left behind fine homes and fine friends, but they spared no expense in bringing along an amazing selection of luxuries and belongings they simply could not do without.

The two women took more than a thousand pounds of household goods and provisions on their Klondike adventure, even though they planned to be gone only a few months. In the days before their departure, dozens of trunks and crates filled with clothing, linen, cutlery, dishes, reading material, acetylene lamps, air mattresses, and hammocks were loaded onto the steamship that would carry them north. A gramophone, a music box, and a collection of records and music box cylinders that ranged from Italian opera to the marches of John Philip Sousa were carefully stowed away in their stateroom, along with Mary's mandolin and zither.

The three most unusual items in their great volume of baggage were a portable bowling alley, a magic lantern with views of naval heroes and battle scenes, and an animatoscope with two dozen films of various subjects, ranging from a recent military funeral procession to the Corbett fight. These were not for their own use, but had been packed on the advice of a friend who thought they could make money offering novel entertainment in Dawson.

The idea held great appeal to both women. "I shall be a thousand times more proud of going back with an inexhaustible sack of gold earned by my own efforts than if the [time] had been passed in idleness in New York, Paris, or London," declared Mary, while Edith wished to show her family she knew how to do something practical. "It would be a proud moment for me to carry home a bag of my own earnings," she remarked, "and I want it all in gold dust, too."[2] Unfortunately, their entrepreneurial plans were ultimately thwarted by delays in shipping, damage to the equipment, and lack of experience.

When Edith and Mary boarded the *St. Paul* on June 12, 1898, they were accompanied by a parrot, two dozen pigeons, a pair of canaries, and two Great Danes named Queen and Ivan. Neither woman was the type to pay any attention to the curious stares and whispered comments of their fellow passengers. They had wealth, position, and an abiding belief in their own infallibility. Mary, in her mid-forties, was the daughter of a prominent Virginia family and the widow of a senior naval officer. Edith, a few years younger and never married, had also been born and raised in refined circumstances. Her great-uncle, Martin Van Buren, had been president of the United States; her father was the former American ambassador to Japan.

Nevertheless, the two tourists failed to impress Della Banks, a prospector's wife who shared a steamer cabin with Mary and Edith on their way south from Skagway at the end of the summer, much to the chagrin of the eminent ladies who had been promised a stateroom to themselves. Della found them "conspicuous in a place where respectable women tried to be as inconspicuous as possible."[3] Although they were very much her social superiors, she responded to their overtures with polite reserve and pre-

Like many Klondike tourists, these two unidentified women brought their new portable roll-film cameras.

ferred not to be seen in their company during a stop-over in Sitka.

Both Edith and Mary were seasoned travellers. Among other places, they had been to Egypt, China, and Japan, and they approached their Klondike adventure with confidence and excitement. Except for the death of one of the canaries on their fourth day at sea, the journey from San Francisco to St. Michael passed without incident. They enjoyed private accommodations and first-class service aboard the *St. Paul,* and the two-week journey afforded Mary ample opportunity for writing. She was a dedicated diarist and upon her return home at the end of the summer turned her journals into a "narrative of their daily life in that terrible Wonderland of the North" entitled *Two Women in the Klondike.*

When the *St. Paul* arrived at the end of its journey, passengers discovered they could not proceed up the Yukon River because of low water. Mary and Edith passed the time by exploring St. Michael and taking snapshots. Relatively inexpensive and easy-to-operate portable roll-film cameras had become readily available by the 1890s; as a result, amateur photography was growing increasingly popular. Stampeders and tourists alike carried their Kodaks to the Klondike, but it was the latter who had the most time for picture-taking.

Finally, on July 7, they boarded the *Leah* and continued on their way to Dawson. The *Leah*'s slow pace was ideal for sight-seeing, and the boat's owners, the Alaska Commercial Company, thoughtfully provided passengers with a pamphlet that described the points of interest along the way.

Frequent stops to take on wood for the boilers gave the women a chance to go ashore and pick flowers, gather berries, practise their gold-panning technique, and exercise Ivan. Queen had been sent home from St. Michael after Edith heard stories of vicious Klondike curs and began fearing for the safety of her pet.

As Della Banks observed, Mary and Edith were conspicuous women, so their arrival in Dawson on July 27 did not go unnoticed. Those who wondered about their presence soon learned from the *Klondike Nugget* that the pair were "simply 'doing' the Klondike country."[4] The newspaper also identified them as the owners of the forty-by-seventy-foot tent sprawled across the hillside on the opposite shore of the Yukon River in West Dawson.

Mary and Edith's famous tent dwarfed all but the largest cabins in the neighbourhood. It took four men to transport the four hundred pounds of canvas over to Dawson and several more to raise it. It did not, however, live up to their expectations. One week after moving in, Mary and Edith returned from town to find their home almost collapsed from wind and rain. They consoled themselves with the fact that, because it was so large, they could always find a dry place inside. "Still," Mary grumbled, "here it stands waving, swaying, swelling, dropping with the different light winds which take it in charge, looking a most slovenly affair, and criticized by people on both sides of the river."[5]

Eventually, after nearly a month of trying to sleep with cold drafts blowing under the bottom of the walls and rain dripping down from the pockets where it pooled, they borrowed a smaller tent and pitched it inside their marquee as a bedroom.

The large tent did have its uses, however, particularly as a venue for church services. Shortly after their arrival, Reverend Andrew Grant approached Mary and Edith about holding Sunday services in their tent, thus allowing the Presbyterians to be the first to preach in West Dawson. The women were happy to oblige, and also offered the use of their Criterion music box to play the hymns.

On Sunday, August 7, a small group of West Dawsonites gathered in Mary and Edith's home. The service began with singing, accompanied by the tinny music of the Criterion as it cranked out "The Lost Chord," "Nearer My God to Thee," and "Prayer from Moses." Then Reverend Grant began his sermon.

Halfway through a reading about Joseph and his many-coloured coat, one of the pigeons that had been fluttering about landed on the music box and the tent was suddenly filled once more with the sombre strains of "Nearer My God to Thee." Since the machine could not be stopped, minister and congregation waited in dignified silence until the song finished, and then carried on as if nothing had happened. On following Sundays the birds were shooed outside before services began.

The day after the first church service, Mary and Edith set off on a four-day guided excursion along the creeks to see the mines and stake a few claims of their own. They had obtained their free miners' certificates, and Edith, who planned to make the tour on horseback, had purchased a cowboy hat to complete her outfit. Good boots would have been a better investment, however, as riding proved impractical and both women ended up with severely blistered feet. Yet, despite sore feet, weary limbs, and getting soaked to their waists during a stream crossing, they declared the trip a success, because they did not return empty-handed.

At the first claim on Bonanza where they were allowed to pan they shouted with joy as the glittering golden flecks separated out from the sand and gravel. Later that day, Edith clambered down a steep bank to see the panning at another site and was rewarded with a gift of a couple of nuggets, while a disappointed Mary stayed on top nursing her blisters. The next day Mary felt unable to face walking at all and remained in camp, while Edith was taken to visit more mines. She returned full of stories about the wonders she had seen, including an Eldorado claim where she only had to poke the bank with her umbrella and gold would tumble down.

The two women stayed in tents and roadhouses during their excursion, but there were limits to their tolerance of rough conditions. Mary refused to use the towels provided in one roadhouse, noting in her journal that "one should always travel with one's own linen, no matter what else has to be left behind."[6] She also objected when their homeward journey took them through Lousetown for fear of becoming infested with lice.

⁓

Proper Victorians though they were, Mary and Edith were as interested in the Klondike nightlife as they were in gold-mining operations. They spent several evenings out on the town with gentlemen friends. The first establishment they visited was the Oatley Sisters' Concert Hall, which they entered through a private door leading directly into an enclosed box. Peeping

through the curtains they watched as the percentage girls and their partners danced waltzes, polkas, and military schottisches. In Mary's estima-
tion, "nothing could have been more highly proper than the dancing." Polly
and Lottie Oatley then took the stage and sang a couple of numbers, after
which the tourists moved on to the Monte Carlo Theatre, where they took
in a "thoroughly respectable variety show."[7]

When they visited the Combination Theatre a week later, Mary and
Edith felt well enough protected by their six male escorts to enter the building through the public entrance and walk through the barroom, instead of
wading through ankle-deep mud to reach the side door. This time the show
they watched from their curtained box was "of the usual variety order, not
very refined, with plenty of coarse jokes, but nothing absolutely vulgar."[8]
They found it more interesting to observe the other members of the
audience.

After several rounds of drinks had been ordered—the ladies sipping
only lemonade—Mary heard one of their companions giving the waiter an
instruction which he seemed reluctant to obey. Finally, the waiter turned to
the two women and handed them each a pile of percentage chips. Seeing
their perplexed expressions, their escort laughingly explained that they had
earned them by "entertaining the gentlemen in the boxes."[9] Worried that he
might have offended them, the waiter apologized, but they were delighted
with these unique souvenirs.

Although Edith and Mary found the theatres and dance halls an amusing diversion, dinner parties were more their style. On August 12, they gave
their first Klondike dinner, co-hosted by their neighbour, ethnologist Alice
Rollins Crane. The evening's guest of honour was the American consul-
general, who was stationed in Dawson. "Under ordinary circumstances it
would be bad form for a hostess to give her menu," Mary wrote in *Two
Women in the Klondike* as she recalled the event, "but I really must state how
well we lived in that corner of the world."[10] She then described their seven-
course meal, which included mock-turtle soup, roast moose, and aspara-
gus salad. Dessert was peach ice cream, which they made themselves in the
ice-cream freezer they had brought from the south.

Between their own provisions and the gourmet items stocked in many
of Dawson's stores to satisfy the whims of the Klondike Kings, Edith and
Mary could easily produce dinners they would have been proud to serve at
home. They were frustrated, however, by their inability to find good help.

They had regretfully left their maid behind in San Francisco because they felt the responsibility of taking a young, attractive girl into an area populated by so many men was too onerous. As for a chef, they assumed someone suitable would turn up when they got there.

Three days after their arrival they still had no cook. That night they managed with great difficulty to open a tin of butter and another of sardines and Edith made soda-biscuits. The next day, in desperation, they hired Mr. Isaacs. The failed prospector was eager for a job, but never reconciled himself to his menial position as their cook and general attendant and always resented being called a servant.

Although Isaacs's culinary skills were adequate, he infuriated Mary. She expected servants to follow orders, stay out of sight when guests were present, and not talk back. He, on the other hand, thought Mary put on airs, and he did not understand why she preferred writing in her notebook to chatting with him. Little did he realize she was recording many of his words for posterity, and that exchanges like the following would pepper the pages of *Two Women in the Klondike*:

> "Isaacs, *do* try and keep the butter covered; here it is open again with all the dust and dirt falling into it; and you've been requested so many times to cover it."—"See here, I wish you ladies would find something complimentary to say once in a while."—"You must not be impertinent."—"I'm not impertinent, I'm only just speakin' the truth; it's rather painful sometimes."[11]

Isaacs finally had his fill of being "bossed around" and quit, although after his parting speech—"I don't call it impertinent; you've 'ad your say, and by golly, I'm goin' to 'ave mine"[12]—it is unlikely he would have been welcome to stay.

By the time Isaacs departed, Mary and Edith were already beginning to make arrangements for their homeward journey. Because it was difficult to secure passage on outbound steamers at that time of year, they worried for several weeks that they would have to endure a winter in the Klondike. Finally they managed to get a place on one of the last boats of the season, and on September 23 they gaily waved good-bye to Dawson.

Rather than retracing their steps by returning to St. Michael, they went up the Yukon River to Lake Bennett and walked out via the White Pass. Once over the summit, they could almost imagine themselves back in civilization as they boarded the elegant passenger coach of the partially completed White Pass and Yukon Railway. They rode the final miles to Skagway in comfort and style, then travelled south by steamer and were soon back home with clean towels and well-trained servants.

Mary Hitchcock and Edith Van Buren may have been the Klondike's most colourful tourists, but they were not the first. Illinois society matron Mrs. M.L.D. Keiser and her twenty-two-year-old niece, Georgie Osborne, started planning their trip almost as soon as news of the Bonanza Creek discovery reached the outside world. "It had been my intention for some years to visit the Yukon valley," Mrs. Keiser told a reporter after having reached Dawson.

> I had travelled extensively, but always felt that I would not be satisfied until I visited the great river of Alaska. When the Klondike excitement came up I saw my opportunity and at once publicly announced that I

Before leaving Dawson, Mary Hitchcock and Edith Van Buren bought souvenir pictures of famous Klondike sights, such as this one of Five Finger Rapids.

would accompany any gentleman and his wife who chose to take me down the Yukon. . . . My niece, Miss G.L. Osborne, decided to accompany me.[13]

Mrs. Keiser's offer was quickly taken up by a couple from St. Louis, and the four set off from Seattle in late August 1897. By the time they reached Skagway, Mr. and Mrs. Mitchell had reconsidered the wisdom of the whole endeavour and decided to go back home. Undaunted, the two women joined another party. Mrs. Keiser, who had previously climbed in the Swiss Alps, never hesitated about tackling the Chilkoot Pass or the trail beyond, and made little of their achievement.

Mrs. Keiser and Georgie went fully prepared to spend the winter in the Klondike and to do a little mining speculation to pass the time. Having survived the rigours of the journey, they settled into a cabin in Dawson. Mrs. Keiser noted with satisfaction that although their friends had been opposed to their unconventional excursion, "we came and are not disappointed. . . . We are now here safe and sound and I rather like the town. It wasn't society, you see, that I came for, but novelty."[14]

Novelty was, ultimately, the lure for most Klondike tourists, even those who were not seasoned globe-trotters. For Lulu Craig, the Missouri school teacher who went to Dawson to get a break from her job, it was "the beautiful scenery, the novel life, the pleasant episodes, and the interesting people" she met that made her trip so exceptional.[15] Lulu was also able to satisfy a desire to expand her horizons. Her year in the Klondike, she said later, gave her "a wider experience and deeper knowledge than almost any other" trip she might have taken.[16]

Lulu, her brother, his wife, and their nine-year-old daughter left home on January 27, 1898. They traversed the Chilkoot Pass early in March, but were then forced to linger for three months at Lake Lindeman waiting for spring thaw. Unlike the genuine stampeders, Lulu felt no sense of urgency and enjoyed the novelty of camping. Her days were filled with domestic duties, reading, writing, walking, and socializing with friends. It was a routine that would become very familiar to her during her stay in the north.

Despite being on vacation, Lulu was not one to sit idle. In Dawson she shared housekeeping and child-minding duties with her sister-in-law, and still had time for "brisk, invigorating" daily walks, even in the coldest weather.

A portion of every day was devoted to writing letters, recording events in her journal, reading novels, and working on the university course in literature she had brought with her. The long winter evenings were spent with whichever friends stopped by the Craigs' cabin for "music and conversation on Art and Literature and the current topics of the day."[17]

The joy of watching spring return to the north was tempered by the knowledge that soon she would have to go home. When Lulu left Dawson in mid-June 1899, she noted with regret that the wild roses were budding but not yet in bloom. It was time to go, however, for she was expected back in her Missouri classroom by September.

Lulu's year in the north was exactly what May Sullivan was looking for when she went to the Klondike in 1899. May was bored with life in San Francisco: "Neither home nor children claimed my attention [and] my husband, travelling constantly at his work, had long ago allowed me carte blanche as to my inclinations and movements."[18] So, inspired by stories of northern gold, she decided to join her father and brother who were already in Dawson.

The White Pass and Yukon Railway began daily runs between Skagway and the south end of Lake Bennett in July 1899. Two weeks later May had the privilege of being among the first women to travel to the headwaters of the Yukon River without muddying her skirts or straining a muscle. She stepped down from the train in Bennett and strolled onto a waiting steamer. When she reached Dawson on July 30, only fourteen days had passed since her departure from Seattle.

Despite being a member of the leisured class, May had not set out with a mere pleasure trip in mind. She had left California with "a firm determination to take up the first honest work that presented itself . . . and in the meantime to secure a few mining claims."[19] Unfortunately, her father and brother were not as liberal-minded as her husband. Dawson, they thought, was still far too rough a place for her to be.

Although May's father and brother refused to let her stay in Dawson and look for a job, they had no objection to her taking over domestic duties in their home while she was there. For the next six weeks May "baked and boiled and stewed and patched and mended, between times writing in [her] note book, sending letters to friends or taking kodak pictures."[20]

On September 16, May and her brother boarded the last steamer heading down the Yukon River. The reluctant tourist, who would have preferred

Dogsleds on the city streets were one of the northern novelties that attracted tourists to Dawson.

to stay for the winter, watched ruefully as Dawson disappeared around a bend in the river. "I felt a very distinct sense of disappointment. The novelty of everything, the excitement which came each day in some form or other, was as agreeable as the beautiful summer weather with the long, quiet evenings only settling into darkness at midnight."[21]

Nevertheless, May could console herself with having gathered enough material to write an account of her travels, a time-honoured tradition among Victorian tourists. In 1902, *A Woman Who Went to Alaska* joined Mary Hitchcock's *Two Women in the Klondike* and Lulu Craig's *Glimpses of Sunshine and Shade in the Far North* on the shelves of those who dreamed of making such exotic journeys. Yet even as books like these were enticing other adventurous women to see the famous Klondike region for themselves, life in the gold fields was changing. Dawson was fast becoming just another small Canadian town.

10
WOMAN
—holds—
THE FIELD

The early years of the Klondike gold rush were characterized by great optimism. Everyone from prospectors to government officials believed the Yukon River valley was a region of unlimited potential. When London *Times* correspondent Flora Shaw stated in 1898 that there was no apparent reason why the Yukon would not soon be counted among the most pleasant and prosperous centres of British settlement, she spoke for many. But things did not turn out as planned. The Klondike's glory days were spectacular but short-lived.

The Klondike gold rush began with the discovery of gold on Bonanza Creek in 1896. Most of the world knew nothing of the excitement until eleven months later, and it took another year for the stampede to reach its peak. Then, in a sudden reversal, the region's population began to decline. By 1906, gold production and population were both falling steadily, and the Klondike era was clearly at an end. Nevertheless, many of those who remained in the region after 1898 considered this its best time.

After its first frenzied years, Dawson moved beyond its origins as a frontier town. It gained a look of permanence with a courthouse, territorial commissioner's residence, and other impressive new buildings befitting the seat of territorial government. Private citizens demonstrated their commitment to the community by funding construction of churches, the Carnegie Library, and a large meeting hall for the Arctic Brotherhood. Roads were improved and neat, frame houses replaced cabins and tents. The biggest change, however, was in the social realm: as the Klondike entered the twentieth century, it became "civilized." More than one commentator of the time attributed this transformation to the influx of women from the south.

As Dawson settled down, white picket fences and frame houses replaced the rough log cabins of the town's early days..

In a September 1900 *Yukon Sun* article about "The Dawson of Today," former Toronto *Globe* correspondent Faith Fenton Brown upheld the view that an increase in the female population had naturally led to a refinement of society.

> There are more homes today in Dawson than ever before, and in consequence, social and religious interests, those chief factors in civilization, are advancing by leaps and bounds. . . .
>
> In the summer of '97 Dawson could count only forty women. The summer of 1900 sees at least one thousand, and the large majority of these are wives and mothers who have come to make homes for husbands and sons. The presence of good women means homes, and each home forms a social centre.[1]

Women did not, of course, single-handedly bring "civilization" to the north. Yet the Klondike did change as it became less of a bachelor society, though wives were not the only women who contributed to this transformation. Before marrying Dr. Elliott Brown and joining the ranks of the homemakers, Faith Fenton had been a shining example of the kind of respectable, unmarried woman who could occupy a prominent place in

Dawson society. These women were instrumental in organizing genteel social activities. Their presence as potential spouses also apparently put mar-
riage-minded men on their best behaviour. According to a November 5,
1898 *Klondike Nugget* article about "Our Lady Friends," the feminine presence even had a salutary effect on men's habits of dress and grooming.

> While it is undoubtedly a fact that there are not as many ladies in Dawson
> as many of us would like to see, still they are here in sufficient numbers
> to add color and life to many an assembly that otherwise would go down
> in history as one of those unspeakable affairs denominated in ordinary
> parlance "stag." It is a remarkable fact and a tribute to the refining in-
> fluence of the members of the gentler sex that since their advent in
> Dawson the tone of the camp has undergone a decided change. . . .
> Dawson is a much better dressed city than it was a year ago. When men
> are isolated from the society of women they become careless as to their
> appearance and neglectful of themselves. It is the potent spell of the
> name "woman" that restores them to a proper appreciation of the pro-
> prieties of life.

A year later, a *Klondike Nugget* editorial noted further signs of women's
"influence for good in the community."

> The refining influence of woman is already felt in our midst and the
> change worked by the arrival of a thousand wives and daughter[s] the
> past summer is apparent on every hand. Tinware on the table is being
> exorcised and the stores are selling white tablecloths, even to miners
> who never had a wife.[2]

While the *Nugget* writers focused on superficial ways that women improved the tone of Klondike society, others were more interested in questions of morality. One Dawson man opined that women's "personal attrac-
tions and cheerful homes, not to mention their culinary abilities, have a
marked moral effect which acts as a bracing tonic to their acquaintances
among the sterner sex."[3]

In a speech to England's Royal Colonial Institute a few months after her
return from the Klondike, Flora Shaw took the orthodox Victorian position that a house without a woman's touch was not a home, and men de-
prived of the comforts of home were more likely to frequent drinking
establishments and other places of ill repute.

Nowhere does one see so plainly as in districts of new settlement the need of woman as a home-maker. The majority of men in the Klondike, excepting, perhaps, the very young, were in the literal sense of the term, "home" sick. They wanted a place as much as a person, but it needed a person to make the place: someone to minister to the common needs of life, to clean the spot in which they lived—even though it were only a tent or shack—to wash the clothes, to cook the food, to give one's fireside a human interest which should make it, rather than another, the magnet of their daily work. The rougher the man the more imperative the need appeared. The absence of homes in such a place as Dawson explains to a great extent the existence of saloons; and in noting the contrast between the splendid qualities exercised in the effort to acquire gold and the utter folly displayed in the spending of it, it was impossible to avoid the reflection that in the expansion of the Empire, as in other movements, man wins the battle, but woman holds the field.[4]

Flora herself had travelled to the Yukon—and around the world—as a single woman pursuing a career. Nevertheless, in one of her dispatches from the Klondike she wrote, without a trace of irony, of the great need for the presence of women "in their best capacity as home-makers." She noted, however, that the absence of "all civilized conveniences" was part of the reason Dawson remained "a town of men."

The men who are most appreciative of the comforts of home are precisely those who will not bring their wives into the country until the conditions of transportation are such as to permit of bringing with them the accompaniments of decent household life. . . . Under present conditions only those [women] specially adapted by habits of courage, activity, and good temper should attempt to cope with the difficulties of the position [of home-maker in the north].[5]

Indeed, the formidable challenges of northern travel and the lack of amenities in Dawson and out on the creeks did discourage many women from going to the Klondike in the early days of the gold rush, alone or with their husbands. But conditions changed rapidly. While many stampeders continued to travel downriver from Bennett in hand-crafted scows and rowboats, at least a dozen small steamers were operating on the route by the summer of 1898. By July 1899, the White Pass and Yukon Railway had

Regular steamer service on the upper Yukon River encouraged more women to make the journey to Dawson.

eliminated the trek from Skagway to the headwaters of the Yukon River. A year later, the tracks reached Whitehorse.

The railway company then turned its attention to linking Dawson with the outside world in winter, establishing a weekly stage service in the fall of 1902. Nine years later, when Dawson kindergarten teacher Laura Thompson took the overland stage on her return from a visit to her family in Toronto, little had changed. Her 330-mile journey began as countless others had in the early hours of a cold, February morning.

> Four o'clock in Whitehorse . . . the mercury at forty below . . . the little town dead and sleeping under its mantle of winter fog . . . a group of sleepy passengers huddled in furs at the White Pass station . . . the great sleigh with its four champing horses waiting.
>
> Off we went into the silent night and into the silent world of white. For five days we would sit in this open sleigh, our noses icicled, our feet warmed by hot bricks and charcoal, while we crossed the Yukon Territory in a wavering diagonal line north.[6]

The stage stopped four times a day, at roadhouses located every twenty-two miles along the way. The horses were changed while the passengers warmed up with hot food and recovered from the hours spent sitting on the hard, low-backed seats. At night the single men slept in bunks in the main room; couples and single women were assigned to small cubicles. It was still an arduous journey, but it was a decided advancement over the days when winter travel was only possible by dogsled.

While the Klondike was becoming increasingly accessible, Dawson was also gaining more trappings of civilization. In 1898, the Dawson Electric Light and Power Company began serving homes and businesses and Dawson's first street lights were installed. This was the same year that telephones came to town. In 1899, street names were posted on every corner and houses were numbered as in more established urban centres. This change was the work of a Los Angeles woman, Maria Ferguson, who was granted a concession by the Yukon council to produce a directory for Dawson and the creeks. In order to do this she had to create a system of street addresses for homes and businesses in town, a task she had previously carried out for the Southern Pacific Railway in California.

The problem of inadequate sewage disposal, which had contributed to the 1898 typhoid epidemic, was addressed in 1899 when the government began digging drainage ditches. These were completed the following year. A waterworks system was also constructed in 1899, making clean drinking water easily available throughout the year and improving the fire department's fire-fighting capability. Another step towards making Dawson a healthier and more pleasant place to live came in 1900, when the government began collecting garbage and systematically disposing of it in the Yukon River, a solution which pleased the town's citizens but not their downstream neighbours.

Paradoxically, the improvements in transportation links between Dawson and the outside world and the introduction of amenities coincided with the Klondike's decline. In the absence of official census figures, best estimates suggest that the Yukon population at the height of the gold rush was around forty thousand. Stampeders continued to make their way to the Klondike throughout the final years of the century, but the number of newcomers steadily decreased. By 1901, there were just over twenty-seven thousand people in the territory, one-third of them Dawson residents and most of the rest living on the Klondike creeks. The discovery of gold in Nome in 1898 had drawn thousands away to Alaska, while many others had given up their prospecting dreams and returned to their homes in the south.

In 1902, gold strikes on Alaska's Tanana River and its tributaries prompted more people to pack their bags and leave the Klondike for the new Tanana mining district and the flourishing town of Fairbanks. When the next census was conducted in 1911, the Yukon's population had plummeted to 8,500, with the greatest concentration still in Dawson and the surrounding area.

As the population of the Yukon declined, the number of non-native women in the territory increased in both relative and absolute terms. At the height of the stampede, women probably represented less than 10 percent of the population. In 1901, 15 percent of all Yukoners were female. Separate statistics were not gathered for Dawson until 1911, when women comprised 24 percent of the population of both the territory and its capital city. Twenty-three hundred men and 710 women lived in Dawson, while on Bonanza Creek—the most populated of the Klondike creeks—there were only 49 women, less than 7 percent of the population.

The fact that the majority of female newcomers were wives had a significant economic impact on the women already living in the Klondike. Women who made their living as cooks, laundresses, and housekeepers found their services were no longer in such high demand. Similarly, business dropped off for the dance hall women and prostitutes. In addition to giving men a greater incentive to stay home, the wives also campaigned vigorously to rid the town of vice. Women, however, were not solely responsible for restricting the activities of the demi-monde; many of the most vocal opponents of the percentage system and prostitution were men.

The women who reaped the greatest financial benefit from the increased female population were the dressmakers, milliners, and store owners who specialized in women's clothing. While on the trail, abbreviated skirts, bloomers, and even the odd pair of men's pants had been the norm for incoming stampeders. In Dawson, however, fashions were as orthodox as anywhere in North America and new arrivals "suddenly found themselves the observed of all observed from the awful brevity of their garments."

A number of ladies who reached Dawson in 1897 and 1898 found themselves in very much of a predicament. Following the advice of newspaper correspondents they had fitted themselves out very nicely with knee high dresses and neat half-boots. . . . On the trail they patted themselves on the back for their sageness in procuring the costumes for they

Dawson ladies prided themselves on being as fashionably attired as women in Montreal or New York.

were undoubtedly a great convenience. But imagine their chagrin upon making for the first time a tour of the populous streets of Dawson to find themselves the only ladies . . . wearing short skirts. There being no bicycles in Dawson, the sight of short skirts is much rarer than even upon the streets of Seattle or Chicago. . . . needless to say that even at Dawson prices, the ladies proceeded at once to lay in a stock of ordinary wear."[7]

Dawson women were extremely fashion-conscious, seeming determined to prove by their dress that they were not rough northerners. In "The Dawson of Today" Faith Fenton asserted that "a woman walking down Dawson streets might be stepping across Broadway or Fifth avenue, New York, as far as her costume is concerned. The tailor-made suit, the lawn blouse and sailor hat, even the fresh-ironed pique or muslin form the ordinary summer dress."

Long after the gold rush ended, ladies' wear importer Mrs. Hutcheon was still able to conduct a lucrative business in Dawson. In July 1904, she left on an extended buying trip to Asia, Europe, and America. While in Paris she planned to "personally select a large stock of novelties in ladies' wear which, when added to the goods secured in Japan and China, will even excel in elegance anything . . . brought to Dawson in the past."[8] Her return was eagerly anticipated by women planning for the next winter's round of dances and dinner parties.

In Dawson's early days, most respectable women had no reason to purchase Paris gowns and few opportunities to dress up. As their numbers increased, however, the new class of Klondike matrons began planning "entertainments" which provided an alternative to the dance halls and theatres. Single women were welcome to help organize and attend these events provided their reputations were untarnished.

One of the first indications that a major shift was occurring in the Klondike's social sphere was a masquerade ball held in November 1898 as a benefit for the volunteer fire department. "The sympathies of Dawson ladies have been enlisted in a good cause," reported the *Klondike Nugget* a few weeks before the event. "When the ladies take a hold of anything it always goes with a 'whoop' and the masquerade is predestined to be the biggest thing of its kind ever seen in these parts."[9] Afterwards the newspaper declared the ball "the biggest success of the year" and heaped praise on the organizers.

> Mrs. W.M. Huston, Mrs. C. Yager and Miss Florence Hamburg must be congratulated most sincerely for the indefatigable energy and rare good judgement in the management of the affair. If there was anything left undone which might have added to the success of the affair it was not apparent; if there was anything missing which might have increased the sum of the enjoyment of attendants it did not appear. The energy of the committee had infected the town, and the result was seen at a glance in the costumes of the dancers—especially the ladies. The graceful draperies on sinuous forms showed consummate good taste and skill in the making of costumes, and the impression made by the gathering upon the observer was of being transported to some eastern metropolis upon some occasion of carnival.[10]

Among the 150 costumed revellers who crowded into the Pioneer Hall were men dressed as Uncle Sam, Santa Claus, Mephistopheles, a troubadour, and a sourdough in a parka trimmed with stale flapjacks. The women's costumes included the Queen of Hearts, Red Riding Hood, a butterfly, a "Moosehide squaw," and an Irish washerwoman. Dawson's leading female entrepreneur, Belinda Mulrooney, and her friend, Miss Pelkington, appeared as a bride and groom, with Belinda making "a dapper little husband in regulation broadcloth and silk hat."[11]

The Fireman's Ball was followed by the week-long Christmas benefit

Dancers at the St. Andrew's Day Ball in 1900 show no sign of flagging at 4:00 A.M.

for St. Mary's Hospital and other gala events, each one more elaborate than the last. For the St. Andrew's Day ball in December 1899, the Palace Grand Theatre was decorated with dozens of yards of bunting and a Gaelic greeting spelled out in electric lights. One hundred and eighty couples danced until the early hours of morning to the music of the Yukon Field Force's military band, with a break at midnight for a feast of Scottish and northern delicacies at the McDonald Hotel. Many of the men appeared in "swallow tail" evening dress, and the women's silk and satin gowns with their fashionably low-cut necklines were, according to the December 2 *Klondike Nugget,* "equal to those worn on similar occasions in New York or Montreal."

Respectable women objected strongly when those whose virtue they questioned showed up at these events. Like many others, Clare Boyntan, who had reluctantly slept in a White Pass roadhouse with her head under the bar, made allowances for conditions on the way to the Klondike, but held to rigid standards once she arrived. Within weeks of reaching Dawson in June 1898, Clare had found her niche, working in one of the downtown stores, singing in the Presbyterian church choir, and regularly attending both morning and evening Sunday services. She was strait-laced yet fun-loving and she especially enjoyed dancing.

Clare was delighted with her first Dawson ball, a benefit for St. Mary's Hospital in October 1898. "I did not miss a dance," she confided to her diary the next day. "Enjoyed the evening immensely and met some lovely people."[12] On Christmas eve, however, she attended a ball which was "queered" by the presence of dance hall girls. To spare themselves the distasteful necessity of contact with such women of ill repute, Clare and a group of like-minded friends organized their own private dancing parties under the auspices of the Dawson Social Dancing Club. The club, one of several such associations, met every Saturday evening.

"Our dancing club is progressing fine," she wrote a few months later. "We have the nicest times imaginable and just enough couples to make dancing a pleasure and holding them at the Family Theatre adds to the comfort and convenience. . . . The greatest of all pleasures is dancing without being obligated to mix with that element."[13]

Dances were not the only places where lines of respectability were drawn. The construction of a skating rink in Dawson sparked a bitter controversy over whether dance hall women should be allowed to use it. A ruling in their favour was finally proclaimed, accompanied by a stern warning that any woman caught smoking or swearing in the dressing room would be banned from the rink for the remainder of the season.

For those who wished it, and who had the proper credentials, life in Dawson from 1898 onwards was a whirl of masquerades, regular dances, dinners, afternoon teas, picnics, card parties, sledding parties, ice carnivals, and tennis tournaments. There were also Dawson Philharmonic Orchestra concerts, plays performed by professional troupes travelling on the northern circuit, and amateur theatricals. Dawsonites prided themselves on being as sophisticated as any urban-dwellers in the south and, as usual, gave much of the credit to women. "Dawson society is especially fortunate," wrote Faith Fenton in the *Yukon Sun,*

> in having at its head women of more than ordinary culture and standing—wives of the N.W.M.P. officers, of the Territorial judges and the Government officials, of several able and high-ranked Canadian lawyers, of mining capitalists, and of the great trading companies. Many of these are women of travel and taste who form a little social world quite equal in brilliance and intelligence to any of the monde in bigger cities.

The Dawson women's hockey team prepares to play visiting rivals, 1904.

Mrs. W. Sampson, the wife of a British American Company employee, expected the worst when she went north with her husband in 1898, but found Dawson less primitive than she had feared. "On the whole, the hardships are not so great," she told a *New York Times* reporter upon her return south. "Mine was a most pleasant residence in the north. There is no reason why any lady should not be happy there. . . . no one need hesitate to follow a husband into Dawson or even up the creeks."[14]

Frequent dances, parties, and musicales helped pass the long, winter nights, Mrs. Sampson explained, while on Sunday afternoons, dogsledding around town or out to the mining camps was a favourite pastime. As well, there were five o'clock teas, which were "most jealously attended by the gentlemen and universally dear to the ladies."

Afternoon teas and "at-homes" became cherished traditions in Dawson as the town settled into respectability. Married women in particular were expected to participate in this Edwardian social ritual. On January 8, 1900, a week after Faith Fenton's wedding, an announcement appeared in the *Dawson Daily News* informing all and sundry that "Mrs. J. Elliott Brown (Faith Fenton) will be at home to her friends on Wednesday and Thursday of this week and every succeeding Wednesday at her residence corner of Mission street and Seventh avenue."

Unmarried women who had sufficient social standing also attended and held at-homes. As Laura Thompson learned shortly after her arrival in 1907, "anybody who was anybody, and some who weren't, had a day."

For those with the proper credentials, life in Dawson at the turn of the century was a whirl of social engagements.

On one's day, one was at home to the entire town during the hours of the late afternoon and early evening. One spent many days before *the* day salting almonds, preparing the olives, churning the sherbert in the freezer, preparing trays of home-made candies. One made sure the proper people were honoured by being allowed to "pour" or "pass", and the coefficient of success was calculated in direct ratio to the number of people who turned up. Thus it was possible to compute the social standing of the entire upper crust of Dawson City mathematically.[15]

In her home town of Toronto, a kindergarten teacher like Laura would have never gained admittance to the upper echelons of society, but Dawson, with its paucity of women, was less discriminating. In contrast to the protocol in southern towns, teachers and nurses in Dawson were deemed as socially acceptable as the wives and daughters of judges, senior North-West Mounted Police officers, civil servants, ministers, bankers, and lawyers. They were even a cut above the merchants, labourers, and lower-ranked policemen, and their spouses. Laura and the other teachers with whom she lived began hosting at-homes on the second Tuesday of the month. This continued to be Laura's day after her marriage to Frank Berton in 1912 and until the Bertons left Dawson and moved south twenty years later.

Women also came together for more serious purposes, such as establishing Dawson's first public library. The day after its opening on January 1, 1900, the *Dawson Daily News* congratulated the women who had carried out this project. The new Free Reading and Recitation Room was praised as being

> so pleasing to the eye, so warming and comforting to the heart and the senses that from this day forward no man or woman in Dawson may say he or she has "no place to go" of an evening. In the equipment of this free reading room there is no hint of the cheapness and general offensiveness that is associated with "free" things generally. The place is well lighted with electricity, well provided with tables, chairs and even lounges, the windows are hung with heavy chenille curtains and there is an air of warmth, comfort and homelike hospitality about it. Besides, there is a first class library of 900 volumes ranged along the wall.

Later in 1900, the more comfortably positioned women of Dawson turned their efforts to helping their less fortunate sisters. A meeting on November 5, convened for the purpose of devising ways and means of assisting the town's homeless women, led to the formation of the Ladies' Relief Association. As the gold rush subsided fewer people were arriving in the Klondike with false expectations and ending up destitute, but there was concern for those who had insufficient resources to see them through the winter. Everyone remembered the previous December when only a neighbour's kindness had saved Mrs. Hecht, a widow with a baby and three other children under the age of sixteen, who had been unable to find work. Upon learning of Mrs. Hecht's desperate circumstances, her male neighbour had rented a cabin for the family and bought them firewood, clothing, and other provisions.

A survey conducted by the Salvation Army the week after the Ladies' Relief Association's first meeting turned up only one woman in immediate need. There was speculation, however, that others in the same position had not come forward because they were too proud to seek help. The association decided to begin by setting up an employment bureau for women rather than simply distributing charity.

As communication with the rest of Canada improved, chapters of national organizations like the Imperial Order of the Daughters of the Empire (IODE) were also established in Dawson. In addition, each of the churches had a women's guild which carried out various good works, such as furnishing hospital wards and supplying them with linen. For their members, the Anglican Women's Auxiliary, the Catholic Ladies' Altar Society, and other church groups also served a valuable social function, "making Dawson women known to one another and engendering the friendly feeling which in this territory is so desirable."[16]

Of course, that friendly feeling did not extend to all women. Dance hall girls and prostitutes, both past or present, were still beyond the pale, and native women had gained little status since Kate Carmack's day. But for the majority of women, post-gold rush Dawson was a good place to live.

Dawson and the surrounding communities had undergone a remarkable transformation from 1896 when Ethel Berry, the Bride of the Klondike, stepped off the steamer from Forty Mile. By the end of the Klondike decade women were no longer isolated in a male-dominated society, yearning for news from home, and wearing fashions that were at least a year out of date. Set down in any medium-sized town in North America most would have been indistinguishable from the rest of the female population. Only their stories—those they told and those they held secret—set them apart from the women who had not dared to follow their dreams and go searching for gold, of one sort or another, in the land of the midnight sun.

NOTES

Chapter 1

[1] James Albert Johnson, *Carmack of the Klondike* (Seattle: Epicentre Press, 1990), p. 94.
[2] "From Klondike to Paris," *Seattle Post-Intelligencer*, Sept. 1, 1898, p. 5.
[3] Julie Cruikshank, *Athapaskan Women: Lives and Legends* (Ottawa: National Museum of Man Mercury Series, Canadian Ethnology Service Paper No. 57. National Museums of Canada, 1979), p. 48.
[4] Johnson, p. 111.

Additional Sources

Carmack, George. *My Experiences in the Yukon*. Published posthumously by Marguerite P. Carmack, 1933.
Cruikshank, Julie. *Life Lived Like a Story: Life Stories of Three Yukon Native Elders*. Lincoln: University of Nebraska Press, 1990.
Cruikshank, Julie. "Images of Society in Klondike Gold Rush Narratives," *Ethnohistory*, Winter 1992, pp. 20–41.
McClellan, Catharine. *Part of the Land, Part of the Water: A History of the Yukon Indians*. Vancouver: Douglas and McIntyre, 1987.
Wilkie, Rab and the Skookum Jim Friendship Centre. *Skookum Jim: Native and Non-Native Stories and Views about his Life and Times and the Klondike Gold Rush*. Whitehorse: Heritage Branch, Dept. of Tourism, Govt. of the Yukon, 1992.

Chapter 2

[1] Lillian Agnes Oliver, "My Klondike Mission," *Wide World Magazine*, Apr.–Sept. 1899, p. 43.
[2] Ibid., p. 44.
[3] Ibid., p. 54.
[4] Frances Gillis, "The Lady Went North in '98," *Alaska Sportsman*, Feb. 1948, p. 13.
[5] Emily Craig Romig, *A Pioneer Woman in Alaska* (Idaho: Caxton Printers, 1948), p. 18.
[6] "Belles of Tacoma to Start for Dawson," San Francisco *Examiner*, Feb. 8, 1898, p. 3.
[7] Barbara E. Kelcey, "Lost in the Rush: The Forgotten Women of the Klondike Stampede" (master's thesis, Dept. of History, University of Victoria, 1989), pp. 28–30.
[8] Martha Louise Black, *My Ninety Years* (Anchorage: Alaska Northwest Publishing Co., 1976), p. 20.
[9] Ibid., p. 28.
[10] "The Outfit a Woman Should Take North," San Francisco *Examiner*, July 22, 1897, p. 2.
[11] "Letter From L.B.," *Seattle Daily Times*, June 24, 1898, p. 3.
[12] Georgia Powell, "The Klondike Nurses," Toronto *Globe*, Oct. 1, 1898, p. 5.
[13] Gertrude Bloss, "Saga of the Klondike," *Canadian Home Leaguer*, July–Aug. 1972, p. 5.
[14] Romig, p. 59.
[15] Oliver, p. 45.
[16] Lulu Alice Craig, *Glimpses of Sunshine and Shade in the Far North* (Cincinnati: Editor Pub. Co., 1900), p. 5.
[17] Black, p. 22.
[18] Annie Hall Strong, "From Woman's Standpoint," *Skaguay News*, Dec. 31, 1897, p. 9.

NOTES

[19] Alice Rollins Crane, "Our Klondike Success," *Wide World Magazine*, June 1901, pp. 180–81.
[20] Virginia P. Boyntan Nethercott, ed., *Klondike Tenderfoot: From the Diaries of Clare M. Stroud Boyntan Phillips* (Starrucca, Pennsylvania: Self-published 1992), p. 14.
[21] Ibid., p. 16.
[22] Ibid., p. 15.
[23] Della Murray Banks, "Rainbow's End," *Alaska Sportsman*, Feb. 1945, p. 22.
[24] Oliver, pp. 46–47.
[25] Ibid., p. 47.
[26] Ibid.
[27] Ibid., pp. 48–49.
[28] Alice Edna Berry, *The Bushes and the Berrys* (San Francisco: C.J. Bennett, 1978), p. 52.
[29] Emma L. Kelly, "A Woman's Trip to the Klondike," *Lippincott's Monthly Magazine*, Nov. 1901, pp. 625–26.
[30] Ibid., p. 627.
[31] Crane, p. 182.
[32] Kelly, p. 630.
[33] Gillis, p. 30.
[34] Faith Fenton, "A Scow Trip Down the Yukon River," Toronto *Globe*, Oct. 22, 1898, p. 24.
[35] Kelly, pp. 631–33.

Additional Sources

Ash, Lulu. "Crossed Chilcoot in Bloomers," San Francisco *Examiner*, Aug. 27, 1897, p. 2.
Berton, Pierre. *Klondike: The Last Great Gold Rush.* Toronto: McClelland and Stewart, 1972.
Garner-Knott Family. Family Papers. Whitehorse: Yukon Archives, Acc. No. 82/224 Pt. 1, MSS 40.
MacGregor, J.G. *The Klondike Rush Through Edmonton, 1897–1898.* Toronto: McClelland and Stewart, 1970.
White, Georgia. Diary, 1898. Whitehorse: Yukon Archives, Acc. No. 82/53, MSS 4.

Chapter 3

[1] Ethel Berry, "How I Mined For Gold on the Klondyke," San Francisco *Examiner Sunday Magazine*, Aug. 1, 1897, p. 1.
[2] Ibid.
[3] Ibid.
[4] Ibid.
[5] E. Blanche Norcross, *Pioneers Every One* (Canada: Burns and MacFachern Ltd., 1979), p. 57.
[6] A.C. Harris, *The Klondike Gold Fields* (Chicago: Munroe Book Co., 1897), p. 238.
[7] Berry.
[8] Ibid.
[9] Harris, p. 229.
[10] John William Leonard, *The Gold Fields of the Klondike: Fortune Seekers' Guide to the Yukon region of Alaska and British Columbia* (Chicago: A.N. Marquis and Co., 1897), p. 154.

NOTES

11 Rebecca and Solomon Schuldenfrei. Correspondence 1897–98, Sept. 6, 1897. Whitehorse: Yukon Archives, Acc. No. 84/87, MSS 166.

12 Ibid., Oct. 19, 1897.

13 Ibid., Oct. 28, 1897.

14 Ibid.

15 Ibid., Jan. 21, 1898.

16 Ibid., Nov. 18, 1897.

17 Georgia White. Diary, June 27, 1898. Whitehorse: Yukon Archives, Acc. No. 82/53, MSS 4.

18 Martha Louise Black, *My Ninety Years* (Anchorage: Alaska Northwest Pub. Co., 1976), p. 20.

19 Ibid., p. 40.

20 Ibid., p. 45.

21 *The Official Guide to the Klondyke Country and the Gold Fields of Alaska* (Chicago: W.B. Conkey Co., 1897), p. 187.

22 Catherine Winslow, *Big Pan-out* (New York: Newton, 1957), p. 70.

23 Harris, p. 449.

24 Ibid., p. 448.

Additional Sources

Becker, Ethel Anderson. "Little Girl in the Klondike Gold Fields," *Alaska Sportsman,* Nov. 1962, pp. 22–24, 34, 36–38.

Berton, Pierre. *Klondike: The Last Great Gold Rush.* Toronto: McClelland and Stewart, 1972.

Dare, Helen. "The Child of the Chilcoot," San Francisco *Examiner,* Sept. 18, 1897, p. 5.

Gates, Michael. *Gold at Fortymile Creek: Early Days in the Yukon.* Vancouver: UBC Press, 1994.

Kessler-Harris, Alice. *Out to Work: A History of Wage-earning Women in the United States.* New York: Oxford University Press, 1982.

Klondike Nugget, "A Klondike Romance," Nov. 25, 1899, p. 3.

Chapter 4

1 Frances Gillis, "The Lady Went North in '98," *Alaska Sportsman,* Feb. 1948, p. 31.

2 A.C. Harris, *The Klondike Gold Fields* (Chicago: Munroe Book Co., 1897), p. 473.

3 Anna DeGraf, *Pioneering on the Yukon 1892–1917* (Hamdon, Connecticut: Archon Books, 1992), p. 3.

4 Ibid., p. 77.

5 Ibid., pp. 83-84.

6 Ibid., p. 109.

7 Harris, p. 476.

8 "The Klondike and Indian River Divisions," *Dawson Daily News,* Golden Clean-Up Edition, 1902, p. 14.

9 "A Successful Business Woman," *Klondike Nugget,* Dec. 25, 1900, p. 15.

10 "A Most Successful Lady Miner," *Dawson Daily News,* Mining Edition, Sept. 1899, p. 27.

11 Alice McDonald, "As Well As Any Man," *Alaska Journal,* Summer 1984, p. 42.

NOTES

[12] "No More Washtub For Her," *Seattle Post-Intelligencer,* July 31, 1899, p. 5.

[13] "Will Open June 1," *Klondike Nugget,* May 31, 1899, p. 3.

Additional Sources

Adney, Tappan. *The Klondike Stampede.* Vancouver: UBC Press, 1994.

Bolotin, N. *Klondike Lost: A Decade of Photographs by Kinsey and Kinsey.* Anchorage: Alaska Northwest Pub. Co., 1980.

Kelcey, Barbara E. "Lost in the Rush: The Forgotten Women of the Klondike Stampede." Master's thesis, Dept. of History, University of Victoria, 1989.

Klondike News. "Women in the Klondike," Apr. 1, 1898, p. 1.

Klondike Nugget. "Miss Mulroney to Leave," Sept. 30, 1899, p. 4.

Loftus, Audrey. "Lady Stampeder," *Alaska,* Nov. 1977, pp. 38–40.

New York Times. "A Woman's Life in Dawson," Nov. 26, 1899, p. 24.

Wells, E. Hazard. *Magnificence and Misery.* New York: Doubleday and Co., 1984.

Wertheimer, Barbara Mayer. *We Were There: The Story of Working Women in America.* New York: Pantheon Books, 1977.

Chapter 5

[1] Robert Coutts, *The Palace Grand Theatre, Dawson, YT: An Interpretive History* (Ottawa: Parks Canada, Manuscript Report Series No. 428, 1981), p. 27.

[2] Martha Louise Black, *My Ninety Years* (Anchorage: Alaska Northwest Pub. Co., 1976), p. 48.

[3] Luella Day, *The Tragedy of the Klondike* (New York: Self-published, 1906), p. 72

[4] Pierre Berton, *Klondike: The Last Great Gold Rush* (Toronto: McClelland and Stewart, 1972), p. 367.

[5] "The Stroller's Column," *Klondike Nugget,* Oct. 21, 1899, p. 4.

[6] Chad Evans, *Frontier Theatre* (Victoria: Sono Nis Press, 1983), p. 177.

[7] *Dawson Daily News,* Mining Edition, Sept. 1899, p. 14.

[8] Evans, p. 241.

[9] "The Girl Who Danced at Dawson," *San Francisco Examiner,* Sept. 26, 1897, p. 7.

[10] "Swiftwater Bill of Dawson City Illustrates a Proverb," *Seattle Daily Times,* Feb. 2, 1898, p. 1.

[11] Laura Beatrice Berton, *I Married the Klondike* (Toronto: McClelland and Stewart, 1954), p. 122.

[12] "She Blew Out Her Brains," *Klondike Nugget,* Dec. 14, 1898, p. 3.

[13] "All For the Love of a Woman," *Klondike Nugget,* Mar. 25, 1899, p. 1.

[14] Dawson City Dance Halls. Letter from Kate Heaman on behalf of the WCTU to Clifford Sifton, June 27, 1900. Whitehorse: Yukon Archives, Gov. 1619, File 1443, Pt. 3.

[15] Dawson City Dance Halls. Letter from William Ogilvie to Clifford Sifton, Sept. 12, 1900. Whitehorse: Yukon Archives, Gov. 1619, File 1443, Pt. 3.

[16] *NWMP Annual Report 1902,* pp. 71–72.

[17] Mary Lee Davis, *Sourdough Gold* (Boston: W.A. Wilde Co., 1933), p. 189.

Additional Sources

Beebe, Iola. *The True Life Story of Swiftwater Bill Gates.* Self-published, 1908.

Berton, Laura Beatrice. *I Married the Klondike.* Toronto. McClelland and Stewart, 1954.

Dawson City Dance Halls. Letter from NWMP Superintendent, Y.T. to William Ogilvie, July 21, 1900. Whitehorse: Yukon Archives, Gov. 1619, File 1443, Pt. 3.

— 197 —

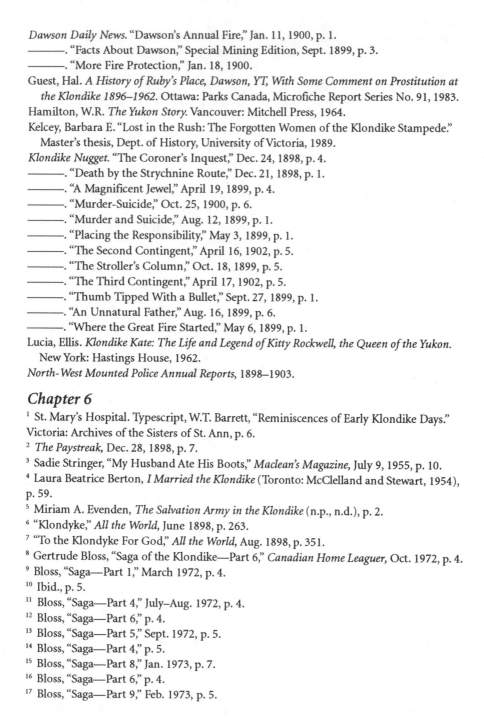

Dawson Daily News. "Dawson's Annual Fire," Jan. 11, 1900, p. 1.
————. "Facts About Dawson," Special Mining Edition, Sept. 1899, p. 3.
————. "More Fire Protection," Jan. 18, 1900.
Guest, Hal. *A History of Ruby's Place, Dawson, YT, With Some Comment on Prostitution at the Klondike 1896–1962.* Ottawa: Parks Canada, Microfiche Report Series No. 91, 1983.
Hamilton, W.R. *The Yukon Story.* Vancouver: Mitchell Press, 1964.
Kelcey, Barbara E. "Lost in the Rush: The Forgotten Women of the Klondike Stampede." Master's thesis, Dept. of History, University of Victoria, 1989.
Klondike Nugget. "The Coroner's Inquest," Dec. 24, 1898, p. 4.
————. "Death by the Strychnine Route," Dec. 21, 1898, p. 1.
————. "A Magnificent Jewel," April 19, 1899, p. 4.
————. "Murder-Suicide," Oct. 25, 1900, p. 6.
————. "Murder and Suicide," Aug. 12, 1899, p. 1.
————. "Placing the Responsibility," May 3, 1899, p. 1.
————. "The Second Contingent," April 16, 1902, p. 5.
————. "The Stroller's Column," Oct. 18, 1899, p. 5.
————. "The Third Contingent," April 17, 1902, p. 5.
————. "Thumb Tipped With a Bullet," Sept. 27, 1899, p. 1.
————. "An Unnatural Father," Aug. 16, 1899, p. 6.
————. "Where the Great Fire Started," May 6, 1899, p. 1.
Lucia, Ellis. *Klondike Kate: The Life and Legend of Kitty Rockwell, the Queen of the Yukon.* New York: Hastings House, 1962.
North-West Mounted Police Annual Reports, 1898–1903.

Chapter 6

1 St. Mary's Hospital. Typescript, W.T. Barrett, "Reminiscences of Early Klondike Days." Victoria: Archives of the Sisters of St. Ann, p. 6.
2 *The Paystreak,* Dec. 28, 1898, p. 7.
3 Sadie Stringer, "My Husband Ate His Boots," *Maclean's Magazine,* July 9, 1955, p. 10.
4 Laura Beatrice Berton, *I Married the Klondike* (Toronto: McClelland and Stewart, 1954), p. 59.
5 Miriam A. Evenden, *The Salvation Army in the Klondike* (n.p., n.d.), p. 2.
6 "Klondyke," *All the World,* June 1898, p. 263.
7 "To the Klondyke For God," *All the World,* Aug. 1898, p. 351.
8 Gertrude Bloss, "Saga of the Klondike—Part 6," *Canadian Home Leaguer,* Oct. 1972, p. 4.
9 Bloss, "Saga—Part 1," March 1972, p. 4.
10 Ibid., p. 5.
11 Bloss, "Saga—Part 4," July–Aug. 1972, p. 4.
12 Bloss, "Saga—Part 6," p. 4.
13 Bloss, "Saga—Part 5," Sept. 1972, p. 5.
14 Bloss, "Saga—Part 4," p. 5.
15 Bloss, "Saga—Part 8," Jan. 1973, p. 7.
16 Bloss, "Saga—Part 6," p. 4.
17 Bloss, "Saga—Part 9," Feb. 1973, p. 5.

Additional Sources

Cantwell, Sister Margaret with Sister Mary George Edmond. *North to Share: The Sisters of Saint Ann in Alaska and the Yukon Territory.* Victoria: Sisters of St. Ann, 1992.

Coates, Ken S. "Send Only Those Who Rise a Peg: Anglican Clergy in the Yukon, 1858–1932," *Journal of the Canadian Church Historical Society,* April 1986, pp. 3–18.

Dawson Daily News. "Noted Pioneer Woman of the North Passes Away," April 23, 1923.

Friedrich, Bruno. "Our Klondyke Expedition," *All the World,* Oct. 1898, pp. 459–62.

Five Pioneer Women of the Anglican Church in the Yukon. Whitehorse: Yukon Diocesan Board, Women's Auxiliary, Anglican Church of Canada, 1964.

Guest, Hal. *A History of the City of Dawson, Yukon Territory 1896-1920.* Ottawa: Parks Canada, Microfiche Report Series No. 7, n.d.

Hamilton, W.R. *The Yukon Story.* Vancouver: Mitchell Press, 1964.

Klondike Nugget. "A Meritorious Work," Sept. 3, 1898, p. 1.

———. "Local Brevities," Aug. 31, 1898, p. 1.

———. "A Most Worthy Institution," July 2, 1898, p. 3.

St. Mary's Hospital—Dawson, Y.T. 1897–98—1947–48: A Golden Jubilee in the Land of the Midnight Sun. Victoria: Sisters of St. Ann, 1948.

St. Mary's Hospital. Memoir, Sister Mary Joseph Calasanctius, *Reminiscences of the Klondike,* pp. 1–4. Victoria: Archives of the Sisters of St. Ann, File No. 569-7.

St. Mary's Hospital. Typescript, C.H. Higgins, "Sisters of St. Anne of Lachine, Province of Quebec In the Gold Fields of the Klondike." Victoria: Archives of the Sisters of St. Ann, File No. 569-7.

Chapter 7

1 Georgia Powell, "The Klondike Nurses," Toronto *Globe,* Oct. 1, 1898, p. 5.
2 Ibid.
3 John Murray Gibbon and Mary S. Mathewson, *Three Centuries of Canadian Nursing* (Toronto: MacMillan, 1947), pp. 261–62.
4 Ibid., p. 264.
5 Ibid., p. 263.
6 Alice Kessler-Harris, *Out to Work: A History of Wage-Earning Women in the United States* (New York: Oxford University Press, 1982), p. 116.
7 "Women on Humboldt," *Seattle Daily Times,* Aug. 17, 1897, p. 8.
8 Dawson City Schools. School Inspection Report, Sept. 4, 1902. Whitehorse: Yukon Archives, Gov. 1615, YRG 1, Ser. 1, Vol. 9, File 505.
9 Kessler-Harris, p. 233.
10 E. Hazard Wells, *Magnificence and Misery* (New York: Doubleday and Co., 1984), p. 157.
11 Faith Fenton, "Packing on the Trail," Toronto *Globe,* Aug. 20, 1898, p. 11.
12 Brereton Greenhous, ed., *Guarding the Goldfields: The Story of the Yukon Field Force* (Toronto: Dundurn Press, 1987), p. 90.
13 Barbara E. Kelcey, "Lost in the Rush: The Forgotten Women of the Klondike Stampede" (master's thesis, Dept. of History, University of Victoria, 1989), p. 142.
14 Flora Shaw, "Klondike," *Journal of the Royal Colonial Institute,* Jan. 31, 1899, p. 196.
15 E. Moberly Bell, *Flora Shaw* (London: Constable and Co. Ltd., 1947), p. 209.
16 Flora Shaw, "Letters From Canada: IV," London *Times,* Sept. 23, 1898, p. 10.

[17] Helen Dare, "But One Cry Heard, and That Gold," San Francisco *Examiner*, Aug. 29, 1897, p. 13.
[18] Helen Dare, "Rumpled, Grimy and Unkempt," San Francisco *Examiner*, Sept. 14, 1897, p. 3.
[19] Helen Dare, "Homeward Bound on the Bosom of the Golden Yukon," San Francisco *Examiner*, Oct. 22, 1897, p. 3.
[20] Alice Rollins Crane, "Our Klondike Success," *Wide World Magazine*, June 1901, p. 180.

Additional Sources
Alaska-Yukon Directory and Gazeteer, 1902.
Becker, Ethel Anderson. "Little Girl in the Klondike Gold Fields," *Alaska Sportsman*, Nov. 1962, pp. 22–24, 34, 36–38.
Berton, Laura Beatrice. *I Married the Klondike*. Toronto: McClelland and Stewart, 1954.
Cantwell, Sister Margaret with Sister Mary George Edmond. *North to Share: The Sisters of Saint Ann in Alaska and the Yukon Territory*. Victoria: Sisters of St. Ann, 1992.
Day, Luella. *The Tragedy of the Klondike*. New York: Self-published, 1906.
Fergusen's Directory, 1901.
Fenton, Faith. "Mail Carrying on the Yukon," Toronto *Globe*, Feb. 18, 1899, p. 5.
Fenton, Faith. "Winter Days in Dawson," Toronto *Globe*, Jan. 28, 1899, p. 6.
Klondike Nugget. "It Didn't Cost Her a Cent," July 30, 1898, p. 1.
———. "A Private Dancing Party," Mar. 11, 1899, p. 4.
———. "A Sad Death," Jan. 7, 1899, p. 3.
———. "Adopted the Child," Jan. 18, 1899, p. 3.
McLellan, Winifred. Whitehorse: Yukon Archives, Acc. No. 82/32, Pt. 2, MSS 001.
Mills, Thora McIlroy. "Rachel Hanna's Diary," Bracebridge *Herald-Gazette*, April 11, 1974, pp. 13, 20–21.
Morgan, Henry James, ed. *Canadian Men and Women of the Time: A Handbook of Canadian Biography of Living Characters*. Toronto: Wm. Briggs, 1912.
New York Times. "Women Fortune Hunters," Nov. 8, 1897, p. 5.
———. "Women Going to Alaska," Feb. 13, 1898, p. 4.
North-West Mounted Police Annual Report 1899.

Chapter 8

[1] "'A Woman' Who Helped Her Husband Dig $84,000 in the Klondike," *Seattle Daily Times*, July 25, 1897, p. 1.
[2] Alice Edna Berry, *The Bushes and the Berrys* (San Francisco: C.J. Bennett, 1978), p. 65.
[3] Juliette C. Reinicker, ed., *Klondike Letters: The Correspondence of a Gold Seeker in 1898* (Anchorage: Alaska Northwest Pub. Co., 1984), p. 50.
[4] John P. Clum, "Nellie Cashman," *Arizona Historical Review*, Jan. 1931, p. 25.
[5] "A Most Successful Lady Miner," *Dawson Daily News*, Mining Edition, Sept. 1899, p. 27.
[6] "Miss Gates off for Nome," *Dawson Daily News*, Jan. 29, 1900.
[7] Ibid.
[8] Ibid.
[9] *The Official Guide to the Klondyke Country and Gold Fields of Alaska* (Chicago: W.B. Conkey Co., 1897), p. 50.
[10] Ibid., p. 180.

NOTES

Additional Sources

Bolotin, N. *Klondike Lost: A Decade of Photographs by Kinsey and Kinsey.* Anchorage: Alaska Northwest Pub. Co., 1980.

Cashman, Nellie. Govt. Records, Application for a fractional claim on Monte Cristo Hill, Jan. 31, 1900, and Letter from Gold Commissioner Senklar to Secretary of Dept. of the Interior, Aug. 29, 1901. Whitehorse: Yukon Archives, YRG 1, Ser. 1, Vol. 73, File 37.

Coutts Collection. Typescript. William Douglas Johns, "The Early Yukon, Alaska and the Klondike Discovery as They Were Before the Great Klondike Stampede Swept Away the Old Conditions." Whitehorse: Yukon Archives, Coutts Collection, 78/69, Box F-89, Folder 20, p. 135.

Dawson Daily News, Golden Clean-up Edition, 1902, p. 47.

Hunt, William R. *Whiskey Peddler.* Missoula: Mountain Press Pub. Co., 1993.

Klondike Nugget. "Carbonneau-Mulrooney," Oct. 2, 1900, p. 2.

McKay, Wallace Vincent. "The Saga of Belinda Mulrooney," Seattle *Times Magazine,* Aug. 12, 1962, pp. 4–6.

Mulrooney, Belinda. Belinda A. Carbonneau vs Charles Eugene Carbonneau, U.S. District Court, Alaska, Dec. 10, 1906. Whitehorse: Yukon Archives, Biography File.

North-West Mounted Police. Judicial Returns of Yukon Detachment, Aug. 1, 1895 to May 31, 1896. Ottawa: National Archives of Canada, Record Group 18, Vol. 140, File 447.

Ogilvie, William. *The Klondike Official Guide.* Toronto: Hunter Rose Co. Ltd., 1898.

Seattle Post-Intelligencer. "Lotta Burns in Seattle," Sept. 28, 1898, p. 5.

———. "No More Washtub For Her," July 31, 1899, p. 5.

Victoria *Daily Colonist,* "Pioneer Woman Miner," Feb. 15, 1898, p. 8.

Zazlow, Morris. *The Opening of the Canadian North.* Toronto: McClelland and Stewart, 1971.

Chapter 9

[1] Mary Hitchcock, *Two Women in the Klondike* (New York: G.P. Putnam's Sons, 1899), p. 3.

[2] Ibid., p. 248.

[3] Della Murray Banks, "Rainbow's End," *Alaska Sportsman,* Feb. 1945, p. 26.

[4] "Personals," *Klondike Nugget,* Aug. 6, 1898, p. 4.

[5] Hitchcock, p. 147.

[6] Ibid., p. 188.

[7] Ibid., pp. 104–6.

[8] Ibid., p. 143.

[9] Ibid.

[10] Ibid., p. 166.

[11] Ibid., p. 206.

[12] Ibid., p. 212.

[13] E. Hazard Wells, *Magnificence and Misery* (New York: Doubleday and Co., 1984), p. 127.

[14] Ibid., p. 128.

[15] Lulu Alice Craig, *Glimpses of Sunshine and Shade in the Far North* (Cincinnati: Editor Pub. Co., 1900) p. 3.

[16] Ibid., p. ix.

[17] Ibid., p. 68.

[18] May Kellogg Sullivan, *A Woman Who Went to Alaska* (Boston: James H. Earle and Co., 1902), preface.

[19] Ibid.

[20] Ibid., p. 30.

[21] Ibid., p. 41.

Additional Sources

Brendon, Piers. *Thomas Cook: 150 Years of Popular Tourism.* London: Secker and Warburg, 1991.

The Official Guide to the Klondyke Country and the Gold Fields of Alaska. Chicago: W.B. Conkey Co., 1897.

Chapter 10

[1] Faith Fenton Brown, "The Dawson of Today," *Yukon Sun,* Special Number: *The Dawson of Today,* Sept. 1900, n.p.

[2] Editorial, *Klondike Nugget,* Oct. 28, 1899, p. 2.

[3] J.H. MacArthur, "Health of Dawson," *Yukon Sun,* Special Number: *The Dawson of Today,* Sept. 1900, n.p.

[4] Flora Shaw, "Klondike," *Journal of the Royal Colonial Institute,* Jan. 31, 1899, pp. 189–90.

[5] Flora Shaw, "Letters From Canada: IV," London *Times,* Sept. 23, 1898, p. 10.

[6] Laura Beatrice Berton, *I Married the Klondike* (Toronto: McClelland and Stewart, 1954), p. 98.

[7] "Some Klondike Clothing," *Klondike Nugget,* Special Edition, Nov. 1, 1899, p. 14.

[8] "A Successful Merchant," *The Northern Light,* July 1904, pp. 29–30.

[9] "Fireman's Ball," *Klondike Nugget,* Nov. 2, 1898, p. 1.

[10] "Biggest Success of the Year," *Klondike Nugget,* Nov. 26, 1898, p. 3.

[11] Ibid.

[12] Virginia P. Boyntan Nethercott, ed., *Klondike Tenderfoot: From the Diaries of Clare M. Stroud Boyntan Phillips* (Starrucca, Pennsylvania: Self-published, 1992), p. 44.

[13] Ibid., p. 47.

[14] "A Woman's Life in Dawson," *New York Times,* Nov. 26, 1899, p. 24.

[15] Berton, pp. 44–45.

[16] Brown.

Additional Sources

Black, Martha Louise. *My Ninety Years.* Anchorage: Alaska Northwest Pub. Co., 1976.

Coates, Ken S. and William R. Morrison. *Land of the Midnight Sun: A History of the Yukon.* Edmonton: Hurtig, 1988.

Dawson Daily News, "A Nobel Act of Charity," Dec. 14, 1899, p. 1.

Fourth Census of Canada, 1901, vol. 1, pp. 5, 22, 142.

Fifth Census of Canada, 1911, vol. 1, pp. 169–70.

Guest, Hal. *A History of the City of Dawson, Yukon Territory 1896-1920.* Ottawa: Parks Canada, Microfiche Report Series No. 7, n.d.

Klondike Nugget. "Attacking a Lady," Sept. 27, 1899, p. 2.

———. "Ladies Relief Association," Nov. 8, 1900, p. 1.

———. "To Care For the Homeless," Nov. 2, 1900, p. 2.

SELECTED BIBLIOGRAPHY

Adney, Tappan. *The Klondike Stampede*. Vancouver: UBC Press, 1994.

Becker, Ethel Anderson. "Little Girl in the Klondike Gold Fields," *Alaska Sportsman*, Nov. 1962, pp. 22–24, 34, 36–38.

Berry, Alice Edna. *The Bushes and the Berrys*. San Francisco: C.J. Bennett, 1978.

Berton, Laura Beatrice. *I Married the Klondike*. Toronto: McClelland and Stewart, 1954.

Berton, Pierre. *Klondike: The Last Great Gold Rush*. Toronto: McClelland and Stewart, 1972.

Black, Martha Louise. *My Ninety Years*. Anchorage: Alaska Northwest Pub. Co., 1976.

Bloss, Gertrude. "Saga of the Klondike," *Canadian Home Leaguer*, Mar. 1972 to Feb. 1973.

Bolotin, N. *Klondike Lost: A Decade of Photographs by Kinsey and Kinsey*. Anchorage: Alaska Northwest Pub. Co., 1980.

Cantwell, Sister Margaret with Sister Mary George Edmond. *North to Share: The Sisters of Saint Ann in Alaska and the Yukon Territory*. Victoria: Sisters of St. Ann, 1992.

Carmack, George. *My Experiences in the Yukon*. Published posthumously by Marguerite P. Carmack, 1933.

Clum, John P., "Nellie Cashman," *Arizona Historical Review*, Jan. 1931, pp. 9–34.

Coates, Ken S. and William R. Morrison. *Land of the Midnight Sun: A History of the Yukon*. Edmonton: Hurtig, 1988.

Coutts, Robert. *The Palace Grand Theatre, Dawson, YT: An Interpretive History*. Ottawa: Parks Canada, Manuscript Report Series No. 428, 1981.

Craig, Lulu Alice. *Glimpses of Sunshine and Shade in the Far North*. Cincinnati: Editor Pub. Co., 1900.

Crane, Alice Rollins. "Our Klondike Success." *Wide World Magazine*. June 1901, pp. 180–84.

Cruikshank, Julie. *Life Lived Like a Story: Life Stories of Three Yukon Native Elders*. Lincoln: University of Nebraska Press, 1990.

DeGraf, Anna. *Pioneering on the Yukon 1892–1917*. Hamdon, Connecticut: Archon Books, 1992.

Gates, Michael. *Gold at Fortymile Creek: Early Days in the Yukon*. Vancouver: UBC Press, 1994.

Gillis, Frances (as told to Patricia McKeever), "The Lady Went North in '98," *Alaska Sportsman*, Feb. 1948, pp. 12–13, 30–32.

Greenhous, Brereton, Ed. *Guarding the Goldfields: The Story of the Yukon Field Force*. Toronto: Dundurn Press, 1987.

Guest, Hal. *A History of the City of Dawson, Yukon Territory 1896–1920*. Ottawa: Parks Canada, Microfiche Report Series No. 7, n.d.

Hitchcock, Mary. *Two Women in the Klondike*. New York: G.P. Putnam's Sons, 1899.

Johnson, James Albert. *Carmack of the Klondike*. Seattle: Epicentre Press, 1990.

Kelcey, Barbara E. "Lost in the Rush: The Forgotten Women of the Klondike Stampede." Master's thesis, Dept. of History, University of Victoria, 1989.

Kelly, Emma L., "A Woman's Trip to the Klondike," *Lippincott's Monthly Magazine*, Nov. 1901, pp. 625–33.

SELECTED BIBLIOGRAPHY

Lucia, Ellis. *Klondike Kate: The Life and Legend of Kitty Rockwell, the Queen of the Yukon.*
New York: Hastings House, 1962.

McClellan, Catherine. *Part of the Land, Part of the Water: A History of the Yukon Indians.*
Vancouver: Douglas and McIntyre, 1987.

McDonald, Alice. "As Well As Any Man," *Alaska Journal,* Summer 1984, pp. 39–45.

MacGregor, J.G. *The Klondike Rush Through Edmonton, 1897–1898.* Toronto: McClelland
and Stewart, 1970.

Nethercott, Virginia P. Boyntan. Ed. *Klondike Tenderfoot: From the Diaries of Clare M.
Stroud Boyntan Phillips.* Starrucca, Pennsylvania: Self-published, 1992.

The Official Guide to the Klondyke Country and the Gold Fields of Alaska. Chicago: W.B.
Conkey Co., 1897.

Oliver, Lillian Agnes. "My Klondike Mission." *Wide World Magazine,* April to Sept. 1899,
pp. 43–54.

Romig, Emily Craig. *A Pioneer Woman in Alaska.* Idaho: Caxton Printers, 1948.

Shaw, Flora. "Klondike," *Journal of the Royal Colonial Institute,* Jan. 31, 1899, pp. 186–235.

Wells, E. Hazard. *Magnificence and Misery.* New York: Doubleday and Co., 1984.

Wilkie, Rab and the Skookum Jim Friendship Centre. *Skookum Jim: Native and Non-
Native Stories and Views about his Life and Times and the Klondike Gold Rush.*
Whitehorse: Heritage Branch, Dept. of Tourism, Govt. of the Yukon, 1992.

PHOTOGRAPH CREDITS

Abbreviations
BCARS: British Columbia Archives and Records Services
Glenbow: Glenbow Archives, Calgary, Alberta
KNHS: Klondike National Historic Site, Dawson, Yukon
NAC: National Archives of Canada, Ottawa, Ontario
PAA: Provincial Archives of Alberta, Edmonton
SAHC: Salvation Army Heritage Centre, Toronto, Ontario
SSA: Archives of the Sisters of St. Ann, Victoria, B.C.
UW: Special Collections Division, University of Washington Libraries, Seattle
VPL: Vancouver Public Library
YA: Yukon Archives, Whitehorse

Page number

4: YA, Al Johnson Coll. 82/341-15
6: YA, Al Johnson Coll. 82/341-21
7: YA, McBride Museum Coll. 3866
8: YA, McBride Museum Coll. 3873
15: BCARS D-4420
16: UW, E.A. Hegg photographer, 2467
20: Glenbow NA-949-55 (original held in RCMP Museum, Regina, Saskatchewan)
21: PAA, Ernest Brown Coll. B5241
27: BCARS D-2077
31: BCARS C-4999
34: Glenbow NA-891-5
37: Glenbow NA-4412-20
41: Courtesy of Joan White
44: YA, H.C. Barley Coll. 4929
51: KNHS, Anita John Coll. 611
57: KNHS, Anita John Coll. 604
65: KNHS, Anita John Coll.
68: NAC, E.A. Hegg photographer, PA-13406
71: UW, E.A. Hegg photographer, 3006
72: VPL 32661
75: BCARS B-6749
80: UW, E.A. Hegg photographer, B461
86: YA, MacBride Museum Coll. 3880
87: J.B. Tyrrell Papers, Thomas Fisher Rare Book Library, University of Toronto
89: NAC PA-013326
93: YA, MacBride Museum Coll. 3793
94: Glenbow NA-3439-2
100: NAC, E.A. Hegg photographer, PA-013284
104: YA, MacBride Museum Coll. 3795
107: NAC C-020314
115: YA, Jacobsen Coll. 84/18-1
116: SSA P69-2-17
125: SAHC
128: SAHC 2983
134: YA, MacBride Museum Coll. 3769
136: SSA P69-2-21
139: UW, E.A. Hegg photographer, 458
141: Glenbow NA-1466-52
143: BCARS D6932
155: Glenbow NA-1786-8
157: KNHS, Anita John Coll. 610
158: SSA
163: KNHS, Anita John Coll.
169: YA, H.C. Barley Coll. 4800
174: BCARS C-4966
177: Glenbow ND-15-16
180: NAC PA-20547
183: NAC, H.J. Woodside photographer, PA-016201
186: VPL 33008
188: BCARS A-5117
190: Glenbow NA-2883-31
191: Glenbow NA-1466-42

INDEX

Photographs are in **bold**.

INDEX

Lowe, Mrs. G.I., 80, **80**
Lugard, Sir Frederick, 147

McDonald, Alex, 156
McDonald, Alice, 76–78, 79
McDonald, Dan, 78
McDonald, Donald, 155–56
Mackenzie River, 22
Mackie, Miss R.A., 140
McLellan, Winifred, 140
Magnet City, Yukon, 72–73
Mahoney, Mrs., 120
Maloof, Freda, 93
Marcus, H.B.S., 95
Mary Angel Guardian, Mother, 120
Mary Benedict, Sister, **116**
Mary Coeur de Jésus, Sister, **116**
Mary Edith, Sister, **116**
Mary John Damascene, Sister (Agnes Ouimette), 113, 117, 118, **136**
Mary Joseph Calasanctius, Sister, 113, 120, 121
Mary Jules of the Sacred Heart, Sister, **116,** 120
Mary of the Cross, Sister (Mary Peterson), 113, 118, 120
Mary Pauline, Sister, 114, **116,** 120
Mary Prudence, Sister, **116**
Mary Prudentienne, Sister, 114, **116,** 121, **136**
Mary's Place, 71, **71**
Mary Zenon, Sister, **116, 136**
Mary Zephyrin, Sister, 114, 116, 117, 120
Meadows, Mae and Charley, 103
Mellett, Susan. See Bowen, Susan
Methodist church, 99
Miles Canyon, Yukon, 34–35, **34**
Miller Creek, Yukon, 41, 42
Mining and prospecting, 3, 153–65, 171
Minor, Mrs. E.P., 154–56
Mitchell, Mr. and Mrs., 175
Mitchell, Pearl, 103
Montana Steam Laundry, 81–82
Montreal Marie (prostitute), 111
Moore, Mrs., 64
Moosehide, Yukon, 7
Mosher, Dr. Mary, 137–38

Mulrooney, Belinda (Carbonneau), 73–75, 160–62, 187
Munger, George, 53, 54, 55
Murders, of women, 102–3

National Council of Women, 132
Native peoples, 5, 7, **7,** 8, **8,** 10, 17, 73, 79, 122, 123, 143, 149, 193
   Han, 7
   Tagish, 1, 5, 8, 10, 144
   Tlingit, 5, 8
Newman, Marjorie (Margie), 90–91
News Publishing Company, 149
Nome, Alaska, 163, 184
North American Transport and Trading Company, 53, 58, 142
North-West Mounted Police (NWMP), 14, 34, 80, 93, 105, 106, 108, 109, 134, 189, 191
Nuns. See Sisters of St. Ann
Nurses, 20, 117, 124, 131–37, **134, 136,** 151, 191. See also Victorian Order of Nurses

Oatley, Lottie and Polly, 91–92, 172
Oatley Sisters' Concert Hall, 91, 171–72
Ogilvie, William, 105
Oliver, Lillian, 11-13, 23, 25, 29–31, 34
Osborne, Georgie, 165, 174–75
Ouimette, Agnes. See Mary John Damascene, Sister

Pantages, Alex, 89–90
Payson, Margaret, 132–35, **143**
Paystreak, The, 119, 120, 145
Payton, Priscilla Hetherington Hanby (Sid), 98
Peace River, 21, 22
Pelkington, Miss, 187
Pelly River, 21
Percentage girls, 87–89, **87.** See also Dance hall women
Peterson, Mary. See Mary of the Cross, Sister
Phillips, Clare M. Stroud Boyntan. See Boyntan, Clare
Police. See North-West Mounted Police

ABOUT THE AUTHOR

When Frances Backhouse began her freelance writing career in 1984, she drew on her training as a biologist and experience as an interpretive naturalist to write about nature and the environment. Later she realized writing would also allow her to indulge her passion for history. In addition to articles about women Klondikers published in *The Beaver* and *Up Here*, her magazine credits include *Canadian Gardening, Canadian Geographic, Equinox, Harrowsmith,* and *Nature Canada.*

Frances lives in Victoria, British Columbia, in a house built shortly before gold was discovered on Bonanza Creek. She balances work with cycling, kayaking, hiking, and gardening.

Photo crédit: Sylvia Harron